To Professor Mazrui,

Thank you for the help and support you have given me.

[illegible signature]

Genocide at the Dawn of the Twenty-First Century

Previous Publications

Who Influenced Whom? Lessons from the Cold War.
Lantham, MD: University Press of America, 2002.

Genocide at the Dawn of the Twenty-First Century

Rwanda, Bosnia, Kosovo, and Darfur

Dale C. Tatum

palgrave
macmillan

GENOCIDE AT THE TURN OF THE TWENTY-FIRST CENTURY

First published in 2010 by
PALGRAVE MACMILLAN® in the United States – a division of
St. Martin's Press LLC, 175 Fifth Avenue, New York, NY 10010.

Where this book is distributed in the UK, Europe and the rest of the world, this is by Palgrave Macmillan, a division of Macmillan Publishers Limited, registered in England, company number 785998, of Houndmills, Basingstoke, Hampshire RG21 6XS.

PALGRAVE MACMILLAN is the global academic imprint of the above companies and has companies and representatives throughout the world.

Palgrave® and Macmillan® are registered trademarks in the United States, the United Kingdom, Europe and other countries.

ISBN: 978–0–230–62189–3

Library of Congress Cataloging-in-Publication Data

Tatum, Dale C.
Genocide at the dawn of the 21st century: Rwanda, Bosnia, Kosovo, and Darfur / Dale C. Tatum.
p. cm.
ISBN 978–0–230–62189–3 (alk. paper)
1. Genocide—History—21st century. 2. Genocide—Prevention—History—21st century. 3. United States—Politics and government—2001–2009. I. Title.
HV6322.7.T36 2010
364.15'109049—dc22

2009045429

A catalogue record of the book is available from the British Library.

Design by MPS Limited, A Macmillan Company

First edition: July 2010

10 9 8 7 6 5 4 3 2 1

Printed in the United States of America.

In loving memory of my parents,
Norris Tatum and Lenora Tatum,
and
in memory of all victims of genocide.
We still have not learned.

Contents

PREFACE

In 1940, while he was a student at Harvard, John F. Kennedy published his bachelor's thesis, *Why England Slept*. In his book, Kennedy examined one of the fundamental questions of his day—why the mighty British Empire slept while Hitler rearmed Germany for the takeover of the world. Great Britain had the largest empire in the history of mankind, and was an active player in international affairs. Yet, Britain watched as the Nazi and Italian war machines expanded, and failed to take firm action to prevent these events from occurring.

Today, the United States is in a similar situation. It is the only remaining superpower. But it slept as tragedies unfolded in Rwanda, Bosnia, Kosovo, and Darfur. Some of the fundamental questions of our day are: Why did these atrocities occur? Could the United States have prevented them from happening? Why did the United States sleep when genocide was being committed? The answers to these questions are not simple.

Yes, the United States slept as these tragedies unfolded, but there are multifaceted reasons why she slept. The United States slept because it was not ready to take on the responsibilities that it faces in the post–Cold War era. In other words, the United States is not sufficiently prepared to deal with the global challenges of the twenty-first century. It has failed to learn from the past. Essentially, the legacy of World War II has been forgotten. World War II was a watershed event in the history of mankind. It was a war fought in defense of principles. World War II was a war against racism and genocide. It was a war that signaled to the world that a common humanity exists and that no person or state has the right to humiliate, abuse, or intimidate others. A consensus emerged after the war that every person, no matter what his or her station in life, nationality, religion, or race, has inherent worth.

To fulfill these ends, human rights were inscribed in the United Nations Charter, the Universal Declaration of Human Rights, and the Convention on the Prevention and Punishment of the Crime of Genocide. It was said that "never again" would the world stand by and allow genocide to happen. Sixty-five years have now passed since the end of World War II, and genocide has happened "again" and "again." It happened in East Timor as the writing of this book began, and it is still happening again in Darfur as the writing of this book concludes. What has happened to bring this situation about? How can this still be happening? And, why does the United States consistently sit by and watch and wait as innocent people are slaughtered?

The fundamental reason why this book was written was to answer the questions stated above. But the most important question that we have yet to answer is why we have not learned from the past. Fifty million people died during World War II. But today, World War II has become a distant memory with no relevance. Therefore, it is no longer a part of the United States' collective consciousness.

Rwanda, Bosnia, Kosovo, and Darfur have come to symbolize all the lessons that have been forgotten from World War II. They have been the scenes of genocide, torture, rape, ethnic cleansing, and the death of our collective consciousness. These tragedies could have been prevented if the United States had acted sooner and had taken bolder action. Why did the United States sleep as the world beckoned her? Why did she sleep and play the role of Nero and watch as bodies filled Lake Victoria during the massacre in Rwanda, as Bosnian women were raped, and as Kosovo was ethnically cleansed? Why does she fail to take action as atrocities are being committed in Darfur? These are the questions that we must ask ourselves and find answers to. For they will surely be asked by future generations.

This book argues that the United States slept while these atrocities occurred not out of malice or contempt for the rest of the world, but because the United States is not prepared to deal with the world and the crises it faces in the twenty-first century. The United States' educational system, political leaders, and civic leaders have not adequately prepared it for the challenges the world faces at the dawn of the twenty-first century. And, until changes are made, genocide will continue to occur in the future.

Los Angeles
2010

Acknowledgments

Writing a book is seldom a solemn act, nor is it done in isolation. There are many people whose contributions helped to make this book possible. First, I would like to thank my parents, Norris and Lenora Tatum, who passed away shortly before this book was completed, for their encouragement, love, and support. Without them, this book could not have been written.

This book developed as the result of a series of conversations held with the late Omari H. Kokole, the former assistant director of the Institute for Global Cultural Studies at Binghamton University, Binghamton, New York. He encouraged me to explore the topic of genocide and to write a book about it.

I would also like to acknowledge the contributions of the late Harold K. Jacobson who served as the Jessie Siddal Reeves Professor of Political Science and the director of the Center for Political Studies at the University of Michigan, Ann Arbor. "Jake" (i.e., Harold K. Jacobson) was kind enough to read several drafts of chapters, and gave me some helpful suggestions before he passed away.

A major debt of gratitude is also owed to Ali A. Mazrui, the Albert Schweitzer Professor for the Humanities and the director of the Institute for Global Cultural Studies at Binghamton University, Binghamton, New York, for his encouragement, support, and suggestions that helped to improve this work. Without him this book could not have been completed.

I would also like to thank Rachel L. Johnson who did some preliminary research for this book; Dwayne R. Coleman Jr., my research assistant; Dr. William Leiter of the Department of Political Science; and Dr. Ikaweba Bunting of the Department of Africana Studies at the California State University, Long Beach, California. Their suggestions helped me to clarify my thoughts.

I would also like to thank Dr. Alosi Moloi, the chairman of the Department of the Africana Studies at California State University, Long Beach, and his assistant Monique Hedrick Walters for their support and the use of facilities that enabled me to complete this book. The moral support of friends and family members such as Lalani Tatum, Dwayne Coleman Sr., Homer Tan, Joseph K. Dumas, and Kijana Mahdi was essential and enabled me to complete this project.

Finally, I would like to thank Linda Taite , Rachel D. Williams, and Lawaynia Tatum-Coleman for their editorial assistance. I would also like to thank Robyn Curtis, the editorial assistant, and Farideh Koohi-Kamali, the academic editorial director at Palgrave Macmillan, for their support. It was because of them that this project was finally able to come to fruition. I am solely responsible for any errors or omissions in this work.

Introduction

Genocide is deeply embedded in America's history. When European settlers came to North America, they found a land that was occupied by approximately ten million Native Americans. However, due to genocide, war, starvation, and disease, that population was reduced to one million. Even after the annihilation of millions of Native Americans had taken place, the U.S. government passed the Indian Removal Act of 1830. This was the modern-day equivalent of ethnic cleansing. Most Native Americans were forced to move to an area west of the Mississippi River. Many were forced to walk this long journey on foot. As a result, thousands perished while walking this "Trail of Tears" away from their ancestral land to reservations. It is ironic that at the Constitutional Convention of 1787 the Iroquois League had served as the blueprint for the U.S. federal government.

Today American society is more democratic than it was in the past. Therefore, it is perplexing why genocide is still tolerated by the United States, a country that has denounced genocide and made strides toward achieving equality among all of its citizens. The United States fought World War II to defend its democratic ideals: liberty and justice for all.

The End of World War II, the Promise

When the guns fell silent over Europe and the mushroom clouds cleared over Asia, fifty million people had perished. World War II was the most destructive event in the history of mankind. But, amidst the death and destruction that had taken place, new hope began to spring and bloom in the souls and minds of the peoples of the world. Studs Turkel has referred to World War II as the "Good War." It was a war fought to liberate mankind from tyranny. However, the legacy of World War II has been forgotten.

World War II and Its Meaning

World War II fundamentally changed the world. It helped to shatter the myth that there was a master race. British troops, unlike the U.S. troops, were racially integrated. People from different racial and ethnic backgrounds were brought together and worked together for a common cause. This had earth-shattering ramifications for many people who lived in British colonies. The British may not have espoused an ideology based on the concept of a master race, but they certainly acted as if a master race existed in their colonies.[1] Segregation and racial humiliation were common practices in British colonies. This seemed to lend credence to the notion that Europeans were superior to other races. Nevertheless, World War II brought this myth to a crashing halt. Many of the soldiers from British colonies lived, fought, and ate with Europeans, noticed their flaws, and therefore learned of their humanity. Thus, the armor of the demigod was stripped away.

World War II also helped to disprove the notion that there was a master race in other ways as well. Japan had carved up much of Asia. It had taken Indo-China away from the French, had driven the British from Myanmar, and the United States from the Philippines. Before leaving the Philippines, General MacArthur made the prophetic statement, "I shall return." But, before his return, he was forced to leave the islands by a strong Japanese fighting force. Japan was a formidable opponent who, in the end, could only be subdued by the ultimate weapon, the atomic bomb.

World War II also fostered the seeds of hope for a better tomorrow. On August 10, 1941, President Franklin D. Roosevelt and Prime Minister Winston Churchill signed the Atlantic Charter. This document held out the hope for self-determination after the war concluded. For the British prime minister, it meant that European countries that had been the victims of Nazi aggression would have the opportunity to determine their own fate after they were liberated. On the other hand, Sir Winston did not believe that the charter applied to people under British colonial rule. However, to the U.S. president, Roosevelt, it had a different meaning. He believed that it applied to all.[2] In the long run, it was Roosevelt's view that prevailed.

After World War II, the United Nations was established as an international institution to prevent another world war. It was established as a forum for dialogue between countries, and to uphold the dignity and worth of the individual. The United Nations Charter was based on the principles that are embodied in the Constitution of the United States. The preamble of the Constitution of the United States begins:

> We the People of the United States, in Order to form a more perfect Union, establish Justice, insure domestic Tranquility, provide for the common defense, promote the general Welfare, and secure the Blessings of Liberty to ourselves and our Posterity, do ordain and establish this Constitution of the United States of America.

On the other hand, the preamble of the United Nations Charter begins:

> We the peoples of the United Nations determined to save succeeding generations from the scourge of war, which twice brought untold sorrow to mankind, and to reaffirm faith in fundamental human rights, in the dignity and worth of the human person, in the equal rights of men and women and nations large and small.

Within one generation two world wars had been fought. The establishment of this house of peace held out hope that another generation could be spared the ravages of another world war.

The prospects for the United Nations to succeed seemed bright. The United Nations did not appear to be hamstrung by the disadvantages that the League of Nations had faced earlier. The League of Nations was doomed at birth, because the United States never joined and because the Soviet Union did not join until 1934. The United Nations did not face these shortcomings. Both of the world's superpowers, the United States and the Soviet Union, joined the United Nations at its inception and seemed dedicated to the effort of maintaining international peace. Therefore, the future looked bright.

The world also watched as justice was meted out at Nuremberg and Tokyo. Leaders of the Axis were charged with "crimes against humanity" for the atrocities they had committed. The Charter of the International Tribunal at Nuremberg defined these crimes as "murder, extermination, enslavement, deportation, and other inhumane acts committed against any civilian population before or during the war, or prosecutions on political, racial, or religious grounds."[3] These trials established an international precedent for human rights. State sovereignty or claims of following orders could not be used as a convenient shield to justify abusive behavior. Leaders of countries were now held accountable for their behavior by the international community.[4]

These principles were incorporated in the Universal Declaration of Human Rights as well. The influence of the United States can be seen in the wording of the Declaration, which was heavily influenced by the U.S. Declaration of Independence. The Declaration of Independence begins:

> We hold these truths to be self evident, that all men are created equal, that they are endowed by their creator with unalienable Rights, that among these are life, liberty, and the pursuit of Happiness.

Similar ideals are expressed in the Universal Declaration of Human Rights:

> Whereas recognition of the inherent dignity and the equal and inalienable rights of all members of the human family is the foundation of freedom, justice, and peace in the world.

The Declaration basically spells out the rights of the individual. No country, no matter how large or small, rich or poor, can justify violating the Declaration, or will be willing to admit that it had violated it.

Hope that countries would be held to higher standards of human rights than in the past was also bolstered by the adoption of the Convention on the Prevention and Punishment of the Crime of Genocide by the United Nations in 1948. Article 2 of the convention states that:

> In the Present Convention, genocide means any of the following acts committed with the intent to destroy, in whole or part, a national, ethnical, racial, or religious group as such.

Moreover Article 3 of the convention warns potential violators:

> The following acts shall be punishable:
>
> (a) Genocide;
> (b) Conspiracy to commit genocide;
> (c) Direct and public incitement to commit genocide;
> (d) Attempt to commit genocide;
> (e) Complicity to commit genocide.

This was meant to insure that acts of genocide would never be committed again. And that never again would the world stand by and watch in silence. It seemed that the world was committed to take action for preventing the mass destruction of human lives.

After World War II, a human rights movement also swept the globe. Decolonization commenced. After all, the troops from various colonies had fought the Nazis, the Fascists, and the Japanese in the name of freedom and racial equality. Now the colonized were able to quote the Atlantic Charter and work toward getting a taste of freedom for themselves. The struggle for liberation in the colonies was both violent and nonviolent. India led the way in 1947 through the nonviolent struggles of Mahatma Gandhi. Other colonies watched Gandhi and adopted his methods. Ghana and Nigeria were ultimately able to obtain their independence by using these methods. However, in the settler colonies where ex-patriots had a higher standard of living than in their native land, violent wars of liberation took place. This occurred in colonies such as Algeria and Kenya, because the ex-patriots did not want to give up the good life. People wanted freedom and saw no reason why they should not be free to rule themselves, given the fact that a victorious war that dispelled the notion of a master race had just been fought.

In addition to the impact that World War II had on the British and the French Empires, it also had a major impact on the United States. Millions of Americans from various racial and ethnic backgrounds had fought in World War II. They too had heard the rhetoric about liberty, justice, and equality. Yet, many were not truly free in their own land. Something had to change, because they "were not going to take it anymore." Hence, World War II helped to give a new push to the struggle for civil rights in the United States. This movement was part of a larger global human rights movement, as witnessed in the decolonization struggle, and did not solely happen as a result of Rosa Parks refusing to give up her seat on a bus.

World War II also elevated the stature of the common man. It seemed to signify that all people are important, no matter what race, creed, or color. Everyone was entitled to basic rights, and the international community would protect those rights. Political lessons were also to be learned from World War II.

Political Lessons

Foremost among the political lessons that it taught us was the importance of military preparedness. After World War I, Great Britain virtually disarmed itself while Germany's arsenal grew.[5] As a result, Germany was able to bully and bluster its weaker neighbors into concessions, and Great Britain could do nothing but capitulate because it was not ready for war. The other political lesson was that one cannot appease a dictator. Appeasement became a word of scorn. And the architect of the appeasement policy with Hitler, Neville Chamberlain, became an international symbol of weakness and naiveté. No statesman wants to be perceived by his opponent or fellow countrymen as an appeaser. One wants to be perceived as standing strong.

Lessons Remembered

Today it seems that the main lesson remembered from World War II is the military-political one about appeasement. Countries such as the United States devote an inordinate amount of resources to military preparedness and try to avoid being perceived as appeasers. Everyone seems to remember Neville Chamberlain's blunder at Munich. But this seems to be the only lesson from World War II that has been remembered. However, even this lesson seems to be a bit hazy. The Pentagon is prepared militarily. The problem is not that it fails to spend enough money on weapons. The problem is how the Pentagon spends money. Bureaucratic inertia has set in, and the Pentagon is still building and buying the same type of weapons that it did during the Cold War. The air force has procured the F-22 Raptor and the army the Crusader artillery systems, and the navy has built a fleet of New Attack submarines.[6] Apparently, the Pentagon is still preparing for a Cold War enemy that no longer exists. It claims that it is preparing a more mobile force. However, the rhetoric of the Pentagon has not matched its actions. Recent defense budgets do not reflect the post–Cold War needs of the United States. More resources are not being devoted to peacekeeping missions or for the rapid deployment of forces to troubled areas. The Cold War ended more than two decades ago, but the Pentagon is still doing things the same old way. The Pentagon continues to focus on the deployment of big-ticket items like a missile defense system.

If the military imperative is all that remains today of what has been learned from World War II, then the lessons forgotten are those regarding human values. At the end of World War II, the world seemed closer to forming a bond of common humanity and collective responsibility for the enforcement of human rights. Today this bond between the peoples of the world has been broken. The response to atrocities is often to do nothing or to let the situation get worse before acting. Once the possibility that a wider war will occur or a threat to a western ally emerges, the United States then takes action. But right now, the United States is sleeping. It has turned its back on the very values that its society is based upon. Why does the United States sleep yet dream about a better world? Why has the United States forgotten the lessons that so many of her sons had to shed their blood to teach us?

The answers to these questions are not simple ones. The United States went to sleep and watched its moral authority eroded not out of spite, contempt, or hatred of the rest of the world. The United States has slept through the greatest tragedies of the post–Cold War period because of the constraints of culture, information, and the lack of preparation among her people that prevented the United States from taking bold action when it was needed. The fault lies both with the people and with the political system. But it is a situation that can be changed. The connection between human values and military preparedness has been broken. The very reason why one should keep one's gunpowder dry at all times is to protect the international values that were established at the end of World War II from violation by the Hitlers, Mussolinis, and Tojos of the world. By forgetting this valuable lesson, an appeasement of human rights takes place, and that is exactly what allows the dictators of the world to gain ground. Putting a halt to the policy of appeasing human rights requires more than military preparedness. It requires remembering what one is fighting for; otherwise one is merely fighting without a cause. This is the greatest legacy of all from World War II. The best defense of democracy is a supportive international environment.

Part I

Setting the Stage for Genocide

Chapter 1

The Cold War with the Third World

Introduction

The term "Cold War" was used to describe the tension between the United States and the Soviet Union that was based on social, philosophical, economic, and political differences. The Cold War between the superpowers began to wind down in the mid-1980s, and finally ended with the collapse of the Soviet Union in December 1991. Yet, another Cold War remains. This one is between the West and the Third World. Like the Cold War with the Soviet Union, it also began after World War II, and is based on the social, philosophical, economic, and political differences between the Third World and the West. Yet, there has been scant acknowledgment that it even exists.

Nevertheless, a de facto acknowledgment of the Cold War between the Third World and developed countries exists. Earlier, the study of Third World countries, even within a global context, was considered "low politics," while the study of the United States, the Soviet Union, Europe, and the Cold War was considered "high politics."

The tension and problems between the West and the Third World were viewed as insignificant until the Soviet Union collapsed. Then they exploded onto the international scene. Sometimes they are misconstrued as a "clash of civilizations." However, it is more than a clash of cultures. These are problems that have existed for a long time but have long been ignored. It is a full-blown Cold War now.

This is a war undertaken by the Third World for respect and recognition. The nature of this war differs by region. Africa has achieved cultural accommodation and compromise with the West. Africa's conflict with the West is mainly economic. On the other hand, Asia has reached economic accommodation with the West. Its conflict with the West is cultural. Furthermore, Latin America's conflict with the West is political. Most of the conflicts between the West and the Third World are not recent. They are long-standing. However, due to negligence, they have not been resolved but have been allowed to reach the point of critical mass, and have exploded onto the international scene in recent years. To label the conflicts as a clash of cultures is a failure to understand them. The nature of the conflicts and how they have affected the Third World's relations with the West and how they can be resolved will be discussed below.

POSTDECOLONIZATION ERA

After World War II, the United States and the Soviet Union became engulfed in a Cold War. Both superpowers made overtures to the independent, newly decolonized, and soon-to-be decolonized regions of Africa, Asia, and Latin America. Some states, such as Ethiopia, became an ally of the United States, while other states, such as Guinea, aligned with the Soviet Union.[1] Still others such as Ghana, Egypt, Yugoslavia, and Indonesia felt that it was in their best interest to avoid alliances and to judge various issues on a case-by-case basis. This latter group met in Bandung, Indonesia, in 1955.

The Bandung Conference in 1955 gave birth to the Non-Aligned Movement (NAM). This conference of Afro-Asian solidarity was a declaration of independence by Third World leaders. They were letting everyone know that they did not intend to become pawns in the superpowers' game of global competition. The western response to this act of defiance was swift and immediate. Many in the West such as John Foster Dulles, the U.S. secretary of state, believed that "those who are not with us are against us" and viewed nonalignment as immoral.

Thus, the Cold War between the developed world and the Third World had begun, and Egypt was its first casualty. To convince Third World countries of their folly, the United States deployed a carrot-and-stick policy. However, the stick was deployed as a weapon against Egypt, which had been promised a loan to build the Aswan High Dam. Gamal Abdul Nasser, the president of Egypt, had angered the West by buying arms from Czechoslovakia, a communist country. In turn, the West punished Nasser by canceling the Aswan Dam loan as a means of showing Third World countries the price they would have to pay for defying the West.

Most of the economic cards were in the hands of the United States and its allies. While natural resources such as oil and minerals are located in Third World countries, the capital and technology needed to develop them are in the West. The United States and its allies are in firm control of the world's international economic regimes, such as the International Monetary Fund (IMF), the International Bank for Reconstruction and Development (World Bank), and the U.S. Export-Import Bank (Ex-Im Bank). Third World countries are in a subordinate position. They did not create these regimes, nor do they control them. Yet, they are often dependent on them for loans to advance their economic development.

To the West, leaders of Third World countries are perpetual beggars. However, this dependency presents the West with an opportunity to influence policy in Third World countries. Aid is often given with "strings attached" (tied aid). For example,

> in 1977. The Egyptian government sought and obtained assistance from the International Monetary Fund. In exchange for the assistance, Egypt was required to increase the price of food, cooking fuel, and other items. In all, Egypt was required by Western institutions to cut food subsidies by $1 billion.[2]

The European Union also dictated the terms of trade with its former colonies through the Lomé Agreement. The Lomé Agreement allowed primary products from African, Caribbean, and Pacific countries to be imported into the European Union duty-free. However, this generosity did not extend to manufactured products from these countries. The purpose of the agreement was to supply Europe's needs and to give these countries an incentive not to industrialize so they would not become competitors with Europe. The West was trying to use its economic resources to co-opt the leadership of Third World countries and to move them in a direction that best suited the West.

THE FAILURE OF CO-OPTATION

Third World leaders had few choices; they had to cooperate with the Western countries that controlled economic resources or risk access to capital and technology that their countries needed for economic development. Abiding by the conditions attached for economic assistance was a bitter pill for many Third World leaders to swallow, because they believed it was a form of neocolonialism.

To overcome the shackles of tied aid, the Third World formed a united bloc at the first United Nations Conference on Trade and Development (UNCTAD) in 1964. The Group of 77 emerged from this meeting. It sought the reform of the international economic system. It is a system that they are beholden to and a system that they played no role in creating. They now wanted to play a role in its decision-making process and demanded a greater transfer of economic resources and technology to their countries. This was a move to free themselves from western control.

Third World leaders found support for their demands in *North-South*, the report of an independent commission headed by former West German Chancellor Willy Brandt. The Brandt Commission urged reform of the international system and argued that the transfer of resources was not charity. The commission stated that the transfer of economic resources and technology to Third World countries would advance the economic development of Third World countries and provide developed countries with additional markets. The report seemed logical, plausible, and beneficial to all. However, it did not take into consideration the international political situation. Those who have power are often reluctant to give it up. In addition, the peoples of the Third World are not viewed as equals by the West, and are hence unlikely to be accorded equal status now or in the near future. Initially, globalization had a negative impact on the underclass in western countries. In recent years, it has also had a negative impact on the middle class in western countries. These events were not anticipated by the Brandt Commission. The conflict between the West and the Third World will continue until it is resolved.

Africa's Conflict with the West

Africa demonstrates that the conflict between the West and the Third World is not simply due to a "Clash of Civilizations."[3] Africa has accommodated Western and Islamic cultures. Both live side by side with indigenous African traditions. The clash between Africa and the West is economic. Africa wants a greater share of the profits extracted from its natural resources that are processed by western interest as well as better terms of trade for its primary products. Africa also wants more aid and technology from the West.

Africa has made cultural accommodation with the West. As Ali Mazrui pointed out in his series *The Africans: A Triple Heritage*, western culture has left a lasting impression on Africa. In his series, Mazrui noted that Africa has borrowed western tastes but not western techniques. Western religion, consumption patterns, ideology, dress, cars, and other western products are prevalent throughout the African continent. The first generation of African leaders from Nkrumah to Kuanda was heavily influenced by western thought. Africa's accommodation with western culture could be observed in Senegal. It is 80 percent Muslim, yet it elected Leopold Senghor, a Christian, as its first president.[4] Many African countries have a western language as their official language and have a western style of government. Africa has not rejected western culture. It has embraced it, perhaps too much.

Africa's main conflict with the West is economic. It has seen a steady decline in its terms of trade with the West. Africa receives relatively low prices for the primary products—tea, coffee, cocoa, and bananas—that it sells to the West. On the other hand, the cost of its imports has gone up steadily. Africa is rich in minerals. Yet it is poor. The downstream production and processing of many of its minerals takes place in the West. Therefore, western countries are able to reap the benefits of the "value added" through the production and refining process. It has also been argued that the West has tried to prevent Africa and the Third World from developing so that it will not have to deal with a potential economic competitor and can continue to have access to cheap minerals and primary products.[5]

Despite what has been stated above, not all African countries have made cultural accommodation with the West. In the seventh century, Khalid ibn al-Walid conquered Egypt during the reign of Abu Bakr. This started the dual process of Islamization and Arabization in North Africa. The parts of Africa where Arabs are predominant have not made cultural accommodation with the West. They are at odds with the West. Pan-African rhetoric aside, these regions have more of an Arab identity than an African one and often identify more with the Middle East than with Africa. Like the Middle East, the conflict between these countries and the West is cultural.

THE CONFLICT BETWEEN THE WEST AND THE MIDDLE EAST

The Middle East is part of Asia. Yet, political scientists treat it as if it is a separate region. Similarly, North Africa is treated as if it is a part of the Middle East. This is done for purposes of analysis. Both Islam and Arab culture are dominant in these regions. Hence, the Islamic

Middle East is separated from the rest of Asia and lumped with North Africa to accommodate generalization.

The conflict between the Islamic Middle East/North Africa and the West is cultural and not economic, unlike the conflict between the West and Africa. The Middle East has embraced capitalism. In fact, Ali Mazrui argues that Islam helped to give birth to capitalism.[6] The formation of the Organization of Petroleum Exporting Countries (OPEC) and the relative scarcity of oil have allowed the oil-producing states of the Middle East and North Africa to turn the tables on the West and strip it of a substantial portion of its wealth. OPEC even trades in dollars. Charles Hugh Smith has pointed out that every time the purchase of U.S. Treasury bonds by Japan and China has fallen off, Arab OPEC members have stepped in to purchase U.S. Treasury bonds from offshore accounts. Smith speculates that this is done by Arab OPEC members to keep the U.S. economy afloat so that the demand for oil will remain high.[7] This enables OPEC to maintain high prices for oil. A drop in the demand for U.S. Treasury bonds triggers high interest rates, thereby causing a recession or decline in the U.S. economy. The Arab Middle East and North Africa are economically wedded to the West.

Capitalism has deep roots in countries such as Algeria and Egypt. Algeria is one of the most industrialized countries in the Arab world. Capitalism is also the basis of the economy of Egypt, the most populous Arab country. Hosni Mubarak, the president of Egypt, has also adopted a plan of capitalist economic development for Egypt. The governments of Algeria and Egypt have faced attacks from Islamic militants who prefer the Shari'a (Islamic law) to secular western-style governments. Note, the resistance arises from opposition to the style and form of government, and is not opposed to capitalism per se. Also, Libya is privatizing its economy and is welcoming foreign investors.

It is on the cultural front that the interest of the Arab Middle East, Iran, and the West diverge. Western culture has become global culture. Western dress, food, entertainment, music, cars, and lifestyles have gone global. This is why many in the Middle East rail against the West. When Muhammad Reza Pahlavi reigned as the Shah of Iran, he began a program to modernize Iran. His plan resembled that of Kemal Ataturk, the founder of modern Turkey. Ataturk believed that for Turkey to catch up with the West, it would have to secularize and adopt western culture. In a similar vein, the Shah of Iran attempted to modernize and westernize his country as well. He was even willing to allow his secret police, ZAVAK, to use terrorist tactics and torture against those who opposed him. The end result was an Islamic revolution that was not a revolution against modernity but a revolution against western culture. As Elbaki Hermassi has pointed out, "They did not even recognize themselves in their own clothes."

The conflict between the Middle East and the West is also a Cold War that has turned hot. Hot conflicts between the West and the Third World, such as wars of colonial conquest, have historically taken place on the soil of Third World countries. However, the current conflict between the West and the Middle East is different. A change in this conflict began when Muammar Gaddafi adopted a new tactic in the 1980s. Gaddafi declared that the West interfered in the affairs of Third World countries all the time; therefore, he felt that he had the right to interfere in the affairs of the West and funded organizations such as the Irish Republican Army (IRA). He also used his embassies in western countries, so-called "People's Bureaus," as centers of terrorism. Gaddafi's Libya was also responsible for the bombing of Pan-AM Flight 103 over Lockerbie, Scotland.

Today, Gaddafi has made peace with the West. Nevertheless, many Islamic terrorists have followed the example he set, and have initiated a hot war with the West that often takes place on western soil. They initiated attacks in the United States, the United Kingdom, Spain, and the Middle East. These religious terrorists want to bring down the West, and rid their region of decadence, secularism, and immorality.

THE CONFLICT WITH THE REST OF ASIA

The conflict between the rest of Asia and the West, like the conflict between the West and the Middle East, is not economic. It is also cultural. Unlike the conflict between the West and the Middle East, the conflict between the West and the Far East has not turned hot and is not likely to do so.

Capitalism has been embraced by Japan, China, Taiwan, Hong Kong, Singapore, India, and other Asian countries. Capitalism seems to meld particularly well with Chinese culture. Economic prosperity, diligence, and the acquisition of material goods are viewed as signs of success in traditional Chinese culture. Capitalism affords an individual the opportunity to fulfill these goals. However, capitalism was not such a natural fit with Japan, which adopted a crash course in capitalism. During the Meiji Restoration in the nineteenth century, Japan was forced to make a decision—industrialize or be conquered like China. Japan chose to industrialize but not to westernize. It opted to borrow western techniques and technology but to retain its own cultural identity. Even today, elements of this can be seen in Japan. The Japanese have rejected the individualism of western culture as the basis of their version of capitalism.

> Most Japanese have never accepted the view that the Adam Smithian "invisible hand" would guide the selfish, profit maximizing behavior of maximum output and the lowest prices for the benefit of the consumer. Rather, they have accepted the "visible hand" of government guidance and business cooperation to produce satisfying results.[8]

In a similar manner, China has embraced capitalism, but it has not embraced western values, especially human rights. According to Human Rights Watch, political repression in China has increased. It is still a police state where torture is used to coerce confessions from the accused, and where freedom of speech and freedom of religion are not tolerated. It obviously has not embraced western values. Yet, its embrace of capitalism is a tight one. China has become a regular customer at the monthly bond auctions that help to finance the United States' deficit. Also, China has the fastest growing economy in the world and manages to attract foreign investors from many western countries. When the Chinese stock market fell by 8.8 percent in March 2007, the stock markets in Europe and the United States tumbled as well. China has become a major factor in the world capitalist economy. Asian countries have also become a major factor in the U.S. economy as well. Currently, Japan owns $1 trillion in U.S. debt and China owns $700 billion in U.S. debt. China and the United States do not argue about whether or not capitalism should be implemented in China. They argue about the lack of human rights there. The West—especially the United States—conducts similar dialogues with other countries in Asia as well.

The Conflict with Latin America

The conflict between the West and Latin America is not economic or cultural. It is political. Since the Monroe Doctrine of 1823, the United States has attempted to control the temper, tone, and direction of governments in Latin America. It considers Latin America to be within its sphere of influence.

With the exception of Cuba, Latin America has adopted capitalism. Mexico has joined with the United States and Canada to form the North American Free Trade Agreement (NAFTA), and the United States has joined with Central American countries (Costa Rica,

El Salvador, Guatemala, Honduras, Nicaragua, and the Dominican Republic) to form the Dominican Republic–Central American Free Trade Agreement (DR-CAFTA). A trade agreement between North and South America will be signed in the near future.

The United States has gone to extensive lengths to control Latin America. In 1895, the United States contemplated war with Great Britain during the Cleveland administration because of Britain's infringement of Venezuela's territory. Also, prior to Cuba's independence in 1903, the United States imposed the Platt Amendment on that country. The Platt Amendment forbade Cuba from making any agreements that might impair its independence; it prohibited Cuba from incurring public debt; the amendment granted the United States the right to intervene to preserve Cuba's independence; it forced Cuba to accept all acts of the U.S. military government; the amendment also made Cuba lease land to the U.S. Navy. Hugo Chavez must have wondered if the constitution of Venezuela contained provisions of the Platt Amendment when the George W. Bush administration objected to his decision to nationalize the utility industries in Venezuela. Latin Americans continue to look over their shoulders, wondering if "Big Brother" to the north will intervene in their affairs.

ENDING THE CONFLICT

To end the Cold War between the West and the Third World, there must first be an acknowledgment that a conflict exists. It does. That is why there is indifference and inaction when genocide occurs. The victims of genocide in Bosnia, Rwanda, Darfur, Kosovo, and elsewhere have been causalities of this war. Many more victims will die unless it ends.

A comprehensive blueprint for reconciliation already exists—*North-South*, the report of the Brandt Commission. Essentially it calls for more western aid and more Third World responsibility. However, it needs to be modified to take into effect the negative impact that globalization has had on Third World and western countries.

To end the current Cold War, the world must also be made safe for diversity. There must be a movement away from the imperialist policies of the West. How are these two goals to be accomplished? The answer to this paradox may be found in *The Evolution of Cooperation* by Robert Axelrod. In this book, Axelrod asks an important question, "Under what conditions will cooperation emerge in a world of egoists without central authority?" After analyzing the results of an iterated

Prisoner's Dilemma tournament, he came to the conclusion that "tit for tat" was the most effective strategy to deploy, as it led to cooperation between parties. In a sense, in this strategy, each is able to foil the goals and ambitions of the other; hence, a stalemate is achieved. For any of the parties to accomplish anything, cooperation must be spawned lest they continue to hold each other hostage and nothing is accomplished. For such a system to work in international politics, the parties must be on an equal footing. However, this is not the case between Third World countries and the West. There is an asymmetric relationship between the West and the Third World, with the West holding most of the advantages.

For greater cooperation to emerge between the West and the Third World, the international system and its institutions must be democratized. This scenario seems unlikely since the West holds most of the cards in its relationship with Third World countries. Democratizing the system would mean that they would have to give up power to empower the Third World.

Nevertheless, as unlikely as this scenario seems, it is indeed possible. Colonialism was once viewed as legitimate. At that point, it seemed unlikely that colonial powers would grant independence to their colonies. However, World War II helped to bring about its downfall. While the war was in progress, the United States and Great Britain signed the Atlantic Charter. It reaffirmed the Wilsonian concept of self-determination. In essence, World War II was a war fought in opposition to the idea that there was a master race. Despite Sir Winston Churchill's protest that this did not apply to those in the realm of the British Empire, it was read by colonial subjects in terms of that opposition. It inspired them, motivated them, and enabled them to point out the hypocrisy between the aims behind the war and the colonial policy that was being practiced. In essence, colonialism was based on the very notion that there was a master race.

One of the greatest legacies of World War II was that it delegitimized colonialism and led to decolonization. In a similar vein, the West is currently engaged in a War on Terrorism. One of the purposes of the war is to spread democracy. However, it is obvious that the international system is not democratic. Once more, we see a policy of hypocrisy. The rhetoric used in support of the War on Terrorism is not supported by international democratic policies. It is ironic that one of the greatest legacies of the War on Terrorism is that it might help to democratize the international system. This may be the price that the West has to pay to gain the cooperation of Third World counties in this venture. Otherwise, they may have no incentive to cooperate.

DEMOCRACY AND CHANGE

Democratizing the international system will not only help to end the Cold War with the Third World, but will also change the nature of the international system. It will empower the weak and curtail the strong. Democratizing the international system will change it because democracy is based on compromise. If the international system is democratized, the Third World and the West will be able to engage in the "tit for tat" strategy discussed by Axelrod in *The Evolution of Cooperation*. In other words, neither would be able to achieve the goals it wants unless there is cooperation between the two sides. Democracy breeds cooperation; without it nothing can be accomplished. Therefore, the West and the Third World will be in a position to learn about each other's goals and to receive feedback. Each side will have to respect the goals and aspirations of the other, for without that the international system will not be able to function.

Democratizing the international system will not end the conflict among countries. However, it will provide a forum where not just more voices will be heard but where more countries will be empowered to take action if that is needed. This would help to advance human rights in Third World countries. In recent years whenever genocide occurred in the Third World, the West did not take action because it did not deem that it was in its economic interest to take prompt action to stop it. Most importantly, democratization of the international system will help to end the Cold War with the Third World, because it will help to transform western perceptions of Third World peoples and societies. The Third World is often viewed as an area of dependence and poverty. In reality, the West also depends on the Third World for its natural resources and labor. Democratization will help the Third World to go from dependency to partnership. In the end, this will be in the best interest of all the citizens of the world.

Chapter 2

The End of the Cold War

After forty-six years the Cold War finally came to an end in 1991. This was a notable event. Many people thought that the fall of Communism would lead to a decrease in the abuse of human rights. However, human rights abuses did not decline after the death of Communism. Some of the totalitarian states such as the former Yugoslavia morphed into authoritarian states where human suffering and misery continued unabated. It soon became obvious that Communist regimes were not the only governments that abused their citizens.

As the only democratic superpower, the United States bore the burden of enforcing human rights. Its diligence in fulfilling this role depended on the priorities of the administration in power and the prevailing national mood. At the end of the Cold War, genocide occurred repeatedly because the United States' commitment to the enforcement of human rights was affected by domestic politics, and a lack of empathy for the victims.

Human Rights and the Cold War

During the Cold War, the priority given to human rights by the United States varied. The emphasis on human rights depended on the approach an administration took to international relations. The idealist school of thought was a major influence on the Truman administration. Idealism encompassed the Wilsonian belief that peace can be achieved among nations by building international institutions that foster communication and conflict resolution, facilitate cooperation, and help negotiations. It was assumed that these institutions would also help to defend and preserve human rights. Thus, the Truman administration took a leading role in the founding of the United Nations. As a result, the United Nations (UN) Charter and the Universal Declaration of Human Rights set the international standard for human rights.

There was a competing school of thought, the realist school. It was headed by Han Morganthau of the University of Chicago. Realists believe that international relations should be conducted on an amoral basis and that a country's national interests are defined in terms of power. They believe that a country should strive to achieve a preponderant balance of power. The Truman administration was influenced by idealism; nevertheless, elements of realism could also be seen in its foreign policy as well. For example, the United States gave aid to Yugoslavia, a Communist country, during the Cold War so it could break away from the Soviet Union. Realists view international politics as a zero-sum game. One can only win at the expense of an opponent.

After World War II, right-wing ideologues (Cold Warriors) emerged in the Republican Party. Prior to World War II, the Republican Party tended to be isolationist. Arthur Vandenberg, a Republican senator from Michigan, played a vital role in moving the Republican Party from its isolationist stance and in getting it to embrace a broader global perspective. Like converts to a new religion, some Republicans became zealots (Cold Warriors) for the cause. These Cold Warriors attacked the Truman administration for the "fall" of Eastern Europe and China to Communism. They said that they would "roll back" Communism when they obtained power.

During the Eisenhower administration, Cold Warriors such as Secretary of State Dulles, Vice President Nixon, and Senator Joseph McCarthy used bellicose rhetoric to usher in the era of "the Red Scare." Ultimately, the Cold Warriors lost out as Eisenhower searched for ways to achieve peace with the Soviet Union. Nevertheless, the Eisenhower administration was willing to tolerate human rights abuses by non-Communist governments such as the authoritarian regimes in Latin America.

When Richard Nixon became the president, he transformed himself from a Cold Warrior into a realist. It is ironic that he became the target of the Republican right-wing where he was once a fixture. Cold Warriors such as Ronald Reagan attacked Nixon and later Gerald Ford for pursuing a policy of détente with the Soviet Union.

Also, during the 1960s, a new faction emerged within the Democratic Party (peaceniks). They were disillusioned with the United States' involvement in the Vietnam War, and wanted to focus on domestic issues such as poverty, education, and illiteracy. They believed that the United States' nuclear arsenal was large enough to protect the country, and called for "sufficient defense spending." In the 1970s, Senator George McGovern, the 1972 Democratic nominee, became their spokesman. They would later play a prominent role in U.S. politics during the 1980s, advocating a nuclear freeze during the Reagan administration.

During the Carter administration, human rights was a central part of U.S. foreign policy. Carter's emphasis on human rights and his public diplomacy upset the traditional foreign policy establishment that adhered to the realist school of thought. They viewed Carter's approach to foreign policy as foolish, amateurish, and idealistic. There were some notable successes for Carter, such as preventing the execution of Kim Dae Jung when South Korea was ruled by an authoritarian government. However, there were also glaring failures, such as Carter's inability to prevent or stop crackdowns against Andrei Sakharov and other dissidents in the Soviet Union. The Carter administration is often unfairly maligned as a failed administration. Consequently, the defense of human rights was perceived as unfeasible. However, Carter's emphasis on human rights was selective. The Khmer Rouge in Cambodia resorted to mass executions when Carter was in office. Yet, Carter never denounced the executions or took action against the Khmer Rouge that committed these vile acts. This seems strange for an administration that was committed to making human rights the cornerstone of U.S. foreign policy. It became apparent over time that Carter's national security advisor, Zbignew Brzezinski, a realist, had gained control of the Carter administration's foreign policy. Brzezinski's grand strategy consisted of using "the China card" against the Soviet Union. The Khmer Rouge was backed by China. Therefore, its barbarous acts were not denounced for fear of offending China. The realist vision of Brzezinski clouded Carter's human rights lens.

After Reagan became the president, three factions emerged in his administration: the old Cold Warriors, a new generation of Cold Warriors, and realists. The old Cold Warriors were led by UN Ambassador Jeane Kirkpatrick. Human rights was not a significant issue for the old Cold Warriors. Kirkpatrick often defended abusive authoritarian regimes, because she believed that they were better than totalitarian Communist regimes and had the potential to morph into democracies. Like their allies, the old Cold Warriors, the young Cold Warriors were opposed to negotiations with the Soviet Union and sought U.S. hegemony. Many of them even believed that it was possible to fight and win a nuclear war with the Soviet Union.[1] They also rejected the doctrine of Mutually Assured Destruction (MAD) and supported the Strategic Defense Initiative (SDI) or "Star Wars." A new generation of conservatives (neocons) was beginning to emerge. However, they found themselves in an ongoing battle with the realists in the Reagan administration. As a result of this foreign policy gridlock, Reagan was the first U.S. president not to hold a summit or to sign an arms control agreement with the Soviet Union during his first term in office. Eventually, the realists won out and Reagan held summits with the Soviet Union, started the Strategic Arms Reduction Talks, and signed an agreement with the Soviet Union on intermediate-range nuclear weapons in Europe. Despite their loss, the neocons would be heard from again.

The administration of George H. W. Bush (President Bush I) combined elements of idealism, realism, and imperialism. Aspects of idealism could be seen in Bush's use of the United Nations to mobilize world public opinion against Iraq. Furthermore, he got authorization from the United Nations for the use of force against Iraq as the Cold War was winding down. Elements of realism could also be seen in his foreign policy as well. Overthrowing Saddam Hussein might have split Iraq into three states: a Kurdish state in the north, a Sunni state in the center, and a Shiite state in the south. This would have destabilized the area. A Kurdish state would have been a threat to the United States' North Atlantic Treaty Organization (NATO) ally, Turkey, and encourage the Kurds in Turkey's eastern province to break away and join their kinsmen. A Shiite state in the south would undoubtedly be allied with Iran. The balkanization of Iraq seemed to be of little value to the United States. Bush had encouraged both groups to rise up against Saddam Hussein. Nevertheless, he abandoned them when they rebelled against Hussein, even though the Kurds had repeatedly been subjected to genocide and even though the Shiites had faced repression as well. Imperialism was also part of the foreign policy of President Bush I. On December 20, 1989, Operation Just Cause was launched. Its purpose was to topple Manuel Noriega, the president of Panama. Noriega was ousted for defying the will of President Bush I. Noriega was no longer willing to assist the United States by giving aid and comfort to the Contras who were trying to overthrow the government of Nicaragua.

POST–COLD WAR U.S. FOREIGN POLICY

The end of the Cold War meant different things to various groups within the United States. To some it meant that the United States had prevailed over the evils of Communism. Therefore, they believed it was no longer necessary for the United States to engage in world affairs. Initially, George W. Bush was a member of this group. During the election of 2000, he criticized the Clinton administration's foreign policy in the Balkans. He said that the U.S. Army should not be used for nation-building. Similarly, the peaceniks also rejoiced at the end of the Cold War, because they felt that defense spending could now be slashed and the resulting "peace dividend" could now be spent on domestic programs. These two groups formed the backbone of a neoisolationist coalition. They believed that the United States did not have to be as involved in world affairs as it had been in the past, because there was no impending danger, and that the United States should now look inward.

On the other hand, the neocons believed that the end of the Cold War represented an unprecedented opportunity for the United States to dominate the world since it was now the only remaining superpower. The idealists also felt that the end of Communism did not mean that the United States should withdraw from world affairs and narrow its focus to domestic issues. They realized that Communist governments were not the only governments that abused their citizens. They believed that vigilance had to be maintained if human rights were to be protected around the world. These two groups never formed a coalition, but they formed the core of Americans who maintained an interest in global affairs.

After the collapse of the Soviet Union, a neoisolationist mood prevailed in the United States. Since the late 1940s, the Republican Party had used the Cold War as its trump card against the Democrats. Republican presidential candidates often portrayed Democratic presidential candidates as weak-kneed and lacking the intestinal fortitude necessary to stand up to the Communist threat that the United States faced from the Soviet Union. In the 1952 presidential election, Richard Nixon railed against Secretary of State Dean Acheson's "cowardly college of Communist containment." Nixon implied that a vote for the Democratic candidate, Adlai Stevenson, would mean the continuation of a weak foreign policy. However, with the collapse of the Soviet Union, the Republican Party lost a key issue that it had been able to use effectively against the Democrats.

In 1992, when Bill Clinton challenged President George H.W. Bush for the presidency, he had no major foreign policy credentials compared to President Bush. Bush was a World War II hero; had served as the UN ambassador, head of the U.S. liaison office in China, director of the Central Intelligence Agency (CIA), and as the vice president; and had led the United States to victory in Operation

Desert Storm as the president. Nevertheless, it did not matter to the American people since the United States no longer faced a threat from the Soviet Union. Moreover, most Americans felt that domestic issues were more important than foreign policy issues because the country was in the midst of a recession. These factors made the election of Bill Clinton possible.

To many, the United States' neoisolationism seemed justified by the debacle in Somalia, where General Aidid thumbed his nose at the UN forces and the body of a U.S. solider was dragged through the streets of Mogadishu. It was within this context that genocide in Bosnia and Rwanda occurred.

When genocide began in Bosnia and Rwanda, the Clinton administration, like the rest of the world, failed to act. Clinton did not want to incur the wrath of the American public and risk a chance for a second term in office. When Clinton was more secure in office, he did intervene to bring genocide to an end in Bosnia in 1995. However, by the time Clinton found his political courage, it was too late for the people of Rwanda. After 1994, the Clinton administration sought to advance human rights by joining UN peacekeeping missions. However, U.S. forces were not deployed until hostilities had ceased. The Clinton administration tried to maintain a delicate balance between preserving human rights and avoiding the political fallout from the neoisolationist American public and the Republican opposition. It sought to do this by avoiding the deployment of ground troops in hostile areas and by working within the framework of international organizations. For example, when genocide was being committed in Kosovo, air power was used by Clinton to strike Serb targets in Kosovo and Serbia. The Clinton administration operated within the framework of NATO to carry out these actions. This allowed the Clinton administration to preserve human rights and minimize casualties.

The Ascendancy of the Neocons

The election of Bill Clinton in 1992 was a significant historical milestone because a generational shift had taken place in the leadership of the United States. A similar shift took place in 1960 when John F. Kennedy was elected president. Kennedy noted this shift in his inaugural address: "The torch has been passed to a new generation of Americans—born in this century, tempered by war, disciplined by a hard and bitter peace."[2] Kennedy was noting the shift in U.S. leadership from generation VII, the seventh since the American Revolutionary War, to generation VIII, his generation, the World War II generation. Similarly, the election of Bill Clinton in 1992 saw another generational shift from Kennedy's generation to generation IX, the baby-boomer generation. While this shift took place at the national level of government, it was slow to occur within the Republican Party. Despite Clinton's victory in 1992, the Republican Party's candidate for the presidency in 1996, Bob Dole, was a member of generation VIII. The defeat of Dole in 1996 signified the defeat of generation VIII. The baby boomers were now in full control of the country, including the Democratic and Republican parties. In 2000, both the major parties nominated candidates who belonged to generation IX.

The nomination and subsequent election of George W. Bush, gave the neocons the opportunity they had been waiting for, the chance to become the architects of U.S. foreign policy. The generational torch had finally been passed from the Cold Warriors to them; yet, there was nothing new about them. They espoused the same ideas—American hegemony (Pax Americana)—as the Cold Warriors who had preceded them.

Initially, George W. Bush did not show an active interest in world affairs. His main interest was domestic policy. He wanted to implement a 15 percent tax cut. President Bush II's lack of interest in foreign policy could be witnessed by his initial refusal to appoint special envoys to global "hot spots" such as the Middle East and the Balkans like President Clinton had done. Furthermore, the neoisolationist views of Bush could also be witnessed by his failure to act as the threat to the United States from al-Qaeda grew. On August 6, 2001, Bush received a memo, "Bin Laden Determined to Strike in the U.S." The memo stated the following:

> FBI information ... indicated patterns of suspicious activity in this country consistent with preparations for hijackings or other types of attacks, including recent surveillance of federal buildings in New York.[3]

Perhaps no other event was as responsible for turning George W. Bush around and getting him more involved in foreign policy matters than the tragic events of 9/11. Thus, by the time of his second inauguration, Bush was a converted neocon. In his second inaugural address, he stated:

> So it is the policy of the United States to seek and support the growth of democratic movements and institutions in every nation and culture, with the ultimate goal of ending tyranny in our world.[4]

Bush was putting the world on notice that the neocons were firmly in control of his administration, and he shared their views. The term neocon (new conservative) implies that they are the creators of a new school of thought. On the contrary, there is nothing new about their ideology. The neocons are simply a new generation of right-wing Republicans who seek to impose their ideas and values—Pax Americana—on the world.

Despite giving lip service to the preservation of human rights, this was not a priority for the neocon. Nevertheless, the theme of democracy and human rights was a recurring one echoed by Bush and the prominent neocons in his foreign policy team. President Bush II spoke out against the massive human rights violations and atrocities in Sudan. Bush stated:

> Some crimes are being committed today by the government of Sudan, which is waging a war against the country's traditionalist and Christian peoples. Some 2 million Sudanese have lost their lives; 4 million people have lost their home. Hospitals, schools, churches, and international relief stations have been bombarded over 18 years of Sudan's civil war.[5]

Respect for human rights and the rule of international law were themes evoked by Vice President Dick Cheney as well during the 2004 Vice Presidential Debate. Cheney said:

> We've got sanctions on Iran now, we may well go to the Security Council and ask for tougher sanctions if they don't live up to their obligations under the initial—International Atomic Energy Agency, a nonproliferation treaty.[6]

Upon analysis it quickly becomes apparent that the policies of the Bush II administration were out of sync with its rhetoric. Despite the professed emphasis on human rights and international law, the Bush administration was selective in defending human rights and in enforcing international law. This could be observed by comparing the words of the Bush administration to its deeds. Moreover, the rhetoric of the Bush II administration served as a shield to hide the true motives of the neocons. They wanted to impose their values on the rest of the world.

The neocons appeared to be compassionate conservatives. George W. Bush spoke out against the atrocities in Sudan. Proof of atrocities in Sudan was provided by a UN report that noted that crimes against humanity had been committed in Darfur.[7] Despite this fact,

President Bush II never attempted to use the sword or the shield of the United States to stop or prevent these heinous acts. Unlike his father, President Bush II showed contempt for the United Nations. Instead of building an international consensus, he attacked Iraq. First, he tried to link the invasion to 9/11. *The Report of the 9/11 Commission* clearly showed that there was no link between Saddam Hussein and the tragic events of 9/11. Bush also attempted to base the invasion on Iraq's possession of Weapons of Mass Destruction (WMD). However, Iraq had no WMD. Subsequently, the administration shifted its rationale for the invasion to Saddam Hussein's violation of human rights. Bush's adherence to the enforcement of human rights and international law was selective. In fact, when Kofi Annan was the secretary-general of the United Nations, he said that the U.S. invasion of Iraq was illegal and that it constituted a violation of the UN Charter.[8]

It is unfortunate that in the post–Cold War era U.S. foreign policy is not based on the preservation of human rights. The administration of George W. Bush focused on global domination and perceived threats from Iraq, Iran, North Korea, and Syria (the Axis of Evil), while tolerating genocide in Sudan. Alas, the combination of the ascendancy of the neocons and a neoisolationist public resulted in a U.S. foreign policy that failed to enforce human rights.

The United States will be in a better position to enforce human rights when it awakens from its neoisolationist slumber and when those who value human rights are in ascendancy. It is ironic that the United States did not defend the very principles that its government was founded upon. Ultimately, the international preservation of human rights and the prevention of genocide depend on the prevailing political attitude in the United States and the values emphasized by its leaders.

Chapter 3

Politics Gets in the Way

The perpetrators of genocide often get off because politics gets in the way. At the end of the movie *Judgment at Nuremberg,* the epilogue notes:

> The Nuremberg trials held in the American zone ended July 14, 1949. There were ninety-nine defendants sentenced to prison terms. [By 1961,] not one was still serving his sentence.[1]

The movie is a fictionalized account of the Judges' Trial that took place in 1947. Nevertheless, what is stated in the epilogue was true. The United States wanted to gain the cooperation and the support of the people of West Germany when the Soviet Union blockaded West Berlin during the Cold War. In other words, many who were guilty of genocide were set free and acts of genocide were forgotten, because the United States wanted to forget about the past and focus on the present. This has happened repeatedly in recent years. Such acts help to perpetuate genocide because they disconnect the present from the past. Therefore, the lessons that should be learned from history are forgotten. History itself is deemed unimportant and as a result genocide keeps occurring.

In recent years Serbia has failed to cooperate with international authorities by refusing to extradite Radovan Karadzic and Radko Mladac. Karadzic was the civilian leader of the Bosnian Serbs during the Bosnian Civil War. And Mladac was the leader of the Bosnian Serbs' armed resistance; he was personally responsible for the execution of 8,000 men and boys in Srebrenica. Yet, Serbia faced no international sanctions for harboring perpetuators of genocide.

The United States wanted the cooperation of Serbia, so negotiations regarding Kosovo's independence could proceed.

President Bush II refrained from taking military action against Sudan, even though he acknowledged that its rulers committed genocide because the Sudanese government was cooperating in the War on Terrorism. Also, the Bush II administration offered to normalize relations with Sudan if it ended genocide in Darfur and held elections. In other words, the Bush II administration was willing to let bygones be bygones with a genocidal regime. The genocide in Darfur needs to be remembered and the guilty punished. However, the Bush administration's proposal ignored the victims and let the guilty go free. It was illogical and naïve. Once genocide is committed, genocidal regimes do not morph into democracies. Hitler was elected the chancellor of Germany but once genocide began, democracy ended. Similarly, Slobodan Milosevic was elected the president of Serbia but once genocide commenced, there was no democracy. History teaches us that genocidists have to be stopped by military force.[2] There is no case of their giving up their prey voluntarily. Genocidists are not democrats. They destroy democracy and do not create it.

Letting the culprits who commit genocide go undermines international law. Genocide is a crime against humanity. Letting the guilty get away with it diminishes the severity of the crimes and therefore fails to deter such actions. When politics gets in the way, the victims of genocide are forgotten. When those who commit genocide are pardoned, an implicit message is sent that genocide is not a serious crime. Thus, the penalty for genocide becomes akin to the penalty for stealing a car.

Genocide is being perpetuated today because politics gets in the way. As long as politics gets in the way, the victims of genocide will be forgotten and there will be no justice. When politics gets in the way, we cannot learn from the past or prevent genocide from occurring in the future. Politics needs to stop compromising justice.

Realism, an amoral policy, became the dominant influence on U.S. foreign policy during the Cold War and post–Cold War eras. As a result, human rights has taken a back seat to the "national interest" that all too often is defined in strategic or material terms. Realism has helped create an ugly reality, genocide, by stripping us of our humanity. Realism enables us to rationalize that others are not entitled to the same rights that we in the West enjoy because "they are different."

Part II

The Case Studies

Chapter 4

Rwanda, the United States, and Genocide

In 1994, the beautiful green hills of Rwanda were transformed into a killing field. Within the span of four months, one million people were killed. Many of them were hacked to death with machetes. This was one of the greatest tragedies the world had seen since World War II. Yet, America's weak and inadequate response is unexplainable.

Why did the United States not intervene to stop the killing and mass destruction? This is an important question since there were ample warnings that genocide was going to occur. The answer to this question is quite simple. The domestic political situation in the United States was a major reason for its inaction. Also, the United States is not ready to meet the demands and challenges of the post–Cold War era. Psychologically it is still stuck in a Cold War frame of mind where its national interest is narrowly defined. Another important factor is that Americans do not relate culturally to many of the peoples of the world. As a result, the United States is not able to respond when a prompt response is needed.

The response of the United Nations to genocide in Rwanda was also pathetic. During the height of the crisis, the United Nations packed up and ran away. This was one of the most cowardly moments in the history of that great organization. However, the blame for this tragedy lies largely with the United States. The United Nations is limited financially and militarily in the endeavors it can engage in unless it has the cooperation of the United States. The cooperation of the United States is essential for the successful outcome of UN peacekeeping missions.[1] The effort to save Rwanda collapsed because U.S.

political leaders were not willing to take the necessary risk. Therefore, the screams of one million people for survival were ignored. The United Nations, the United States, and the world tried to pretend that these were silent screams, but this tragedy will forever tarnish the reputation of the United Nations and the United States.

How could this happen at the dawn of the twenty-first century? After all, was the United Nations not created to prevent genocide from occurring? It is also surprising that genocide could occur in the post–World War II era since the Convention on the Prevention and Punishment for the Crime of Genocide was ratified by the international community in 1948. For the answers to these questions, we must look at Rwanda's history, the state of U.S. politics during the crisis, the U.S. media, and American culture.

Rwanda's history shows that a caste system developed among the Hutus and the Tutsi. The system was transformed into ethnic lines of identification during the colonial era, because the colonial authorities perpetuated the myth that the Tutsis were Hamitic descendants, while the Hutus were Bantus.

The growth of isolationism in the United States eliminated the use of force as an option, thereby preventing the United Nations from acting as an agency of collective security. The U.S. media also bears a great deal of the blame for the lack of an American response to the genocide in Rwanda. African affairs are often ignored by the U.S. news media. It seems that the only time that stories about Africa are reported by the U.S. news media is when there is a disaster. Therefore, the American public has scant knowledge of what is happening in Africa. And, when events are reported, they make it seem as if "tribal warfare" is the norm. Thus, the U.S. media implied that the genocide taking place in Rwanda was just another case of tribal warfare and did not require U.S. intervention. There is little cultural affinity between the United States and Africa, despite the fact that a significant percentage of its population is of African descent. As a result, little empathy exists for Africans and their plight in the United States. This has worked to the detriment of Africa—especially Rwanda.

THE MYTH OF RWANDAN HISTORY

According to some accounts of Rwandan history, its ethnic divisions can be traced back to the fifteenth century when Tutsi cattle breeders conquered the indigenous Hutu farmers.[2] The Tutsi were said to be of Hamitic origin. The myth of Tutsi and Hutu origins was perpetuated during the colonial days, first by the Germans and then by the

Belgians.[3] John Hanning Spike helped to create this myth. Others joined in and helped to disseminate it.[4]

When the Germans colonized Rwanda in 1899, they noticed differences between the Hutu and the Tutsi. The Hutu majority who tilled the soil were considered to be of standard Bantu stock since they seemed to resemble people from the surrounding areas of East Africa. However, the Tutsi seemed remarkably different. These cattle herders appeared to be tall, thin, and have narrow faces. Therefore, the Hutu were viewed as typical "Negroes." On the other hand, the Tutsi were viewed as a cut above the rest of the Bantu in the area. "The [Tutsi] … were … designated … 'white coloureds' who represented a 'missing link' between the 'Whites' and the 'Blacks.'"[5] As a result, there was a distinct difference in the way the Tutsi and the Hutu were treated by the colonial authorities. The Tutsi were treated as the superior tribal group and the Hutu were treated as the inferior tribal group.

Germany was defeated during World War I and had to forfeit its colonies. The League of Nations therefore awarded control of Rwanda to Belgium. The Belgians followed the lead of the Germans by also classifying the Hutu and Tutsi as separate ethnic groups, but the Belgians took the process one step further.

> the Belgians … reorganized customary relations between the Tutsi lords and Hutu serfs by introducing chiefdoms and sub-chiefdoms to reinforce Tutsi domination. These administrative reforms, which took place during the 1930s, were used to depose most of the Hutu chiefs. The result was that in 1959, 43 of the 45 chiefdoms and 549 of the 559 sub-chiefdoms were under the control of Tutsis. It was at this time that identity cards were progressively introduced.[6]

How one was categorized determined one's fate. The Tutsi were the chosen ones and given respect, social status, and social benefits. They were the ones allowed by the Belgians to have access to education, and as a result, the Tutsis were in a position to get better jobs.

There was a more subtle purpose behind the Belgians singling out the Tutsis for special favors as well. This policy created a rift behind the Hutu and the Tutsi, thereby preventing a united effort against the European encroachers. It was simply the old policy of "divide and conquer." Ethnicity was simply a way to drive a wedge between the two groups. This policy worked well.

In reality, the Hutu and the Tutsi are not separate ethnic groups in the traditional sense of the word. An ethnic group, or the pejorative term "tribe," usually refers to a group of people who have a common history, speak the same language, share elements of the same religion, have a common myth of origin, and have a sense of belonging among themselves. The two groups share too many similar traits to be classified as separate ethnic groups. The Hutu and the Tutsi speak the same language (Kinyarwanda), live in the same area, intermarry, belong to the same clan, and follow the same traditions. To a great extent, Hutus and Tutsis are separate castes rather than separate ethnic groups.

> Classification by the colonial authorities into one group or the other was often arbitrary.
>
> So it was that German, and later Belgian colonizers developed a system of categories for different "tribes" that was largely a function of aesthetic impressions. Individuals were categorized as Hutu or Tutsi according to their degree of beauty, their pride, intelligence and political organization.[7]

It was also possible for a Hutu to be reclassified as a Tutsi if he acquired more cattle.[8] However, these categorizations would ultimately have far-reaching results. It created a sense of separateness between the groups. And, the separate identities that were created during the colonial days would ultimately be the central source of division that would tear the beautiful country of Rwanda apart.

Tutsi dominance of Rwanda endured as long as the Hutu acquiesced, but the social system that was implanted in Rwanda by the Germans and Belgians was due to erode over time as the Hutus began to close the social gap on the more privileged Tutsis. As more Hutus gained access to education and technology, they began to wonder why people who spoke their language and shared their culture were permitted to dominate them. By the 1950s, Tutsi dominance that had been perpetuated by the Belgians seemed unjustifiable and intolerable to the Hutus. In 1959, the Hutu majority rebelled against Tutsi domination and overthrew it. Now, the Hutu were dominant and 20,000 Tutsis were killed and 150,000 went into exile in neighboring countries.[9] It is ironic that such large-scale violence would occur between two groups who were so culturally similar, but the seeds of destruction were sown by the colonizers—the outsiders. The European colonizers were successful in getting the Hutus and the Tutsis to believe the Hamitic myth of separate origins, even though both groups were indigenous to Rwanda. The Hutus came to view the Tutsis as outsiders, even more so than the Belgians and made them the objects of their frustration. Hutus and Tutsis became separate ethnic groups because they were told they were, and believed the lie. Animosity became the main characteristic of the relationship between the Hutus and the Tutsis when Rwanda gained its independence in 1962.

The tense relationship between the two groups was coupled by economic hard times in the late 1980s and early 1990s. In 1987, Rwanda had to implement an austerity program (structural adjustment) to secure a loan from the International Monetary Fund (IMF). More economic damage was inflicted on Rwanda's economy when the price of coffee fell and the government devaluated its currency by 50 per cent in 1990. This was followed by another currency devaluation in 1992. In addition, not enough land had been allocated for the production of food in Rwanda. As a result, competition for land and other scarce resources was exacerbated between the two groups because of the country's economic problems. Therefore, Hutus opposed to sharing power with the Tutsis used the death of President Juvenal Habyariman as an excuse to wipe out the Tutsis so they could retain power.

The Rwandan Genocide

On April 6, 1994, an aircraft carrying President Juvenal Habyariman of Rwanda and President Cyprien Ntariyamira of Burundi was shot down over Kagali, Rwanda. This event started the chain of events that led to genocide in Rwanda. The resulting slaughter that took place in Rwanda was appalling. Killing on such a massive scale had not occurred since World War II. Nevertheless, the United States did nothing to stop it. In fact, the Clinton administration went out of its way to make sure that the United Nations did not intervene as well.

The slaughter in Rwanda was not the result of an uncontrollable emotional outburst due to the assassination of President Habyariman by the Tutsis. In most cases the killing was premeditated. Orders were passed down from government ministers to the prefects, then to the burgomasters who scheduled meetings with the masses to plan attacks against Tutsis.

> The military and the militia brought essential skills and firearms to the slaughter, but they were too few to kill on a massive scale in a short span of time. Executing an extermination campaign rapidly required the mobilization of hundreds of thousands of ordinary people, tens of thousands to actually slaughter and the others to spy, search, guard, burn, and pillage.[10]

Most of the ordinary people who participated in the slaughter were not acting on a spontaneous basis. They were impoverished and lived in a densely populated state. Genocide represented an opportunity for the Hutus to better themselves economically. It was an opportunity to seize Tutsi land and property such as cattle. Some also engaged in the killing as a form of self-defense.

> In person and on the radio, Shingiro Mbonyumutwa of the MRD-Power, son of the president of the first Rwandan Republic, used his considerable prestige to whip up fear and hatred of the Tutsi. In a use of the now-familiar "accusation in the mirror," he told a Rwandan Radio listener that Tutsi intended to carry out genocide against the Hutu: They are going to exterminate, exterminate, exterminate, exterminate [ugutse-mbatsemba-tsembatsemba]. They are going to exterminate you until they are the only ones left in this country, so that the power which their fathers kept for four hundred years, they can keep for a thousand years.[11]

The Hutus who believed this fictitious appeal believed that it was simply a matter of "kill or be killed" by the Tutsis. So, they launched preemptive attacks that they believed were acts of self defense. Yet, others who engaged in the genocide did so out of peer pressure. They were required by their burgomasters to participate in "civilian self-defense." Those who refused to participate would be threatened with death, violence, and the destruction of their property. And, burgomasters often rewarded those who participated.

> They also offered powerful incentives to draw the hesitant into killing. They or others solicited by them provided cash payments, food, drink, and in some cases, marijuana to assailants.[12]

Many who were killed during the genocide were hacked to death with a machete. This is a slow and tedious process. The perpetuator of such a heinous crime has plenty of time to think about what he is doing. These were not spontaneous acts. They were deliberate. They were premeditated. This makes it perplexing why the United States and the United Nations did not take prompt action.

THE CLINTON ADMINISTRATION AND RWANDA

Genocide is defined as "the systematic killing of, or program of action intended to destroy a whole national or ethnic group."[13] After World War II, an international consensus developed that genocide was a "crime against humanity." This was a crime that the international community was no longer willing to tolerate. When genocide occurred in Rwanda in 1994, the Clinton administration sought to limit the involvement of the United States and the United Nations. The actions of the Clinton administration—at first glance—are hard to explain. Undoubtedly, there are racial and cultural gaps between the United States and Africa, despite the fact that the United States has a significant population that is of African descent. William Jefferson Clinton was close to the United States' African American community. He was often called "America's first black president." The fact that genocide in Rwanda occurred under his watch is all the more shocking, but occur it did. The failure of the United States to prevent genocide in Rwanda is far-reaching, but President Clinton must bear part of the blame, though not all of it.

When Bill Clinton campaigned for the presidency in 1992, he supported a standing army for the United Nations. He envisioned the United Nations as the primary vehicle for crisis intervention. But, as Ali Mazrui has pointed out, there is often a gap between what one professes before one enters office and the actions one takes after entering office.[14] Before one assumes office, one often focuses on policy goals, but after one assumes office, one's main focus is often on retaining power. After Bill Clinton became the president, he sought to restrain the actions of the United Nations and effectively prevented it from intervening in Rwanda. The reasons for this turnabout will be explained below.

On April 12, 1994, President Clinton sent a letter to Congressional leaders, informing them about the evacuation of Americans from Rwanda and Burundi.

> During April 9–10, 275 Marines were airlifted via C-130 aircraft to Bujumbra, Burundi. (A total of 328 U.S. Armed Forces personnel deployed to Burundi, including aircrews.) Their mission was to be in position to link up with American citizens moving from Rwanda to Burundi via overland convoy and to be prepared to proceed to the Rwandan capital of Kagali to assist with their departure, if necessary. On April 9–10, American citizens proceeded to leave Rwanda by several overland convoys to Bujumbura and by other routes. Approximately 240 U.S. citizens were evacuated from Rwanda. Most were then flown by U.S. C-141 aircraft to Nairobi, Kenya. Approximately 21 citizens chose to remain in Rwanda for various reasons. It did not become necessary for the United States to enter Rwanda. (United States C-5 aircraft also airlifted Belgian military forces and equipment into Nairobi to assist Belgian efforts in support of their citizens.) I am

> pleased to report that these operations were successful, that no hostilities were encountered and that no casualties were suffered by U.S. forces in operation. I took these actions pursuant to my constitutional authority to conduct foreign relations and as Commander-in-Chief.[15]

The right of President Clinton to evacuate U.S. citizens from Rwanda is not in question. As his letter stated, he was duty-bound to look after their well-being. Nevertheless, he failed to look after the well-being of the people of Rwanda. The United States did not make an attempt to save their lives. This was a sharp contrast to the efforts of the Swiss and the Belgians who saved hundreds of Tutsi and Hutu politicians, human rights activists, clergy, and other leading citizens of Rwanda.[16] It seemed that Rwandan lives did not matter to the United States.

The president's contradictory actions were also bewildering. He called for action to be taken to end the violence in Rwanda, but he himself was unwilling to take action. In a radio address on April 30, 1994, President Clinton stated:

> I call on the Rwandan army and the Rwandan Patriotic Front to agree to an immediate cease-fire and return to negotiations aimed at a lasting peace in their country.[17]

Closer examination of the ongoing events reveals some answers.

THE UNITED STATES AND THE UNITED NATIONS

President Clinton's lack of responsiveness to the crisis in Rwanda is linked to U.S. action in Somalia. In December 1992, President Bush I committed troops to the United Nations' operation in Somalia, when the Somalian government collapsed. Operation Restore Hope was the United States' contribution to the effort to restore order to Somalia, but that noble gesture collapsed when President Clinton, following the lead of UN Secretary-General Boutros Boutros-Ghali, blamed General Muhammad Farah Aidid for the continuing violence in Somalia. U.S. and UN forces attempted to capture General Aidid. As a result, U.S. forces came under attack, and the American public watched their television sets in anger, as the body of a dead U.S. soldier was dragged through the streets of Mogadishu. This led to the withdrawal of all U.S. forces from Somalia in March 1994. President Clinton was widely criticized for what happened in Somalia. Therefore, he was not ready to make a commitment to another peacekeeping mission in Africa when genocide occurred in Rwanda. Moreover, his health care initiative had collapsed in Congress the previous fall, and public opinion polls showed that President Clinton had a low approval rating with the American public. His job approval rating was 42 percent in April 1994.[18] This was borne out when the Republicans captured both Houses of Congress—an event that had not happened since the Eisenhower administration—during the fall elections of 1994. The president was in a position of political weakness. Once the genocide began, the United Nations decided to withdraw its forces from Rwanda rather than to stay and to stop it. According to Paragraph 17 of the United Nations Assistance Mission for Rwanda (UNAMIR) mandate:

> the force was "morally and legally obligated to use all available means to halt ethnically or politically motivated acts" and that it "will take the necessary action to prevent crimes against humanity."[19]

Nevertheless, the United States supported the withdrawal of UNAMIR. On April 21, 1994, Resolution 912 was introduced in the Security Council; it reduced UN forces from 2,500 to 270. The resolution stated:

> Appalled at the ensuing large-scale violence in Rwanda, which has resulted in the death of thousands of innocent civilians, including women and children, the displacement of a significant number of the Rwandese population, including those who sought refuge with UNAMIR, and the significant increase in refugees to neighboring countries.[20]

The United States and the United Nations acknowledged the death and destruction in Rwanda, but were not willing to act to defend the victims of these inhumane acts. They were, in effect, abandoning the people of Rwanda to their fate, genocide. It was time to act, and there was no action. From April 28–29, 1994, 250,000 refugees from Rwanda flooded Tanzania. The misery in Rwanda was now unbearable. Ironically, on April 27, 1994, the Security Council approved Resolution 914 that expanded the peacekeeping force in Bosnia. To paraphrase George Orwell, all are equal but apparently some are more equal than others.

Radio Mille Collins, the Hutu-controlled radio station, called out for the perpetrators of genocide to complete their work. It carried messages that "the grave is half empty who will help us to fill it?"[21] General Romo Dallaire, the commander of the UN forces in Kagali, later said that with a contingent of 5,000 troops he could have saved 50,000 lives during the critical period between April 7, 1994, and April 21, 1994—instead the United Nations fled. This action was unprecedented.[22] The U.S. Department of Defense opposed intervention in Rwanda.[23] The events in Somalia were a nightmare for the U.S. military. It was apparent that the U.S. military did not want to get tied down in a country that it did not perceive as having any strategic importance and for which it lacked contingency plans. As far as the Pentagon was concerned, this looked like another Somalia, and it did not want to be part of another failed military mission.

On May 3, 1994, President Clinton signed Policy Decision Directive 25 (PDD 25). It indicated that the United States had to be more cautious in undertaking peacekeeping missions and that attention had to be paid to the cost of the missions. In addition, the directive stated that U.S. troops should serve under U.S. commanders and that U.S. participation in peacekeeping missions should be based on the condition of vital U.S. interests being at stake. PDD 25 also sought to reduce the United States' financial contributions to peacekeeping missions, by controlling the number of UN peacekeeping missions and the involvement of the U.S. military in those missions.[24] Leadership to halt genocide in Rwanda would not be forthcoming from the United States.

> The PDD trapped the U.N. in vicious circle: the United States would refuse any new deployment of U.N. Blue Helmets unless all the necessary conditions (logistical, financial, troop deployments, etc.) were fulfilled yet they could never be fulfilled *without* the active support of a superpower.[25]

PDD 25 effectively rendered the United Nations a useless institution.

On May 16, 1994, the Security Council passed Resolution 917 that provided for the deployment of 5,500 UN troops to police Kagali, the capital of Rwanda, and to protect refugees. The Clinton administration favored a smaller force.[26] Because of PDD 25, this resolution had no chance of succeeding. Only Ethiopia, Senegal, and Ghana agreed to provide forces. But what were such small nations to do on their own? They lacked the equipment to be effective. Therefore, they had to depend on other countries to provide the equipment they would need for the mission; however, the equipment was not forthcoming. Due to PDD 25, the United States was concerned about the scope and the cost of the mission, and the necessity for providing Ghana with fifty armored personnel carriers.[27] There was a high human cost for this delay—genocide in Rwanda continued. It was reported that 10,000 bodies drifted from the Kagera River into Lake Victoria in Uganda, and as many as 100 bodies an hour were washed ashore.[28] This created a health hazard for East Africa. Some of the killers offered their victims the opportunity to be executed with a bullet instead of being hacked to death with a machete if the victims would pay for the cost of the bullet.[29] According to one press report:

> Children are skewered on sticks. I saw a woman cut open from the tailbone. They have removed breasts and male genital organs.[30]

Rather than taking action, on May 17, 1994, the Security Council passed Resolution 918 condemning the killing in Rwanda. It stated:

> *Strongly condemning* the ongoing violence in Rwanda and particularly condemning the very numerous killings of civilians which have taken place in Rwanda and the impunity with which armed individuals have been able to operate and continue operating therein.[31]

However, the Security Council refrained from using the term genocide.[32] President Clinton and the members of his administration also refrained from using the term genocide as well.[33] Members of the United Nations and the Clinton administration refrained from using the term genocide for fear of invoking the Convention on the Prevention and Punishment of the Crime of Genocide. UN members are duty-bound to uphold it. Article I of the Convention states:

> The Contracting Parties confirm that genocide, whether committed in time of peace or in time of war, is a crime under international law which they undertake to prevent and punish.[34]

Article II states:

> In the present Convention, genocide means any of the following acts committed with intent to destroy, in whole or in part, a national, ethnical, racial, or religious group, as such:
>
> (a) Killing members of the group;
> (b) Causing serious bodily or mental harm to members of the group;
> (c) Deliberately inflicting on the group conditions of life calculated to bring about its physical destruction in whole or in part;
> (d) Imposing measures to prevent births within the group;
> (e) Forcibly transferring children of the group to another group.[35]

Article III of the Convention was also relevant. It states:

> The following acts shall be punishable:
>
> (a) Genocide;
> (b) Conspiracy to commit genocide;
> (c) Attempt to commit genocide;
> (d) Complicity in genocide.[36]

The term was apparently not used by the Clinton administration until the Tutsi-dominated Front Patriotique Rwandais (RPF) was on the verge of victory in the Rwandan conflict. On July 15, 1994, the U.S. Embassy in Rwanda was closed and the following statement issued:

> The United States cannot allow representatives of a regime that supports genocidal massacres to remain on our soil.[37]

Most of the fighting was now over, so it was apparently safe to come out of the closet and to acknowledge reality; genocide had occurred in Rwanda.

President Clinton emphasized dealing with the aftermath of the slaughter rather than intervention to deter or bring all hostilities to an end. To that end, he stated:

> we also know from not only the Somali experience but from what we read of the conflict between the Hutu and the Tutsis that there is a political and military element to this. So I think we can take the lessons we learned and perhaps do a better job over a longer period of time and perhaps head off the starvation and do those things which need to be done. I hope so.[38]

This action was aimed at giving aid and comfort to the survivors of genocide rather than at its prevention. Most of the slaughter was now over. The hundred days of terror that caused more than two million deaths and more than two million people to abandon their homes was now over. The United States had avoided a long-term military entanglement. The Pentagon avoided being embarrassed, but the cost was too high. The United States effectively sat on the sidelines when millions of lives were at stake. U.S. action could have made a difference and saved lives. But the United States failed to act. The hands of the Clinton administration were partially tied by public opinion, by

Congress, and by its own desire to avoid risk. U.S. involvement in a peacekeeping mission in Rwanda may have led to the downfall of the Clinton administration. This was a risk that no one in the administration was willing to take.

If the United States was unwilling to take action, France was prepared to do so after the collapse of a truce that had been negotiated between the Rwandan government and the RPF. On June 22, 1994, the UN Security Council passed Resolution 929. It endorsed French intervention in the war to provide humanitarian assistance and to provide order. The resolution stated:

> *stressing* the strict humanitarian character of this operation which shall be conducted in an impartial and neutral fashion, and shall not constitute an imposition force between the parties[39]

But the French had ulterior motives for intervening in Rwanda. It was not to protect the lives of the people of Rwanda. It was to preserve France's "national interest." The French government launched Operation Turquoise, and deployed its troops in the western part of Rwanda. French troops first entered Cyangugu. The French eventually established a base six miles from the advancing Tutsi-led RPF forces. They manned their position with Foreign Legionnaires and heavy artillery.[40] France was, in effect, protecting a region that contained Rwandan government forces. It had intervened in the war on the side of the Rwandan government—a government that it had armed and supported over the years.[41] It did not seem to matter to the United States or to the world that it had been deceived by France and that France was trying to save a government that committed genocide. An honest broker was needed to mediate the crisis to bring the hostilities in Rwanda to an end, but one could not be found. France failed and the forces of the RPF marched on to victory, thus bringing the slaughter in Rwanda to an end, but the toll was heavy on Rwanda, the United States, and the world.

These events proved that the signatures on the many documents to preserve human rights and human dignity were now nothing more than hollow promises that went unfulfilled for the people of Rwanda and that would not be fulfilled in the future for any African country. The world that was dreamed of after World War II did not exist, and had turned into a nightmare, for the United States had now entered a deep slumber and did not want to be awakened.

THE CONGRESS

One of the main impediments to the United States taking action during the crisis in Rwanda was the U.S. Congress. Since the Vietnam War, Congress has played a larger role in U.S. foreign policy. This has not always benefited the United States, its neighbors, or the world community at large. It has often delayed the decision-making process during a crisis—especially when non-American lives are at stake. During the crisis in Rwanda, the U.S. government was constrained by a number of factors. First, the Democratic-controlled Congress was in no mood to engage in bold foreign policy moves in an election year. Second, the Cold War had ended. Many in Congress, especially right-wing Republicans, had not adjusted their foreign policy lenses. Beyond winning the Cold War, many conservative members of Congress saw no need for the United States to become entangled in events beyond their country's borders. Inertia had descended upon them. The world was moving in one direction, one of increased ethnic conflicts, and they stayed in their Cold Warrior mode. As a result, Congress was beset by deadlock. Congress is an institution that operates by consensus. Where there is no consensus, there is no action. This was to be the undoing of the people of Rwanda. No help was to arrive from the United States to save their lives.

In January 1994, it became apparent that the Republicans in Congress were going to make the foreign policy arena a political battleground. Representative Henry Hyde, who would later become one of President Clinton's chief nemeses during his impeachment proceedings, attempted to introduce the Peace Powers Act of 1994. This bill sought to limit the role of the United States in UN peacekeeping missions. Representative Hyde set out to tie Clinton's hands. In a speech before the House of Representatives, Hyde stated:

> Mr. Speaker, with the Clinton administration's active support, the United Nations has undertaken to expand traditional international peacekeeping in new and troubling ways. Under the rubric of "assertive multilateralism"—and with little real consultation with Congress—the Clinton administration and the United Nations took a successful humanitarian operation in Somalia and expanded it into an ill-conceived nation-building experiment that has turned to disaster resulting in the loss of nearly 30 American lives.[42]

It was obvious that a faction within the Republican Party was out to get Clinton. His job approval rating was on the decline. President Clinton was elected to fix the U.S. economy. And, before his inauguration, Clinton's support among the American people began to swell. However, during his second week in office, he signed an executive order that caused a great deal of controversy. It instituted the policy "don't ask, don't tell," allowing gays to serve in the U.S. military forces. As a result, Clinton's support among the American people began to decline. Many of his supporters felt betrayed because he did not deal with economic matters first. This wounded him politically. Also, his universal health care initiative subsequently failed. This meant that he did not deliver on one of the key promises that he had made during the 1992 presidential campaign. Therefore, the public was questioning his leadership abilities. In addition, the fiasco in Somalia seemed to confirm the negative image of Clinton that he was a weak leader, building in the minds of many Americans. At this point in his administration, it appeared that Clinton was headed for a one-term presidency.

The Republicans in Congress sought to limit Clinton to one term by withholding their support so that he would not be reelected. To achieve that end, the Republicans in Congress set out to deny him any foreign or domestic policy victories. Therefore, they sought to withhold their support by tying the President's hands, even during a critical period when genocide was in progress. Senator Dole of Kansas, the Senate minority leader who would later run against Clinton for the presidency in 1996, introduced the Peace Powers Resolution in the Senate as well. The resolution called for the imposition of the following measures to curtail U.S. involvement in UN peacekeeping operations:

1. No U.S. troops under foreign command.
2. No U.S. forces could be committed to a U.N. army without Congressional approval.
3. Congress had to be included in "the loop" before the U.S. cast its vote on peacekeeping.
4. Truth in budgeting for U.N. peacekeeping.
5. Bringing accountability to the U.N. process. (An independent inspector general).
6. The U.N. must give the U.S. credit for U.S. non-cash or in-kind contributions (e.g. personnel, transport, and equipment).[43]

The Act also called for the United States to stop providing the United Nations with intelligence information and for U.S. companies to have access to peacekeeping contracts.[44]

It was ironic that Republicans cheered the foreign policy adventures of the Reagan and Bush administrations, yet they sought to hamstring the Clinton administration. The reasons for this paradox are twofold. First, some of the Republicans in Congress, like Hyde, were obviously going after Clinton for political reasons. House Republicans were extremely partisan. This was apparent early on in the Clinton administration, when every Republican in that chamber refused to vote for the president's deficit reduction plan.

Yet, there were other Republicans in the Senate who seemed to have other motivations for tying President Clinton's hands. Many were veterans of the Cold War. For over fifty years their lives had evolved around the Cold War and Europe. The frost of animosity between the United States and the Soviet Union began to melt during the Gorbachev years. Then, on December 25, 1991, the Soviet Union's flag over the Kremlin was lowered for the last time, never to be raised again. The Cold War, which had been the focal point of U.S. foreign policy, was finally over. With the collapse of the Soviet Union in the early 1990s, nothing else seemed important to them. Now that victory had been achieved, and the nation was secure against a nuclear attack, everything else seemed minor and did not seem to matter as much. These Republicans suffered from a form of political inertia. Once the Cold War ended, they failed to adjust their vision to the new reality facing the world—genocide. Ethnic conflicts had become a dominant factor in international politics by the 1990s, but old guard Republicans did not view these conflicts as important because they did not meet their Cold War definition of what constituted the national interest.

Dole also had other ulterior motives. He was attempting to deny the administration any honeymoon period so he could make a bid for the presidency himself. After Clinton had been in office for only a few weeks, Dole, the Senate minority leader, successfully filibustered the president's $16.2 billion economic stimulus plan. It was obvious that the lack of cooperation was politically motivated. A group of Republicans in the House of Representatives attacked Clinton for his inaction on Rwanda. One of the leaders of this group was Representative John L. Mica of Florida's Second District. On May 18, 1994, he stated:

> Mr. Speaker, as history records this past month, unfortunately it will recall another sad chapter in President Clinton's foreign policy.
>
> I am not talking about Bosnia, Haiti, North Korea, or China, I am speaking about Rwanda.
>
> This time the United States failed to act to avert a genocide of our time. This administration not only ignored the wholesale slaughter in Rwanda, it delayed action on creating an international force and allowed the killing to continue.[45]

At first glance, Representative Mica's remarks appear to be on target. The Clinton administration did not take prompt action when genocide occurred in Rwanda. However, Representative Mica never called for any specific action to be taken on behalf of the victims of genocide in Rwanda. Mica was merely engaging in political posturing. Other Republicans in the House of Representatives made similar comments. Representative Connie Morella of Maryland had the following comments placed in the *Congressional Record* to express support for a joint resolution commemorating the fiftieth anniversary of World War II. It stated:

> THE AMERICAN INVOLVEMENT IN WORLD WAR II WAS SUPPORTED BY THE COUNTRY. AS A NATION, WE COULD NOT TOLERATE THE HEINOUS MASSACRE OF MILLIONS AND THE DISSOLUTIONS OF PERSONAL FREEDOM. WARS, TODAY, DO NOT APPEAR TO BE AS CLEARLY GOOD OR BAD, RIGHT OR WRONG AS WORLD WAR II. . . . WITHIN THE PAST FIVE YEARS WE HAVE WITNESSED. THE . . . TRAGIC SITUATION IN BOSNIA, IN SOMALIA, AND IN RWANDA.[46]

Representative Morella, unfortunately, was unable to relate the events of World War II to the crisis in Rwanda. The United States fought World War II because it was opposed to Hitler's concept that there was a master race and opposed genocide. Now, with these principles at stake in Rwanda, they were deemed to be something not worth defending. The lessons of World War II had been forgotten.

A greater sense of bipartisanism prevailed in the Senate than in the House of Representatives. There was a consensus that the genocide in Rwanda merited special attention and should be stopped, but that was as far as the consensus seemed to go. Senate Resolution S207 was introduced. It urged the United Nations and the Organization of African Unity (OAU) to continue their efforts to bring about a cease-fire, and urged President Clinton to continue his diplomatic efforts.[47] The Senate appeared to be divided into various factions. One group of liberal Democrats was headed by Senator Paul Simon of Illinois and Senator Edward Kennedy of Massachusetts. The Democrats expressed concern about the genocide that had occurred in Rwanda, and commended President Clinton for responding to the crisis by sending aid. Nevertheless, they felt that the United States and international agencies needed to do more to stop the genocide and to bring about a diplomatic solution. This was the message contained in the statement made by Senator Moyhihan of New York in the Senate on June 10, 1994. He said:

> I rise today to address matter of the utmost gravity, namely the genocide being committed even as we speak in Rwanda ...
>
> This is not conventional bloodletting ...
>
> The slaughter in Rwanda is continuing because the murderers have no fear of international retribution.
>
> Yes, the United Nations must live within its budget and its mandate. But there are areas where it should—indeed, must—act, and it needs the resources to do so.[48]

The moderate Republicans who formed part of this faction with the liberal Democrats expressed similar views. For instance, Senator Durenberger of Minnesota stated:

> I rise again today to emphasize the continuing need to take steps to assist the peacekeeping effort of the United Nations—and to reduce the suffering in Rwanda and the neighboring countries of Uganda, Tanzania, and Burundi to which thousands of refugees have fled.[49]

While this group advocated action, they did not demand unilateral military action on the part of the United States if the United Nations failed to deal adequately with the crisis. They favored multilateral diplomatic action as a solution.

At first glance, one might not understand the division that had occurred in Congress. For years, conservative Republicans have been at the forefront of U.S. interventionism. They cheered the Reagan administration when it built up U.S. military forces and when Grenada and Panama were invaded. Now, they stood for political inaction. Why the contradiction? Right-wing Republicans do not object to the use of force, but, in the case of Rwanda, force would have to be used for a cause and a people who did not register on the right-wing agenda. Africa was only important to the right wing when groups within countries such as Angola, Namibia, or South Africa—that possesses minerals that the United States and its allies need—were flirting with the Soviet Union. Then, they felt U.S. involvement was justified because U.S. material interests were at stake. American aid to Africa diminished when the Cold War ended. Rwanda has no minerals and is not considered to be located in a strategic area. Therefore, in the eyes of the right wing, it had no value and was not worth the sacrifice of American lives. In general, the right gave more importance to Europe than to the Third World. Now, in the midst of one of the worst human tragedies since World War II, right-wing Republicans withheld their support, for they defined U.S. national interests in economic and strategic terms and not in human terms. It is ironic that this faction of the Republican Party that emphasized morality stood by in silence, and insisted that U.S. national interests were not at stake as one of the most immoral acts of the twentieth century was committed. Moreover, they wanted to expel Clinton from the presidency any way that they could. They were in a partisan mood and did not want to hand the president a foreign policy victory. Here was an issue that the conservatives could use to hem in Clinton.

As the crisis in Rwanda worsened, the bipartisan faction that consisted of liberal Democrats and moderate Republicans seemed to have grasped the magnitude of the events unfolding in Rwanda. They now felt that military action might be necessary to end the genocide in Rwanda; however, they did not want the United States to act unilaterally. The Democrats most likely felt an obligation to defer to the wishes of President Clinton, and the moderate Republicans most likely did not want to be viewed as backing the Clinton administration carte blanche.

Another reason for the weak U.S. response to the crisis in Rwanda was the lack of support for action among the American people. Many Americans had never heard of Rwanda until the crisis developed there. As the British journalist Simon Hoggard of the *Guardian* wrote, "Rwandans are thousands of miles away. Nobody you know has even been on holiday to Rwanda. And Rwandans don't look like us."[50] Rwanda is thousands of miles away from the United States, but psychologically it is light years away from the average American. Even though America's history is intertwined with Africa's and a significant percentage of its population is of African descent, Africa has remained on the periphery of U.S. foreign policy. On April 22, 1994, during a National Security Council meeting, President Clinton inquired if the Congressional Black Caucus had shown interest in Rwanda, and was informed that they had not.[51] Africa has received scant coverage in the U.S. media, therefore the average American does not feel a sense of connection with Africa. Most Americans were not able to relate to the people of Rwanda on a personal level, since their knowledge of Rwanda and its people was so scant.

In general, the people of the United States were also separated from the people of Rwanda by a racial divide due to the portrayal of African affairs by the U.S. media. Very often "tribal warfare" is portrayed as the norm. Stories in the *Los Angeles Times, New York Times, Washington Post*, and other leading newspapers around the country, portrayed the conflict as being "Hutu versus Tutsi." The U.S. media failed to explain to the American public that the Hutu and the Tutsi are not ethnic groups and that there was more at stake than a clash between rival ethnic groups or "tribes." More media coverage was focused on the death of Kurt Cobain, Paula Jones's accusations against President Clinton, and the indictment of O. J. Simpson for murder than the genocide that was occurring in Rwanda. But the U.S. press, like the U.S. president, was slow to use the term genocide, therefore the American public was not truly informed about the scope of the conflict. In effect, "tribal warfare" was portrayed as being pathological among Africans. Lack of familiarity with Rwanda among the American people created a psychological/racial divide that was never narrowed.

American culture and ideology were at odds with each other. American democratic ideology is based on dignity and respect for mankind, but American culture also fears that which is perceived as foreign, and therein lies the problem. America has an ongoing struggle with xenophobia. For the United States to be effective during a crisis, it will have to overcome this problem.

CONCLUSION

The United States slept as a tragedy unfolded in Rwanda. She slept as the world wondered where she had gone. The United States slept when her leadership was needed. She slept because her government was not willing to take action, and her people were not informed about the magnitude of the crisis that was taking place in Rwanda. This was a major failure of U.S. foreign policy. The United States was trapped by indifference and ignorance. The genocide in Rwanda could have been prevented if the United States had been willing and able to lead the world community. A cable from General Dallarie, the head of UNAMIR, warned that Rwanda was on the brink of genocide in January 1994. General Dallarie's cable stated:

> Principle aim of Interhame in the past was to protect Kigali from RPF. Since UNAMIR mandate [our informant] has been ordered to register all Tutsi in Kagali. He suspects it is for their extermination. Example he gave was that in 20 minutes his personnel could kill up to 1000 Tutsi.[52]

The Secretariat at the United Nations knew this but they sought to keep this information from the members of the Security Council, because they feared it might result in the Security Council abandoning Rwanda as it had abandoned Somalia.

The withholding of this information does not exonerate the United States. It was well aware of what was happening in Rwanda.

The CIA completed a study at the end of January 1994 that indicated that if violence erupted in Rwanda, half a million deaths could occur.[53] The United States provided no leadership when its leadership was needed the most.

The Republicans hemmed in President Clinton. Many seemed to resent him from the time he took office. The Republicans had occupied the presidency for the twelve years prior to Clinton's election. They withheld their support on crucial votes such as the president's deficit reduction proposal. The Republicans were not eager to hand the president political victories. He would have to fight for them. It was difficult, though not impossible, for President Clinton to fight for the lives of the people of Rwanda. The U.S. peacekeeping operation in Somalia ended in a fiasco. Many Americans watched their television sets in horror as the body of a dead American was dragged around the streets of Mogadishu, Somalia. Due to the humiliation that the United States had faced in Somalia, President Clinton was reluctant to get involved in Rwanda. Moreover, the Republicans in Congress were also eager to seize the opportunity to prevent Clinton from leading a successful military mission.

President Clinton did send large-scale aid to the refugee camps in the neighboring states, but it was too late. This was tantamount to addressing the matter after the fact. This did nothing to prevent or stop the slaughter that was unfolding in Rwanda. Perhaps this was the best that a politically weakened president who faced upcoming Congressional elections would be willing to do, but one would be hard pressed to explain this to the people of Rwanda. The American public also slept through the genocide in Rwanda, because they were unable to relate to the people of that country. There was a need to cross the cultural divide between the United States and Rwanda so that the American people would understand that the conflict was not "tribal warfare," as conflicts in Africa are often portrayed. This was something extraordinary in the history of mankind—this was genocide. The American public did not seem to grasp this until it was too late. This was not entirely their fault. One of the reasons that they did not understand what was going on was the way that the U.S. government dealt with the crisis. The Clinton administration refused to use the word genocide. This indicated that the matter was less than urgent. And the problem was also compounded by the way the tragedy was covered by the U.S. press. The American public was used to dealing with Africa with indifference, but now was the time when action was needed, but was not forthcoming. John F. Kennedy once wrote, "it takes time to change men's minds, and it takes violent shocks to change an entire nation's psychology."[54] The U.S. press never alerted the people of the United States of the magnitude of the crisis until it was too late. It failed to shock them so that they would wake up.

Some U.S. newspapers such as *The New York Times* gave extensive coverage to the events in Rwanda during the crisis. However, at no time did *The New York Times* or any other major U.S. newspaper call for U.S. intervention—unilateral intervention—when the situation began to deteriorate in Rwanda. Instead, the events that unfolded were viewed as a human tragedy of historic proportions.

As stated previously, U.S. foreign policy essentially failed in Rwanda. This was very ironic. U.S. foreign policy failed at a time when the United States seemed to be at the height of its power. The Soviet Union had collapsed. The United States faced no external threats of destruction. The U.S. economy was also showing new signs of life. The United States appeared to be strong militarily and economically. The awesome power of the United States was rendered useless by divisions and indecisiveness. Therefore, it was rendered useless during a time when it was needed the most.

The crisis in Rwanda also exposed the weakness of the United Nations. During a crisis, it is a weak and ineffective organization without the commitment of the United States. It is an organization that has done much to form international rules and norms, but it cannot take action to make those principles it stands for come to life without the cooperation of the United States, as demonstrated in this chapter and the following chapters.

The crisis in Rwanda also gave us insight about how international society operates. The human rights described in the UN Charter and the various conventions do not apply to Africans. That was the powerful message that was sent by international society as one million Rwandans were abandoned—they were deemed expendable people.

We should open our hearts and our minds to the peoples of the world. That way, when they are endangered, we can see their faces, hear their screams, and acknowledge their humanity. This will prevent genocide from occurring again.

CHAPTER 5

BOSNIA-HERZEGOVINA: THE KITTY GENOVESE OF THE BALKANS

This country is bleeding, and there is not much room for diplomatic hesitation.

—Letter from the Bosnian president, Izetbegovic, to the UN secretary-general, Boutros Boutros-Ghali

INTRODUCTION

Representative Steny H. Hoyer (Democrat-Maryland) saw a stark parallel between the indifference that Bosnia encountered from the international community and the murder of Kitty Genovese that occurred in the Kew Gardens section of Queens, New York, in 1964. Representative Hoyer said:

> it was almost 30 years ago that the cries for help and screams of agony of Kitty Genovese went unheeded by her neighbors as she was brutally slain outside her home. Of the 38 people who later admitted to hearing the young woman's pleas, not one called the police until after Kitty Genovese's 35 minute ordeal had ended, leaving her dead.
>
> According to the *New York Times* report, the murder of Kitty Genovese did not occur swiftly, but spanned more than half-an-hour. During that time, her attacker was twice interrupted by the sounds of neighbors' voices and the flash of apartment lights. Twice, the prospect that someone would come to Kitty Genovese's rescue caused the attacker to flee. But twice, the attacker returned when no neighbors, no police, no assistance actually materialized. Undeterred, Kitty's murderer returned

> a final time to finish what he had started, finding Kitty at the back of her building where she had crawled in hopes of finding safety. Tragically, there was no hope for Kitty Genovese and there, near dozens of her own neighbors, her killer delivered the final blow.
>
> Mr. Speaker, today Bosnia continues to struggle against the repeated assaults of Serbian and now Croatian forces just as Kitty Genovese battled against a senseless act of violence 30 years ago.[1]

The United States' behavior during the war in Bosnia, like the murder of Kitty Genovese, is hard to comprehend. The war began during the Bush I administration[2] and ended during the Clinton administration. It was a brutal war in which genocide, rape, and genital mutilation were common. At times, the United States seemed to do little more than engage in hand-wringing and haranguing about the brutality of the war, and seemed content to follow Europe's lead. This chapter will explain the United States' behavior during the war in Bosnia.

World War II and Lessons Unlearned

The war in Bosnia involved many of the principles that were at stake during World War II. It was about human rights, justice, and equality. Who is equal and who is not? However, the United States often acted with indifference to the war in Bosnia, because important lessons from World War II were forgotten.

During World War II great principles were at stake. World War II taught us that national interest is not solely defined in terms of material goods or strategic areas. World War II was a war against bigotry, racism, and genocide. It was also based on sovereign equality among nations and equality among people. These concepts are what led to the signing of the Atlantic Charter and the Convention on the Prevention and Punishment of the Crime of Genocide.

Another lesson learned from World War II is that it is not possible to appease a dictator. Hitler was appeased by forcing Czechoslovakia to cede the Sudetenland to Germany, and Neville Chamberlain proclaimed "peace in our time." It later became apparent that Hitler was not satisfied when he made another request for a part of Poland. By that time, the Allies realized that they had made a cardinal mistake. Similarly, the international community attempted to appease the dictatorships in Belgrade and Pale by carving up Bosnia in an attempt at appeasement, which did not work then, and does not work now.

World War II also taught us what can happen to a country when it encounters economic hardship. The harsh terms of the Peace

Treaty of Versailles led to the rise of Adolf Hitler. Yet, the lords of the International Monetary Fund (IMF) forgot this lesson. Their insistence that Yugoslavia embrace free market policies to make its economy more efficient wiped out many of Yugoslavia's social guarantees. This led to the economic disintegration of Yugoslavia and the rise of a demagogue, Slobodan Milosevic. The West, particularly the United States, bears some responsibility for this outcome, since it has the largest block of votes in the IMF.

World War II also weakened the concept of state sovereignty. After the war, trials in Nuremberg and Tokyo established that there were crimes that were so heinous that they were not protected by state sovereignty. The international community bore responsibility to prevent genocide, to end it, and to bring those responsible for it to justice. Nevertheless, the United States and its allies watched as genocide took place under the guise of "ethnic cleansing" in Bosnia, did little to prevent it, and waited three years before they made an effort to stop it. Initially, the United States simply adopted the position that it did not have any vital interest at stake in Yugoslavia. Secretary of State James Baker said, "We don't have a dog in that fight." Slobodan Milosevic and his cronies noted the actions of the United States, and soon realized that they could commit genocide without being sanctioned. Hence, the mass graves that were to dot the Bosnian countryside.

New World Order for a New Generation

The end of the Cold War changed the international system. Before the Cold War ended, there were two superpowers. But in December 1991, the flag of the Soviet Union was lowered from the Kremlin for the last time. Now, there was one superpower, the United States. With the end of the Cold War, the United States' national security concerns changed. During the Cold War, the United States went to unparalleled lengths to help Yugoslavia remain free from the Soviet Union. When the Cold War ended, Yugoslavia lost its political significance to the United States. In fact, the end of the Cold War brought on a state of neoisolationism for many Americans who viewed the Cold War as the United States' main foreign policy concern. When the Cold War ended, they felt the only reason for the United States to be involved in foreign affairs was to protect its economic interest. The neoisolationist had forgotten what it means to live up to the responsibility of being a superpower, and what happened prior to World War II when the United States attempted to withdraw from the problems of the world and found its safety and existence threatened. Isolationism cannot act as a substitute for a national security policy.

Another reason for the United States' timid approach was that a generational shift was taking place in the country. The election of William Jefferson Clinton as the president of the United States saw the passing of the torch from the World War II generation (generation VIII)[3] to the baby boom generation (generation IX).[4] World War II was a defining moment for generation VIII. This generation tended to be weary of appeasement, and tended to use World War II as a model of what could happen if firm policies were not adopted in the face of aggression. However, for generation IX, World War II is nothing more than a chapter in a history book. For them, the Vietnam War was the defining war. Generation IX was loath to become involved in a foreign war for fear of getting bogged down in a quagmire with no way out (the Vietnam syndrome). This thinking became prevalent in the Clinton administration and at the Pentagon. As a result, the Vietnam syndrome caused indecisiveness within the United States, helped to prolong the war in Bosnia, and resulted in many unnecessary deaths. Bosnia was not analogous to Vietnam.

FAILED PERCEPTION AND WESTERN PREJUDICE

The international community also failed to understand the conflict in Bosnia. In the United States, the conflict was viewed as an invasion of Bosnia by Serbia. In Europe, the war in Bosnia was viewed as a civil war. It was neither. Both failed to grasp the fundamental issues that were at stake in Bosnia. The conflict was the direct result of the disintegration of the Yugoslavian state. The state had provided economic and social guarantees. One guarantee was subsistence, but the state also protected cultural rights. One had the right to be a Macedonian, Slovenian, Croatian, Serb, Hungarian, Montenegrin, Albanian, and, later, even a Muslim. But with the disintegration of Tito's Yugoslavia, these guarantees no longer existed. Moreover, the problem was compounded by the rise of nationalism in the republics. Minorities in the various republics felt threatened, because no attempt was made to guarantee their rights as citizens. By emphasizing ethnicity, instead of civil liberties and civil rights, the international community helped to impose a system of apartheid on Bosnia, which was one of the most integrated parts of Yugoslavia earlier. This was a notable issue. It was almost as if the United States had forgotten its own struggle to achieve democracy. After the American Revolutionary War, James Madison wrote *Federalist Paper No. 10.* It stated the belief that democracy could not exist without the protection of minority rights, otherwise all one would have would be the tyranny of the majority. This is what existed in the former Yugoslav republics after the disintegration of the federal government. The issue at hand was the protection of individual rights and group identity, not tribal warfare. The United States did not take the lead in trying to rectify this situation. This would have enabled Bosnia to remain intact instead of being partitioned. It is ironic that the United States and its European allies wound up as the ultimate ethnic cleansers.

THE DISINTEGRATION OF YUGOSLAVIA AND THE MYTH OF HISTORY

The war in Bosnia did not have historic roots as many European and U.S. statesmen kept insisting. In fact, history shows us just the opposite. For over four hundred years there was peaceful coexistence between the various ethnic groups in Bosnia. Before the war, one-third of the marriages in Bosnia were between people from different cultural backgrounds.[5] In addition, every block of Sarajevo was integrated. The city was not divided into Muslim, Croat, or Serb sections. The myth of historical conflict was used as an excuse by leaders of the international community to justify a policy of neglect. The British prime minister John Major and other European leaders often made references to ancient rivalries. Americans were not immune from making similar errors. Retired Rear Admiral James W. (Bud) Nance said, "Why are we keeping peace? Let them fight. They have been fighting for a thousand years."[6]

Yugoslavia began to disintegrate, not because of historical rivalries inside the country, but because of external pressures. The austere policies imposed by the International Monetary Fund (IMF) and the end of the Cold War were greater factors in the disintegration of Yugoslavia than the pull of history.

THE FOUR YUGOSLAVIAS

Yugoslavia has essentially gone through four different phases during its brief existence. It was originally created after World War I as the Kingdom of the Serbs, Croats, and Slovenes. National self-determination was one of the forces behind World War I, but Yugoslavia did not benefit from it. The Balkan states were small, and their security was threatened by their neighbors. Therefore, Yugoslavia was created out of a need to provide for the security of small, weak states. Yugoslavia faced territorial threats from Italy, Bulgaria, and Hungary. The Italians wanted control of the Dalmatian coast and Albania. Bulgaria laid claim to Macedonia, and Hungary claimed Banat and a part of Croatia. Post–World War I Yugoslavia was also racked by internal feuds, and its economy collapsed with the decline in the demand for primary products during the Great Depression. As a result, Yugoslavia lapsed into a dictatorship. Democracy returned in 1935, but Yugoslavia's increased dependence on Germany and Italy for trade gave these countries undue influence. In 1941, Yugoslavia joined the Axis pact as a neutral country. When details of the pact were announced, Yugoslavia's army and air force units carried out a coup on March 27, 1941. Subsequently, Yugoslavia was attacked by Nazi Germany and its allies (Italy, Bulgaria, and Hungary).

Yugoslavia was then divided among the Axis powers. Northern Slovenia was annexed by Germany, while Italy occupied the rest of Slovenia, Herzegovina, southern Serbia, the Dalmatian coast, and Montenegro. Hungary annexed the region north of the Danube. Bulgaria finally got Macedonia as well as part of southern Serbia. The Ustashas, a pro-Nazi Croatian group, were allowed to set up their own independent state that consisted of Croatia, Bosnia, and part of Herzegovina. The flag of the Croatian fascist state included the *sahovnica*, Croatia's ancient red and white coat of arms. The fascist Croatian state engaged in the mass killing of Serbs and Jews.

Two resistance groups emerged in Yugoslavia. One was the Chetniks, who were loyal to the Yugoslav monarchy. The other resistance group was the Partisans, the Yugoslav communists. It was led by Josip Broz who was better known as Tito. The Partisans mainly operated in Serbia. The two groups maintained a modicum of cooperation, but they could not agree on the tactics to be used against the fascists. The Nazis punished civilians in towns and villages in retaliation for attacks by the guerrilla forces.[7] Therefore, the Chetniks chose to avoid direct confrontation with the enemy and relied more on sabotaging installations. This caused the Partisans to become suspicious of the Chetniks who were guilty, they felt, of collaborating with the Nazis. Tito continued his battle against the fascists, regardless of the consequences. This conflict eventually resulted in the Chetniks collaborating with the Italians and Germans.

Therefore, the Allies began to back the Partisans. Tito and his Partisan movement emerged from the war in firm control of Yugoslavia. Unlike the other "people's democracies" of Eastern Europe, Tito and his followers had not ridden to power on the back of the Red Army of the Soviet Union. They had liberated themselves from the fascists mainly by their own efforts.

The second Yugoslavia (1945–1980) was Tito's Yugoslavia. Josip Broz Tito was firmly in control of the state, and was unwilling to allow Yugoslavia to become a fiefdom of the Soviet Union, and, consequently, Yugoslavia was expelled from the Communist Information Bureau (Cominform) in 1948. Yugoslavia was able to maintain its territorial integrity, despite the onslaught of hundreds of border clashes with the Soviet Union's allies, because it turned to the West, particularly the United States, for help. From mid-1949 to mid-1955, Yugoslavia received $598.5 million in grants, loans, and sales. Yugoslavia also received $588.5 million in military assistance from the United States. Tito later became a leader of the Non-Aligned Movement (NAM), and someone whom the United States and its allies courted during the Cold War. This enabled Yugoslavia to survive its battle against the Soviet Union. The Cold War thus helped to contribute to Yugoslavia's security, and helped to maintain some internal cohesion in Yugoslavia as well.

The third Yugoslavia (1980–1991) was the communist, post-Tito Yugoslavia. It was governed by an eight-man presidency that consisted of representatives from the six republics and two autonomous regions in Serbia, Kosovo, and Vojvodina. However, Yugoslavia's relationship with the United States began to undergo some fundamental changes during this period. In 1985, Mikhail Sergeyevich Gorbachev became the secretary-general of the Communist Party of the Soviet Union. Gorbachev pursued a policy of glasnost, openness, and perestroika, the restructuring of the Soviet Union's economy. To accomplish these goals, Gorbachev needed the cooperation of the United States. Thus, there was a fundamental shift in the relationship between the two superpowers from confrontation to cooperation.

Ultimately, due to its debt and inability to provide for its citizens' needs, the Soviet Union collapsed. This fundamentally changed the international system. During the Cold War, countries such as Yugoslavia were able to play one superpower off against the other. Yugoslavia was located in the Soviet Union's sphere of influence—central Europe. The United States felt that an independent and unified Yugoslavia would give the other countries of Eastern Europe an incentive to shake themselves free from the grasp of the Soviet Union as well. Warmer relations between the superpowers diminished Yugoslavia's importance to the United States. Therefore, aid was not given as readily as it had been in the past. Yugoslavia no longer held strategic or ideological value for the United States. The Cold War had been won.

Yugoslavia was created to protect the southern Balkan region from the designs of Italy, Bulgaria, and Hungary. By the post-Tito era, these states no longer coveted Yugoslavia's territory, and the Soviet Union too was no longer a threat to Yugoslavia. This weakened the internal cohesion in Yugoslavia, and this too was an important factor in its disintegration.

Within Tito's Yugoslavia, the various constituent nations were accorded proportional distribution of government jobs, budgetary outlays, and cultural rights. Tito's government maintained the appearance of fairness among Yugoslavia's nations. If there was a show trial involving a member of one national group, show trials involving members of other national groups would soon follow. Thus, in Tito's Yugoslavia one had the right to be a Macedonian, Serb, Hungarian, Croat, Montenegrin, Muslim, Albanian, and a Slovenian. One's national identity was not suppressed—it was guaranteed by the state.

> The concept not only conferred language rights and psychological security about the survival of cultural community but also required that all federal activities (from appointments to public office such as army generals or the rotation of the prime minister to the distribution of federal investments and representation at cultural festivals) take directly into account the proportional representation of individuals by constituent nationality—called the national key (kljuc, or quota system).[8]

To ensure fairness, Tito also granted autonomy to Vojvodina in the northern region of Serbia that was inhabited by many ethnic Hungarians, and Kosovo, a province in the southern region of Serbia that was inhabited by ethnic Albanians under the 1974 Yugoslav constitution. And, to maintain the delicate balance among Yugoslavia's nations after his death, Tito created a rotating presidency where the eight different nations of Yugoslavia would be represented.

Tito's social guarantees began to be tested and slowly stripped away in the 1970s and 1980s, so much so that there would be nothing left of them by the 1990s. The Organization of Petroleum Exporting Countries (OPEC) price increases of the late 1970s hit Yugoslavia hard. From 1977–1980, OPEC increased the price of oil from $5 a barrel to $22 a barrel. This plunged Yugoslavia into debt.

> A second oil price rise occurred in 1978–79. Interest rates for U.S. dollars, in which Yugoslav debt was denominated, jumped into double digits. At the same time the country's borrowing from commercial banks at free market rates had reached 58 percent of total debt. Commercial banks lending to Eastern Europe nearly stopped altogether

> after 1978, and that trend was given political impetus in 1978–80 by the Polish crisis and the Soviet invasion of Afghanistan. For Yugoslavia, an economic crisis originating in the foreign sector could no longer be averted by minor adjustments. With seriously depleted foreign reserves, failing exports, and an increasingly intractable foreign debt of about $20 billion, the government had no choice but to focus all its attention on foreign liquidity.[9]

Yugoslavia had few alternatives, therefore it turned to the IMF to finance its foreign debt. The IMF often demands the implementation of austerity programs (structural adjustment) in return for assistance. The IMF is interested in the efficient distribution of resources, but the imposition of these programs often comes at the expense of political stability. IMF riots became common throughout the Third World in the late 1970s and 1980s.

The terms the IMF imposed on Yugoslavia were severe. The public was forced to bear the brunt of these economic reforms.

> For the population this meant austerity as the government sought every possible way to cut domestic consumption and squeeze foreign currency and exports out of the economy. Food subsidies were abandoned in 1982. Prices for gasoline and heating fuel, food, and transportation rose by one-third in 1983. All imports not critical to production were prohibited, including all consumer goods. Two currency devaluations and the decision to allow the currency to float cut the value of the dinar by 90 percent between 1979 and 1985.[10]

The country's economic restructuring was also required. Yugoslavia attempted to bolster its manufacturing industries where exports were lucrative. Slovenia and Croatia were the most prosperous republics, and they opposed efforts to take revenue from their regions to build factories in the less developed regions, such as Serbia, Macedonia, and Bosnia-Herzegovina. They wanted their revenues reinvested in their own regions.

Stripping away Yugoslavia's social guarantees also helped to tear it apart. The socialization process consists of acquired identities at various levels. One is indoctrinated into one's family, ethnic group, and community by acquiring language, customs, religion, myth of origin, social norms, gender roles, and other traditions. This often serves as one's core identity. From there, other social layers such as one's political identity are acquired. At this stage, one is indoctrinated into the political system by learning how it works and what one's role is to be in the system. The system sustains itself by providing its followers with benefits. However, as the Yugoslav economy began to deteriorate and the social safety net was removed, the various layers of its citizens' associations and loyalty began to be stripped away. The federal government's inability to provide for its people caused it to lose legitimacy. All that seemed to remain was the primordial loyalty of the people to their respective ethnic group, while loyalty to their government and fellow citizens from different ethnic groups melted away. This opened the door to nationalist demagogues such as Slobodan Milosevic. The seeds of Yugoslavia's destruction were thus sown by the resulting changes in the international environment, the harsh conditions imposed by the IMF, and domestic factors within Yugoslavia. This was the cause of Yugoslavia's fall from grace, a fall from which it would never recover.

The fourth Yugoslavia (1991–2006) was the rump Yugoslavia. It consisted of Serbia and Montenegro. During its early phase, it was dominated by Slobodan Milosevic and Serbian nationalism, and it was the main source of instability in the Balkans.

The Rise of Slobodan Milosevic

Revitalization movements are common during periods of economic hardship, social change, and political upheaval. They consist of a retreat into one's own culture to give one reassurance and a sense of well-being. Revitalization movements began to take root in the various republics of Yugoslavia when communism began crumbling. And it was during this period of decay in Yugoslavia that Slobodan Milosevic came to power in Serbia, the largest republic in Yugoslavia. Slobodan Milosevic was no nationalist, but he was a crafty politician who knew how to embrace a convenient issue when it could benefit him. Milosevic came to power as the head of the League of Communists of Serbia in 1987. He was the protégé of Ivan Stambolic, the president of Serbia.

Nationalism gave Milosevic the opportunity to grasp power and to replace Stambolic and jump to the front of the bandwagon of nationalism in Serbia, which had now replaced communism as the civil religion of Serbia. The 1974 Yugoslav constitution was at the heart of many Serbians' complaints. It gave autonomy to Vojvodina, a region in Serbia with a significant Hungarian population. It also granted autonomy to Kosovo, a region of Serbia that was predominantly Albanian. Both provinces were given seats on Yugoslavia's rotating presidency. The Serbs believed this diluted their political power. Milosevic's opportunity to grab power came in the form of a memorandum of the Serbian Academy of Sciences and the Arts. The memorandum was written by academics at the well-respected academy. It was published in a newspaper, *Vecernje Novosti*, on September 24, 1986, in draft form. According to the document:

> Serbs were in such an unjust position in post–Second World War Yugoslavia, argued the document, that their very existence was threatened. They were the victims of economic and political discrimination by their Croat and Slovene countrymen. Serbs had the greatest military contribution (and suffered the most causalities) over the last century and, far from being rewarded, were punished during peacetime ... In Kosovo and Metohija, ... Serbs faced genocide.[11]

It blamed Tito and the League of Communists of Yugoslavia for the plight of the Serbs. It was a bombshell. Nationalism was thus fueled further in Yugoslavia. Prominent members of the Serbian League of Communists denounced the document, but Milosevic remained silent. His reasons would later become obvious.

On April 24, 1987, Ivan Stambolic, the president of Serbia, sent his protégé, Slobodan Milosevic, to talk to Serbs in Kosovo. This event was to make Milosevic a Serbian folk hero. He told the Serb minority of Kosovo, who faced abuse at the hands of the Albanian majority, "No one should dare to beat you." Milosevic's popularity soared. By December 1987, Milosevic had driven his mentor, Ivan Stambolic, from power, and he assumed the presidency of Serbia. Then he stripped Vojvodina and Kosovo of their autonomy. Milosevic was loved in Serbia, but despised for his chauvinism in the rest of Yugoslavia. Now, Slobodan Milosevic appeared to be the king of the Serbs; however, later during the war in Bosnia, Milosevic would be exposed as a political opportunist.

By the time that free elections were scheduled for the republics, the Berlin Wall had fallen, and communism was dying throughout Eastern Europe and in the Soviet Union. To the United States and its European allies, this was an encouraging sign. Debate in Yugoslavia appeared to be robust, and the people were going to have an opportunity to vote in free elections for the first time since World War II. Senator Sam Ervin once said that democracy might be mankind's last chance to govern itself decently. However, the founding fathers felt that it had potential pitfalls. In *Federalist Paper No. 10*, James Madison wrote:

> Men of factious tempers, of local prejudices, or of sinister designs, may by intrigue, by corruption, or by other means, first obtain the suffrages, and then betray the interest of the people.[12]

Yugoslavia's institutions for ameliorating social conflicts had atrophied, and nationalism was rampant throughout the republics. Democracy is not a perfect form of government. People sometimes succumb to the rhetoric of demagogues. Adolf Hitler was elected as the chancellor of Germany, and Slobodan Milosevic was elected as the president of Serbia in a free election.

Milosevic's election in 1990 sent shock waves throughout the other Yugoslav republics. He was attempting to centralize control of the federal government. The abolition of autonomy for Vojvodina and Kosovo, along with Milosevic's influence over Montenegro, gave him control of four out of eight seats on the Yugoslav presidency. Slovenia and Croatia were the most prosperous republics. Consolidation of power by the central government meant that they would have to surrender more of their revenue to the central government. This was something that they were not willing to do.

Under Yugoslavia's constitution, the republics had the right to secede. Therefore, President Milan Kucan of Slovenia and President Franjo Tudjman of Croatia began to make plans to secede from Yugoslavia. They could not stand the thought of living in a country dominated by Milosevic and his Serbian chauvinism. The impending secession of Croatia and Slovenia raised problems for Bosnia-Herzegovina (Bosnia). In 1991, the census showed that Bosnia was 44 percent Muslim, 33 percent Serb, and 17 percent Croat.[13] These groups had a long history of cooperation and coexistence. If Croatia and Slovenia left Yugoslavia, there would be no counterweight to balance Serbia. Milosevic would then control four out of the six remaining seats of the Yugoslav presidency. Bosnia's Croats and Muslims would become second class citizens in Milosevic's Serboslavia. The handwriting was on the wall. If Croatia and Slovenia seceded, Bosnia would have to secede as well; otherwise Bosnian Croats and Muslims would find themselves at the mercy of Milosevic.

President Alija Izbetgovic of Bosnia and President Kiro Gligorov of Macedonia sought to put together a proposal that would enable Croatia and Slovenia to remain in Yugoslavia. Their plan called for Serbia and Montenegro to remain the center of Yugoslavia, while Bosnia and Macedonia would be loosely associated as constituent republics, and Croatia and Slovenia would have sovereignty within the confederation. This plan was called a "confederation within the federation" as well as an "asymmetrical federation." President Izbetgovic and President Gligorov were trying to hold back the onslaught of Milosevic, who vetoed the plan. That doomed Yugoslavia and put it on its deathbed and the course of war.

It is ironic that the modern Balkan wars are viewed in the West as an attempt by Milosevic to keep the other republics from seceding from Yugoslavia. In fact, Serbia was the first republic to secede from Yugoslavia. Slovenia and Croatia did not secede from Yugoslavia until June 25, 1991. Serbia seceded from Yugoslavia earlier. When the federal presidency was paralyzed over a decision to declare a state of emergency and to deploy the Yugoslavia Peoples' Army (JNA), Milosevic effectively withdrew Serbia from the federation. On March 16, 1991, Slobodan Milosevic went on television and stated, "Yugoslavia is finished." He then went on to say that he had:

> ordered the mobilization of special reservist and the urgent mobilization of additional Serbian militia units. Yugoslavia has entered into its final phase of agony ... The Republic of Serbia will no longer recognize a single decision reached by the Presidency under existing circumstances because it would be illegal.[14]

The Yugoslav presidency had failed to function, and Milosevic had essentially pulled Serbia out of the federation. Milosevic destroyed Yugoslavia by defying it, denying it, and placing an emphasis on Serbia. His subsequent wars against the republics were not intended to keep them in Yugoslavia, but to take land from them to increase the size of his domain, Serbia. Redefinition of the borders of the Balkan states and protection against the tyranny of the majority were at the heart of the oncoming conflicts.

When war came to Slovenia, it was not overwhelmed by violence. The war lasted for only ten days—forty-four JNA soldiers were killed and Slovenian casualties were in single digits. This "war" was staged more for the television cameras than anything else. Milosevic had agreed to let Slovenia opt out of the federation—it had few Serbs and no cultural ties to Serbia. The purpose of the war was to discredit and humiliate the JNA so Milosevic's political hand would be strengthened. Slovenia's status was finalized under the Brioni Agreement. Croatia, by contrast, was not as lucky. It had a Serb minority of 600,000 out of 4.8 million people (12.5 percent of the population). Many of Croatia's Serbs lived in Krajina. Milosevic figured that this area would make a nice addition to Serbia.

When war came to Croatia, fighting broke out in Krajina. A de facto partition of Croatia took place. The Krajina Serbs, with assistance from Milosevic and the JNA, set up their own government. The Croatian government fought back to prevent this wanton land grab. When the war ended, the United Nations deployed peacekeeping forces to separate the combatants. The rebellion had taken place, because the Croatian Serbs were not convinced that their individual rights and cultural identity would be protected in Croatia. The original draft of the Croatian constitution did not recognize the Serb minority as a constituent nation—a right they had during the days of communism. The final draft of the Croatian constitution passed by the Sabor (Parliament) gave Serbs and other minorities the right to use their own language and to have their own schools in areas where they were the majority. In 1992, laws were passed to guarantee self-government and autonomy where Serbs were the majority as well.

To many Croatian Serbs, this was a farce. They did not trust the Croatian government. President Tudjman originally had not guaranteed the rights of the Serbian minority as a constituent nation within Croatia. At a public rally, Tudjman had once remarked, "Thank God my wife is not a Jew or a Serb."[15] Moreover, once Tudjman took power, a new Croatian flag was unveiled. It displayed the *sahovnica*, the ancient Croatian symbol that was prominently displayed on the Ustashas flag of the Croatian fascist republic during World War II. The Ustashas were responsible for the slaughter of thousands of Jews and Serbs. Croatia should have provided Bosnia a lesson regarding avoiding pitfalls on the road to independence; unfortunately it did not.

Bosnia's Declaration of Independence

Slovenia and Croatia's withdrawal from the Yugoslav federation sealed Bosnia's fate. It had to withdraw from the federation as well or it would have been left at the mercy of Milosevic. Bosnia was Yugoslavia's most integrated republic. Mosques, Catholic cathedrals, and Orthodox churches were in walking distance of each other. The prospect of war spreading to Bosnia seemed dim to most of its inhabitants. As stated previously, one-third of the marriages in Bosnia were between people from different cultures, and many cross-cultural friendships had been formed as well. Bosnia was a social success because the federal government under Tito had guaranteed the social and cultural rights of the people. However, Bosnia's fate was to be influenced by forces outside of its borders as well as within. This was the situation Bosnia faced on the eve of its independence.

A declaration of independence is a solemn occasion. It signals a break with the past and a new beginning for the future. For Bosnia-Herzegovina, its declaration of independence signaled the beginning of its destruction. It would be rebuilt, but the Bosnia that many came to know and admire would cease to exist. On October 15,

1991, the Muslim and Croatian members of the Bosnian parliament (the majority) voted for Bosnia to become an independent state. The Serbian members of parliament had walked out prior to the vote. Ten days later, in their own parliament, Bosnian Serbs voted to remain part of Yugoslavia. From February 29–March 1, 1992, a referendum was held on Bosnian independence. Once more there were social divisions—Muslims and Croats voted for the referendum and Serbs boycotted it. There was a major difference in the perception of the Bosnian government among the Muslims, Serbs, and Croats of Bosnia. To the Muslims and Croats, leaving Yugoslavia was a necessity. Life in a country dominated by Slobodan Milosevic would mean being relegated to the status of second-class citizenship and a crackdown on political rights. For the Bosnian Serbs, remaining in Yugoslavia provided them with a form of psychological comfort. It meant remaining part of a larger unit that contained the Serbian homeland. To them, this was essential, since the web of social and cultural guarantees that were a part of Tito's Yugoslavia no longer existed. Leaving Yugoslavia would be a form of psychological isolation for them. This was the situation that confronted Alija Izetbegovic, the president of Bosnia-Herzegovina.

Alija Izetbegovic, an honest, competent, and capable man, was elected the president of Bosnia in December 1990, but he was hampered by a lack of political experience and indecisiveness. He did not try to take rights away from anyone, but his actions did not reassure the Bosnian Serbs of their rights either. Izetbegovic was the leader of the Muslim-dominated Party for Democratic Action (SDA). He was not a Communist; therefore, he had not held political office prior to the 1990 elections. He was often inattentive to how he was perceived outside of the Muslim community. Serbian nationalists wrongly accused him of wanting to set up an Islamic state in Bosnia. Nothing was further from the truth. Izetbegovic was a committed democrat, but Serbian nationalists often cited events from his past to prove their point. They pointed to his activities during his youth as a member of *Mladi Muslimani* (Young Muslims), when he wrote the "Islamic Declaration" in 1973.[16] It was intended to promote dialogue among Muslims. Izetbegovic's views had evolved over time.

> To judge the six presidents of the former Yugoslav republics by their character of twenty years ago, then Slovenia would have a Stalinist as head of state; Croatia would have a raving anti-Semite; Serbia a bloodthirsty Bolshevik; Montenegro an adolescent; and Macedonia another Stalinist.[17]

Izetbegovic thought that it was folly to set up any semblance of an Islamic government since Muslims did not constitute a majority in Bosnia. He simply wanted to live in harmony with the other national groups in Bosnia.

In politics, it is often perception more than reality that counts. Given the perception that various groups had of Izetbegovic, the burden was on him to prove them wrong. The Bosnian constitution granted the Croats, Serbs, and Muslims the rights of constituent nations, but Izbetgovic never took the initiative to reassure the Bosnian Serbs that their rights would not be violated. He had many opportunities to do so, but appeared to be hampered by his lack of political experience. For example, Izetbegovic was a guest-of-honor at the inauguration of the Serbian Democratic Party (SDS) in Bosnia. At that function, Radovan Karadzic, the leader of the Bosnian Serbs, said Serbs must have equal status and share power in Bosnia.[18] Izetbegovic could have seized the opportunity to say that he agreed with Karadzic's statement, but he did not. Such a gesture would have gone a long way, and might have undercut the support of Karadzic who would later scheme with Milosevic to partition Bosnia.

What the Bosnian Serb community feared was having the umbilical cord with "mother" Serbia cut. They feared the same thing the Bosnian Muslims and Bosnian Croats had feared, when they considered the possibility of Bosnia remaining part of Yugoslavia—being a persecuted minority. These fears were real and were not adequately addressed by the Bosnian government. The Bosnian Serbs felt that if the Bosnian Croats and Bosnian Muslims had the right to self-determination, they should have that same right. If the Bosnian government had been more astute, it would have created institutional safeguards to protect against the tyranny of the majority. As James Madison stated, a democracy cannot exist and sustain itself without such measures. Moreover, this situation raises a question about the limits of self-determination. Is any minority group free to declare itself independent from the majority? The case for the independence of the Bosnian Serbs would be difficult to make, since they were not being subjected to abuse or mistreatment in Bosnia, nor were they being denied political representation. However, they should have been provided with more explicit guarantees than they received from the Bosnian government, since their cooperation was the key ingredient to keeping Bosnia intact. The assistance of the United States could have been helpful in achieving this goal. At this stage, Bosnia needed ideals and principles to build on—these could have been borrowed from the American experience.

The Bosnian government embodied some of the ideals of democracy. It was diverse in its makeup. The government consisted of a representative presidency, parliament, and a judiciary. The Bosnian presidency consisted of two Muslims, two Croats, and two Serbs. Moreover, a Serb, Momelio Krajisnik, served as the speaker of the parliament, and a Croat, Jure Pelivan, served as the prime minister. In addition, Izetbegovic formed a coalition government with the leading Serb and Croat parties, the SDS and HDZ, respectively. In reality, this was a facade of unity. The Bosnian Serbs, led by Radovan Karadzic, sought a pretext to withdraw their support from the Bosnian government.

> The SDS began to undermine government institutions, first, by staging a boycott of parliament. The Party repeatedly declared that Izetbegovic was not entitled to preside over the Serbian people, because under his leadership Bosnia-Herzegovina supported Slovenia and Croatia in their wars against Yugoslavia.[19]

This was nothing more than a convenient excuse. Yugoslavia no longer existed, and everyone knew it. Karadzic had already planned a land grab that would lead to war.

The War in Bosnia-Herzegovina

In John Locke's *Second Treatise on Civil Government*, he stated that during a time of war the safety of the innocent is preferred. In Bosnia, the innocent were targets. Slobodan Milosevic did not cause the war in Bosnia. He just made it more brutal than it had to be. A new term "ethnic cleansing" was added to the vocabulary of the West, and Bosnia became the scene of genocide, mass graves, rape, mutilation, and torture. A brutal war existed on the continent that was supposed to be among the most civilized, Europe. The behavior of the participants was shocking, and serves as an important lesson for humanity.

Bosnia's fate was already determined before it seceded from Yugoslavia. Neither Croatia nor Serbia respected the territorial integrity of Bosnia-Herzegovina. President Tudjman of Croatia and President Milosevic of Serbia met in March 1991 at Karadjordjevo to discuss the partition of Bosnia. Tudjman wanted Herzegovina and Milosevic wanted to add the eastern portion of Bosnia to Serbia. Neither respected the Muslims of Bosnia as a legitimate national group. Many Serbs and Croats believed that Bosnian Muslims were Serbs (Orthodox) or Croats (Catholics) who would return to the fold some day.[20] President Tudjman had referred to Bosnia as a "national state of the Croatian nation."[21]

The Serb-dominated JNA created a plan for the dismemberment of Croatia and Bosnia-Herzegovina in the mid-1980s. The two-page plan was known as RAM and Rampart-91. According to Susan Woodward, it was a contingency plan to protect Serbia from an invasion by the West.[22] But it was more than that. The exact meaning of the acronym is not known but the term Rampart gives us some insight. *Webster's New World Dictionary* defines rampart as: (1) an embankment of earth surmounted by a parapet and encircling a castle, fort, etc., for defense against attack; and as (2) any defense or bulwark.[23] The number 91 apparently refers to Psalm 91, verse 5, that states, "Thou shalt not be afraid for the terror by night; nor for the arrows that flieth by day." Existence of the plan became known during the war in Croatia in 1991. Apparently, the plan envisioned uniting the Serbs concentrated in the regions in Croatia and Bosnia with the Serbian homeland. It was put into effect by Slobodan Milosevic. The plan consisted of massive quantities of arms being delivered to areas of Bosnia inhabited by Serbs.

> In August [1991], when his humiliation was reaching its peak, the federal Prime Minister, Ante Markovic, revealed the existence of RAM and leaked a taped conversation between President Milosevic and General Nikola Uzelac, who ran the Banja Luka corps of the JNA with his own particular touch of evil. During this conversation, Milosevic ordered Uzelac to release weapons to the leader of the SDS, Radovan Karadzic.[24]

Moreover, it was also akin to the Nazis' final solution for the Jews. It included the use of terror, rape, and genocide. The minutes of a JNA meeting on the feasibility of implementing RAM stated:

> Our analysis of the behavior of the Muslim communities demonstrates that the morale [and] will ... of their group can be undermined only if we aim our action at the point where the religious and social structure is most fragile. We refer to the women, especially adolescents, and to the children. Decisive intervention on these social figures would spread confusion among the communities thus causing first fear and then panic, leading to probable retreat from the territories involved in war activity.[25]

Also, Vladimir Srebrov, the founder of the Serbian Democratic Party (SDS), has admitted that he distanced himself from the SDS when he discovered the existence of the plan.

> The plan was drawn up in the 1980s by the General Staff of the Yugoslav People's Army (JNA). It envisaged a division of Bosnia into two spheres of interest, leading to the creation of a Greater Serbia and Greater Croatia. The Muslims were to be subjected to a final solution: more than 50% of them were to be killed, a smaller part converted to Orthodoxy, while an even smaller part—those with money, of course—was to be allowed to leave for Turkey, by way of a so-called "Turkish corridor." The aim was to cleanse Bosnia-Herzegovina completely of the Muslim nation, and to divide the country along the River Vrbas. The very name of Bosnia was to disappear. This was the aim behind the creation of "Republika Srpska."[26]

Furthermore, the *Croatian Herald* discussed the Plan on July 28, 1992.[27] What would be known as ethnic cleansing was the result of a well-thought-out and orchestrated script, first implemented in Croatia and then in Bosnia.

Ethnic cleansing was a new word added to the vocabulary of the international community in the early 1990s. It consisted of Serbian paramilitary forces terrorizing Croatian and Muslim civilians so they would leave their homes, or killing them individually or en masse, to render an area ethnically pure for Serbs. As a result, mass graves would become commonplace in the rural areas of Bosnia. This is what the war in Bosnia was about. It was not just about the control of an area. It was about the elimination of a people from an area to render it ethnically pure by force or by terror.

To outside observers, the war in Bosnia appeared to be a civil war. It was not a civil war in the contemporary sense of the word. In a civil war, there is usually an attempt to co-opt, coerce, capture, or enslave the opposition. In many ways, the war in Bosnia was unique and defied categorization. A civil war also involves acts of what Ali Mazrui refers to as primary violence. He defines primary violence as violence concerning the territorial integrity of the state, when one group does not want to live in the same state with another group.[28] This occurred at various levels. On the one hand, Bosnia did not want to live in Yugoslavia with Milosevic. On the other hand, the Bosnian Serbs partitioned a section of Bosnia for themselves, because they did not want to live in the same state with Croats and Muslims. In this sense it resembled both macro and micro civil wars.

The war in Bosnia also involved the redefinition of the state's identity. Yugoslavia was the state of the southern Slavs. After the collapse of the Titoist state, Milosevic sought to refine Yugoslavia as a Serbian-dominated state (Serboslavia). Serbia sought to attach itself to the Krajina of Croatia and the region of Bosnia-Herzegovina that became known as Republika Srpska.

The war in Bosnia was also unique in that rape was used as a weapon against civilians. In *Rape Warfare: The Hidden Genocide in Bosnia-Herzegovina and Croatia*, Beverly Allen stated that rape was used in Croatia and Bosnia-Herzegovina as a form of genocide. According to Allen, the Bosnian Serbs and the JNA committed three forms of genocidal rape. They took women of different ages from their homes and raped them in public and departed. A few days later, Bosnian Serbs or JNA soldiers offered terrified civilians safe passage away from their homes if they agreed never to return. Also, women held at concentration camps were raped, tortured, and killed. In addition, women at camps were raped for prolonged periods and released from the camps when it was too late for them to have an abortion. Allen makes a convincing point that this is a violation of Article II of the Convention on the Prevention and Punishment of the Crime of Genocide. Specifically this action violates the following sections of Article II,

(a) Killing members of the group;
(b) Causing serious bodily or mental harm to members of the group;
(c) Deliberately inflicting on the group conditions of life and calculated to bring about the physical destruction in whole or in part;
(d) Imposing measures intended to prevent births within the group.

Rape was clearly used as a tool to demean, humiliate, and eliminate Muslims and Croats in Bosnia: a crime for which some are being punished only now, with the victims still suffering from the aftereffects.

The Bosnian Serbs violated virtually every international convention. The Geneva Conventions state that hospitals are to be considered neutral areas, but in this war the Bosnian Serbs targeted hospitals and denied the wounded proper treatment. Moreover, prisoners were starved, denied clothing, medical treatment, and sanitary facilities. Concentration camps and mass graves became the norm after Radko Mladac took over as the commander of the Bosnian Serb forces. On May 22, 1992, he opened prisoner of war/death camps in Bosnia. The existence of these camps was revealed to the West for the first time by Roy Gutman of *Newsday*. Gutman reported:

> In one concentration camp, a former iron-mining complex at Omarska in northwest Bosnia, more than a thousand Muslims and Croat civilians were held in metal cages, without sanitation, adequate food, exercise or access to the outside world.

> In a second improvised camp, in a customs warehouse on the bank of the Sava River in the northeast Bosnian city of Brako, 1,350 people were slaughtered between May 15 and mid-June [1992], ... Guards at Brako executed prisoners by slitting their throats or with firing squads.[29]

At the Omarska camp, the 300 prisoners were put in 700 square-feet cages, and they were stacked four high. "There were no toilets, and the prisoners had to live in their own filth, which dripped through the grates."[30] In the Brako concentration camp, after some of the prisoners were killed and their bodies dumped into the Sava River, one prisoner recounted a gruesome scene from the camp.

> Lujinovic, a 53 year old Muslim, said he was one of only 150 prisoners still alive of the 1,500 who had arrived at the beginning of May. After slaughtering nine-tenth of the prisoners, the guards turned on the townspeople who had not been captured, he told *Newsday* during a two hour interview ...
>
> Then instead of tossing those bodies into the Sava, they had prisoners drive them to an animal feed plant, he said. Lujinov said the prisoners didn't actually throw the corpse into the oven, but they had every reason to believe the bodies were being cremated for animal feed for that day, "the air in Brako would stink so badly you couldn't open a window."[31]

Muslims were also placed in cattle cars and shipped through Banja Luka to death camps.[32] Furthermore, Serb paramilitary forces conducted "Muslim hunts" in which unarmed civilians were hunted down and killed for no reason other than the fact that they were Muslims. This same appalling behavior had previously been witnessed by the world seventy years ago—in Nazi Germany. A holocaust was taking place. The destruction of Croats and Muslims in the area that was to become known as Republika Srpska became the central aim of the Bosnian Serb forces and their JNA allies. Neither the United States nor its Western allies were willing to take bold action to stop the genocide. That is what made this brutality possible. There were no consequences for genocide. After the fall of Srebrenica in 1995, one Serb soldier said, "The world has allowed us to do this ... Tomorrow they will allow us to do the same in Zepa."[33] As we shall see later, the United States and its allies often went out of their way to make it clear that they would not introduce ground troops to bring this savagery to an end. This only gave encouragement to the tormentors.

The West, especially the United States, never seemed to grasp the extent to which the violent acts in Bosnia were premeditated. The leader of the Serbian Democratic Party (SDS) in Krajina (Croatia), Jovan Raskovic, was a psychiatrist and his former student, Radovan Kradzic, was the leader of the SDS in Bosnia. Raskovic bears some indirect responsibility for helping to establish the mindset in Serbia that would tolerate a policy of ethnic cleansing. Before his death in 1992, Raskovic said on television:

> I feel responsible because I made the preparations for this war—even if not the military preparations. If I hadn't created the emotional strain in the Serbian people, nothing would have happened.
>
> My party and I lit the fuse of the Serbian nationalism not only in Croatia but everywhere else in Bosnia-Herzegovina.
>
> We have driven this people and we have given it an identity. I have repeated it again and again to this people that it comes from heaven and not earth.[34]

Psychology played an important role in the way ethnic cleansing was carried out. The memorandum of the Serbian Academy of Sciences and Arts went a long way in feeding the insecurity of the Serbs of the former Yugoslavia. Political leaders, such as Milosevic and Karadzic, grasped it as proof that the Serbs were being exploited. It played into the Serb mythology that they won the war (World War II) but lost the peace. Physically, there is nothing to differentiate a Serb from a Croat or a Muslim. Blue eyes are a common feature in Bosnia. The war was not based on race. The people of Bosnia come from the same racial stock, look alike, and speak the same language. The war in Bosnia, ironically, was brutal because Bosnia was a well-integrated area where people of different nationalities intermarried and cooperated with each other. Ali Mazrui pointed out similar situations in Germany, Rwanda, Burundi, and Zanzibar where there was a high degree of social integration. For example, in Germany the Jewish community was well-integrated into German society and identified with the German state; nevertheless, this did not protect them from the brutality of the Nazis. The reason for the brutality is a perceived wrong by an aggrieved group that seeks to correct the situation by acts of violence against members of another group.[35] At this point, the degree of social integration or social interaction is irrelevant. In fact, the brutality helps to bind the members of the aggrieved group together. It reinforces one's group identity by making those from the aggrieved group rationalize their brutality against others.

> Given the normative orientation which had historically held together the Bosnian community, ethnic cleansing had to be done in ways which were absolute. Given the shared values which integrated the Bosnian society, ethnic cleansing had to be done in ... ways which were absolute and ruthless. Otherwise, the uncertainty and ambivalence of Bosnian Serbs could not be overcome. Thus the objective of ethnic cleansing was to force Bosnian Serbs "to realize there was no retreating, no faltering, no compromising, that they were inextricably bound to their leaders, and could only march with them to 'total victory' regardless of the cost."[36]

In essence, the violence was a way to bind the Bosnian Serbs together. Moreover, Serbs in Serbia were able to rationalize the brutality by maintaining the mentality that the other cultural groups in Yugoslavia had always victimized Serbs.

Moreover, the war in Bosnia was also a convenient way for Slobodan Milosevic to divert the attention of the people of Serbia away from the country's problems. In 1987, when Slobodan Milosevic went to Kosovo, he became the poster boy for Serbian nationalism. By 1991, many of those posters had come down. There was massive opposition to Milosevic's autocratic rule. In March 1991, there were extensive student-led protests against his repression and control of the media.[37] The following year, there were also protests to commemorate the demonstrations of 1991. That same year—1992—the heir to the Serbian throne, Alexander, returned to Serbia. Some saw him as a potential political alternative to Milosevic. There were additional protests, and economic sanctions were imposed against Serbia. Clashes also occurred with ethnic Albanians in Kosovo, and Milosevic had to deal with political opposition from Dobrica Cosic, the president of Yugoslavia, and Milan Panic, the prime minister of Yugoslavia. These events might have toppled Milosevic if the wars in Croatia and Bosnia had not created a core of supporters on whom Milosevic could always rely for support.

During the war in Bosnia, a rift developed between the guardians of Serbian chauvinism, Slobodan Milosevic and his Bosnian Serb clients. Milosevic unleashed an ugly force throughout the Balkans that he was now unable to control. The sanctions imposed on Serbia and Montenegro were beginning to take their toll. When Milosevic attempted to reign in his client, the Bosnian Serbs, he found that he could not. Milosevic attempted to get the Bosnian Serb parliament to accept the Vance-Owens Peace Plan, even though he believed that it would not be implemented. He failed to gain their support. Subsequently, Milosevic implemented a short-lived arms embargo against his clients in Republika Srpska. Moreover, when Milosevic, with the assistance of Russia, was on the verge of getting sanctions against Serbia lifted, the Bosnian Serbs launched an attack on Gorazde in April 1994. "Dr. Milosevicenstein" had created a monster that he could not control.

The Bosnian Serbs had no reason to be flexible. There was no one to stop them. They had gained control of 70 percent of Bosnia. Their actions on the ground determined their strength at the negotiating table. Radovan Karadzic, the leader of the Bosnian Serbs, commented, "Why should we negotiate with the Muslims at all? ... They are militarily defeated, and we have no urgency to negotiate with them."[38] Drunken with the hubris of their battlefield victories, the Bosnian Serbs were out of control.

One of the great ironies of the war was that it was supposed to be a war based on Serbian nationalism to protect Serbs. The war in Bosnia destroyed that myth. No one was crueler to the Serbs of Bosnia-Herzegovina than Radovan Karadzic and Slobodan Milosevic. The Bosnian Serbs and their JNA allies attacked cities, towns, and villages. Many of those killed were Muslims, Croats, and Serbs. Since Bosnia was well-integrated, many of the attacks by the Bosnian Serbs resulted in the deaths of Serbs. The Bosnian Serbs pounded Sarajevo unmercifully during the war. This resulted in the indiscriminate killing of civilians of various nationalities. The bombs that rained down on Sarajevo and other areas killed Serbs, Croats, and Muslims alike. People dedicated to furthering the cause of "their people" would not commit such wholescale killing of "their people." What lay at the heart of Milosevic and Karadzic's actions was not the betterment of the Serbian people, rather nationalism was used to disguise their criminal intent.

One group that had a vested interest in perpetuating the war in Bosnia was the Yugoslav People's Army (JNA). The JNA consisted of 220,000 troops in 1980, and was scheduled to be reduced to 150,000 troops due to budget cuts by 1992.[39] The army was the fourth largest in Europe and had 70,000 officers; 70 percent of them were Serbian or Montenegrin.[40] If Yugoslavia was broken up, such a large army would not be needed; therefore, the soldiers would have to be demobilized, and many would join the growing ranks of the unemployed. Moreover, over 60 per cent of the military industries were in Bosnia.[41] Undoubtedly, the succession of Bosnia would have had a substantial impact on the JNA's military capabilities. Anticipating the war, Milosevic transferred all JNA officers and troops who were born in Bosnia back to Bosnia. He even paid the salaries of the

JNA officer corps in Bosnia. This helped to keep the JNA satisfied and off Milosevic's back. The JNA was a powerful interest group that had to be neutralized. The war in Bosnia accomplished that goal.

The fall of Srebrenica in 1995 underscored the changes that had taken place in the international system. It had become weak and leaderless. The United States and its European allies stood by as Srebrenica fell and Radko Mladac and his cohorts proceeded to execute 8,000 Muslim men and boys. As reports of the massacre filtered into Western countries, condemnations and hand-wringing were the extent of their actions. It had become obvious to all that "never again" was now nothing more than a meaningless slogan. Tito's Yugoslavia was no democracy, but in that country one did have a right to a national identity. In essence, that is what the war was about. It was not a civil war, as portrayed in Europe, and it was not an invasion, as portrayed in the United States. It was about fundamental guarantees for one's cultural identity. By failing to understand the conflict, the United States and its allies became part of the problem.

Democracy in this region was not considered worth defending by the Western world because the end of the Cold War rendered it a nonstrategic area—too bad for the victims. Too bad that the valuable lessons learned during World War II had been forgotten.

The Bush I Administration

It would seem that if anyone would understand the lessons of World War II and the importance of deterring tyrants, it would be George Herbert Walker Bush, the forty-first president of the United States. He was a veteran of World War II and was awarded the Distinguished Flying Cross for the service he rendered to the United States as a navy pilot. President Bush I was also the architect of Operation Desert Storm, a successful war against a tyrant. Therefore, it is hard to understand why the massacre in Bosnia could have begun under his watch, but it did. This section will attempt to explain the reasons for this paradoxical situation.

The Bush I administration's approach to the conflict in Bosnia was timid and an embarrassment to the United States. The United States had led a coalition against the Iraqi dictator, Saddam Hussein, when he invaded Kuwait. The Cold War was grinding to a halt and the United States was the preeminent power in the world, yet it watched as Yugoslavia disintegrated and genocide occurred. This happened because of the lessons President Bush I learned from World War II and the impact the Vietnam War had on the Pentagon. To Bush,

World War II was a significant event. It underscored the importance of standing up to a dictator who posed a threat to the international system. When Saddam Hussein invaded Kuwait, he threatened the world's oil supply. Therefore, President Bush I assembled an international coalition to defeat him.

Nevertheless, what is notable about Operation Desert Storm is what was not done. President Bush I failed to come to the aid of the Shiite Muslims and the Kurds when they rebelled against Saddam Hussein. In Bush's eyes, only actions that posed a direct threat to the United States and its allies deserved to be met with American resistance. Apparently, Hussein's suppression of the Kurds and the Shiites did not meet this criterion.

In addition, since the Vietnam War, the U.S. military had sought to avoid long-term military engagements in foreign countries (the Vietnam syndrome). The United States' military involvement in Vietnam was brought on by the China syndrome. In 1949, China fell to the Communist forces of Mao Zedong. Right-wing critics of the Truman administration erroneously charged that it was responsible the for "losing China." This became a prime motivating factor for United States' military involvement in Vietnam. The U.S. presidents Eisenhower, Kennedy, Johnson, and Nixon did not want to become the presidents who "lost Vietnam." But when Vietnam fell in 1975, the China syndrome gave way to the Vietnam syndrome. The U.S. military was now averse to long-term military commitments and sought to avoid them, at all costs, to avoid the humiliation of another Vietnam.

The fall of Vietnam and the end of the Cold War changed U.S. foreign policy. Previously, the United States tended to undertake foreign military adventures for strategic, economic, political, and ideological reasons. The fall of Vietnam and the end of the Cold War brought the ideological imperative to a close. This meant that intervention for humanitarian reasons, and in defense of democracy, was now unlikely. The perspectives of President Bush I and the U.S. military were in sync on Bosnia, which was viewed as nonessential. Slobodan Milosevic was a regional threat, but posed no threat to the international community at large; moreover, Bosnia has no oil, and therefore the United States adopted a hands-off policy.

Opinions in the Bush I administration regarding Bosnia were not unanimous. President Bush I and the U.S. secretary of state James Baker did not regard Bosnia as anything more than a blip on the foreign policy radar screen. On the other hand, Brent Scrowcroft, Bush's national security advisor, and Lawrence Eagleburger, the assistant secretary of state, seemed to sense the importance of what was at hand. According to Scrowcroft:

> Eagleburger and I were the most concerned about Yugoslavia. The president and Baker were furthest on the other side. Baker would say, "We don't have a dog in this fight." The President would say to me once a week "Tell me again what this is all about"[42]

President Bush I and Baker won out in the formation of administration policy.

Moreover, when Secretary of State Baker went to Yugoslavia, he was ill-prepared for the trip because he did not think the disintegration of Yugoslavia was an important issue. Baker gave mixed signals to the leaders of the republics who wanted to secede from Yugoslavia. He told them not to secede and, on the other hand, he told Milosevic that the United States would not prevent them from seceding. In addition, Baker did not even know who Momir Bulatovic, the president of Montenegro, was, and he did not meet with members of the JNA, even though it was a major factor in whether the Balkans would spin out of control.[43]

Since the fall of the Soviet Union, the Bush I administration believed that the United States' main foreign policy objective had been met, and failed to take advantage of the opportunities it had to influence the turn of events in Yugoslavia. In 1991, there was a notable split among the people of Serbia. Many were fed up with Milosevic's autocratic rule. In March 1991, 100,000 people in Serbia organized a rally to protest against Milosevic. Instead of encouraging the protestors, the Bush I administration took a passive stance. It was reported that:

> After three months of civil war, 100 cease-fires and more than 1,000 dead, Europe and the United States have finally determined their approach to the civil war in Yugoslavia.
>
> They are giving up.[44]

The position of the Bush I administration seemed puzzling. In the midst of the crisis in Bosnia, Secretary of State Baker resigned to assume control of President Bush I's reelection campaign. This demoralized the State Department. However, Lawrence Eagleburger, who speaks Serbo-Croatian and previously served as the U.S. ambassador to Yugoslavia, took over as the secretary of state.

Eagleburger, unlike many in the administration, understood the gravity of the situation in the crumbling Yugoslavia. This makes the actions of the Bush I administration all the more inexplicable, especially in light of the emergence of Milan Panic, the Yugoslav prime minister, as a political alternative to Milosevic. Panic had left Yugoslavia and immigrated to the United States and became a successful businessman. Panic later returned to Yugoslavia to become its prime minister. His was a voice of reason among voices of irrationality. He deplored what Yugoslavia had become and tried to stop the violence. President Bush I and Secretary of State Eagleburger did very little to advance the cause of Panic. The president and Eagleburger could have met with Panic when he challenged Milosevic for the presidency of Serbia in 1992 to boost his status by promising a swift end to the sanction if the rump Yugoslavia returned to democracy and ended its aggression against its neighbors. By most accounts, Panic barely lost the election despite the finagling of the results by Milosevic's forces. Effective involvement on the part of the United States could have prevented the resulting tragedy and, ironically, lessened the commitment to Yugoslavia that the United States would ultimately have to undertake.

The foreign policy adopted by the Bush I administration bore a striking resemblance to the foreign policy of the Nixon administration, as described by Henry Brandon in *The Retreat of American Power*. In that book, Brandon describes how President Nixon staged a military withdrawal and set up regional powers to protect the United States' interests in various parts of the world. Since the disintegration of Yugoslavia had occurred in Europe's backyard, Bush considered it to be Europe's problem and wanted Europe to manage it. It was a problem that Europe could not solve because it lacked the clout and resources that only the United States possessed. In President Bush I's "New World Order," the United States reigned but did not rule. The various regional lords and barons were left to rule their fiefdoms on behalf of the imperial crown. Apparently, the Bush administration suppressed reports it had received from the U.S. embassy in Belgrade.[45] So, the United States took a backseat as a human tragedy unfolded. To members of the Bush I administration, the formulation of the "New World Order" may have been nothing more than an academic exercise, but it was a death warrant for civilians in Bosnia. American Jews recognized the signs of genocide and implored President Bush to work with the United Nations and to shut down the death camps, but their concerns went unheeded.[46]

THE CONGRESS AND PRESIDENT BUSH I

The founders of the U.S. republic established a system of government that operates by consensus. As the tragedy in Bosnia unfolded, a consensus developed in the U.S. Congress that bolder action was needed to stop genocide in Bosnia. Members of Congress were more conscientious than the White House on the need for action to bring the atrocities in Bosnia to an end.

Disturbing accounts of the Bosnian war in the media fueled Congress's call for action. Members of Congress were heavily influenced by U.S. press reports that portrayed the conflict as an invasion of Bosnia by Serbia. *The New York Times* had an unparalleled influence on members of both parties in Congress. One of the leading members of Congress who was calling for a more assertive U.S. policy in Bosnia was Senator Bob Dole (Republican-Kansas), the Senate minority leader and a veteran of World War II. On July 24, 1992, Dole placed an article from the July 18, 1992, edition of *The New York Times*—"A War on Civilians" by Michael T. Kaufman—in the *Congressional Record*. The article stated, "what has been going on is fundamentally a Serbian War of aggression largely against civilians." Dole went on to state "the time is long overdue for the world community to take concrete steps toward bringing peace to Bosnia."[47] Dole's position was a stark departure from the timid posture adopted by the Bush I administration. Other leading Republicans in the Senate took similar positions. Senator Dennis DeConcini (Republican–New Mexico), the cochair of the Helsinki Committee, noted that the United States could do more to help the victims of the war in Bosnia by influencing the United Nations and NATO to create secure zones in Sarajevo.[48]

Democrats in the Senate held a similar position. Senator Claiborne Pell (Democrat-Rhode Island) demonstrated an in-depth knowledge of the conflict when he spoke about it in the Senate. He said, "the United States acting in the United Nations should consider immediate military action to stop the killing now."[49]

As a result of the bipartisan consensus in the U.S. Senate, Serbia was condemned in Senate Resolution 290. It resolved that:

> (1) The United States should hold accountable the Government of Serbia for the attacks on and the occupation of the Republic of Bosnia-Hercegovina and Croatia, and for the extensive and systematic abuse of human rights in Kosovo.
> (2) The United States should withhold recognition of Serbia and its ally Montenegro …

(3) The United States should actively encourage its allies to follow the same course.[50]

The House of Representatives was also concerned about what was happening in Bosnia. The House, like the Senate, was influenced by press reports about the atrocities in Bosnia, and wanted to see a more active policy initiated to bring the violence there to an end. Representative Frank Wolf (Republican-Virginia) called the events in Bosnia genocide, recommended the suspension of the rump Yugoslavia's Most Favored Nation (MFN) trading privileges, and inserted an article from *The New York Times* into the *Congressional Record* that chided President Bush I for not showing the same boldness in Bosnia that he had shown against Iraqi aggression.[51] In addition, Representative Leon Panetta (Democrat-California) condemned the killing in Bosnia, and called on President Bush I and his colleagues to bring the killing of innocent civilians in Bosnia to an end. He said that the United States had an obligation to protect the innocent.[52] However, Representative Helen Bently (Republican-Maryland), who is of Serbian descent, was the odd person out. She acted as an apologist for the Serbs in Bosnia and Serbia. She said:

> I have warned that putting pressure and blame in the Serbs alone would not stop the fighting since they are not the only combatants and not the only invaders of Bosnia soil. There has been evidence aplenty—for at least three months—of Croatian soldiers fighting inside Bosnia, seizing villages and territory for the flag of Croatia.[53]

Representative Bently was in the minority. Most members of both parties, regardless of their ideology, felt that the United States had not done enough to stop the wanton slaughter of the innocent in Bosnia.

A Senate resolution was brought to the Senate floor in August 1992. The resolution urged President Bush I to seek a UN Security Council resolution for the use of force in Bosnia to deliver humanitarian relief, gain access to prisoner of war camps, and to have heavy weapons placed under UN supervision. The measure had strong support but some members of the Senate opposed it. One opponent of the resolution was Senator Robert Byrd (Democrat–West Virginia). He fell into the old trap of using the myth of ethnic rivalry to justify nonintervention. Senator Byrd stated:

> What is our purpose with this resolution? It is policing of ethnic hatred, now in the form of Serbian aggression in Bosnia, in the age old cauldron of ethnic division that we call the Balkans.[54]

However, Senator Byrd did not carry the day. Senate Resolution 330 passed in the Senate on August 11, 1992.

A similar measure came to the floor of the House of Representatives on the same day as House Resolution 554. It urged the UN Security Council to authorize the use of force to deliver humanitarian aid. Both houses of Congress seemed to be in agreement that now was the time for action. Despite the call for action by both houses of Congress, relief would not be forthcoming from the strongest country on earth, the United States.

Congress was not in a position to determine the direction of U.S. policy in Bosnia. First, public opinion was not galvanized around any specific policy. Many people felt sorrow at seeing the graphic pictures of the victims, but felt uncertain about the course of action the administration should take. They looked to officials in Washington, DC, to take the proper course of action in a conflict that many of them did not understand. Moreover, in the absence of public pressure, the president still determines the content of U.S. foreign policy. In *U.S. v. Curtiss-Wright Export Corporation* (1936), the United States Supreme Court stated:

> It is important to bear in mind ... exclusive power of the President as the sole organ of the federal government in the field of international relations—a power which does not require as a basis for its exercise an act of Congress.[55]

Congress cannot dictate the content of U.S. foreign policy. Congress' greatest power is that of naysayer. It can prevent or deny presidential action, because it controls the country's purse strings, but it does not control the actual content of policy. In this realm, the power of Congress is at its height when a major sector of public opinion is mobilized behind a specific policy position as it was during the Vietnam War. At that time, Congress was effective at exerting influence to make the executive abandon a position rather than adopt a particular position.

Also, another factor working against Congress was that 1992 was a presidential election year. President Bush I was politically vulnerable. The country was mired in a recession, and Bush was facing a tough challenge from Bill Clinton, the governor of Arkansas. Many of the Republicans in Congress wanted a more effective policy in Bosnia to be enacted, but they did not want to undermine a sitting Republican president who was fighting for his political life.

During the campaign for the presidency in 1992, William Jefferson Clinton called for the United States to adopt a more aggressive policy in Bosnia. He called for the United States to take the lead in seeking UN Security Council authorization for air strikes to be used against those who attacked UN relief efforts in Bosnia. Shortly after Clinton adopted this position, President Bush I adopted a similar stance. It took the pressure of the political campaign to get Bush to adopt a tougher policy.

In November 1992, William Jefferson Clinton was elected the forty-second president of the United States, but Clinton found himself retreating to the position of President Bush I due to domestic policy concerns. This led to more deaths and destruction in Bosnia. Finally, Clinton learned that only he, as the president of the United States, could bring the carnage in Bosnia to an end. In the process, Bill Clinton learned what it meant to be a leader, but unfortunately it was a lesson that he later forgot and that helped to bring forth yet another Balkan tragedy.

THE CLINTON ADMINISTRATION

The election of Bill Clinton as the forty-second president of the United States was a significant event in the history of the United States. When John F. Kennedy was elected the thirty-fifth president of the United States, he noted in his inaugural address that his election was significant because it symbolized the torch being passed to a new generation of Americans (generation VIII), the first generation born in the twentieth century to take power. It was the generation that had fought World War II and had come of age at the birth of the Cold War. Similarly, Bill Clinton's election had symbolic importance. Clinton was the first member of the baby boom generation (generation IX) to be elected the president of the United States.

World War II was the main reference point for generation VIII, but the War in Vietnam was the main reference point for generation IX. To them, it represented everything that was wrong with the government. It symbolized a government that lied to its people to pursue its owns ends. And, most importantly, it symbolized the futility of violence, and the dangers of becoming an active participant in a foreign war.

The United States was always an optimistic country, but Vietnam changed that. Vietnam changed the United States from a country of optimism into a country of cynics. During the days of John F. Kennedy, Americans believed that they could make the world a better place. After Vietnam, Americans no longer felt connected to the world. The war in Vietnam tore the United States apart and created a credibility gap between the government and its people and between the young and the old. To baby boomers, Vietnam was a mistake that was to be avoided in the future. It is often hard to go against one's own life experiences, but that would be necessary if Bill Clinton was to succeed in Bosnia.

President Clinton advocated a policy in Bosnia that became known as "lift and strike." It called for the United Nations to lift the arms embargo against Bosnia that had been placed on all of the republics of the former Yugoslavia on September 25, 1991, so the beleaguered Bosnian government could arm itself. It also called for air strikes against Serb artillery positions. However, Clinton was fearful of Bosnia turning into a quagmire like Vietnam, and was not prepared to act unilaterally. He sent Secretary of State Warren Christopher on a tour of European capitals to convince the United States' allies to support this policy. From March–April 1993, Secretary of State Christopher visited eleven European leaders and was met with resistance. Great Britain and France led the resistance. They objected because they had peacekeeping troops on the ground in Bosnia, and believed that lifting the arms embargo against Bosnia would escalate the violence, thereby endangering their troops.

Christopher was frustrated. The attempt to form a unified policy with the United States' allies embittered Christopher. He began to refer to Bosnia as "an irretractable problem from hell."[56] He also said that "no vital [American] interest" was at stake in the Balkans.[57] He also referred to "ancient ethnic hostilities" in the Balkans.

Equally disturbing was the change that President Clinton had undergone as well. In *On the Edge*, Elizabeth Drew wrote that President Clinton had changed his mind about "lift and strike" before Christopher returned from his European trip, because he had read the *Balkan Ghost* by Robert Kaplan. Clinton, like many others, came to the false conclusion that the violence in the Balkans stemmed from ancient tribal hatred. As a result, "lift and strike" was abandoned and the United States took a backseat to European leadership.

Another important factor in the retreat of the Clinton administration from Bosnia was the Powell Doctrine. This was the name given to a defense policy enunciated by Pentagon officials, the most notable being General Colin Powell, the chairman of the Joint Chiefs of Staff. It was a legacy of the Vietnam War. The Powell Doctrine was based on the belief that the United States must not become involved in long-term military operations in other countries and that "military force is best used to achieve a decisive victory."[58] Powell opposed military action in Bosnia and was even opposed to the humanitarian airlifts that the Clinton administration began in April 1993.

> When Administration officials prepared a diplomatic protest to the Serbs asking them to stop shadowing relief flights with their combat planes, military and civilian officials at the Pentagon softened the language to remove any implicit threat to take military action to stop the practice.[59]

If this doctrine had been in effect in the 1940s, the United States would not have entered World War II because of its rigid restrictions requiring the certainty of outcome.

President Clinton had already spent some of his political capital fighting the Pentagon over gays in the military, so Clinton pursued his domestic agenda while only giving lip service to "lift and strike." *Balkan Ghost* frightened Bill Clinton and resurrected the ghost of Lyndon Johnson and Vietnam. Johnson's War on Poverty became a casualty to the War in Vietnam. Clinton was elected to deal with the United States' economic problems, and had a full domestic agenda that included deficit reduction, unemployment reduction, and universal heath care. An article in the *Wall Street Journal* written by Arthur Schlesinger Jr. in May 1993 might have influenced the president as well. In that article, Schlesinger, a historian and former advisor to President Kennedy, made an analogy between Bosnia and Vietnam.[60] Therefore, Bosnia was abandoned—it was a mistake. The impact that *Balkan Ghost* had on the president was apparent from the rhetoric he began to use to describe the conflict in Bosnia. In reference to the Vance-Owens peace plan that called for Bosnia to be partitioned into ten cantons, President Clinton said:

> I think this plan shows that a civil war which has roots going back centuries, literally centuries, based on ethnic and religious differences, has not been resolved in the way that I certainly would have hoped.[61]

Clinton also sought to play down the magnitude of the crisis in Bosnia. Terrence Hunt of the Associated Press asked President Clinton if he saw any parallels between ethnic cleansing in Bosnia and the Holocaust. Clinton replied: "I think the Holocaust is on a whole different level. I think it is without precedent or peer in human history."[62] Ethnic cleansing in Bosnia was not of the magnitude of the Holocaust, but it was, nonetheless, a notable tragedy in the annals of twentieth-century history and should not have been ignored.

Furthermore, it was difficult for the Clinton administration to develop a coherent policy toward Bosnia because it was badly divided. Vice President Gore and UN Ambassador Albright favored air strikes against Serb targets. They believed that the United States should resort to unilateral action, if necessary. National Security Advisor Anthony Lake and Secretary of State Christopher believed in a limited "lift and strike" policy to get humanitarian aid through to civilians. On the other hand, Secretary of Defense Aspin favored limited protection of enclaves.[63]

With atrocities continuing to be reported by the media, the Clinton administration was forced from its complacency. It opted for a policy of containment. A contingent of 300 troops was sent to Macedonia and Clinton backed a UN resolution to set up six safe areas. The names of the six safe areas, Tuzla, Bihac, Srebrenica, Sarajevo, Zepa, and Gorazde, would soon become well-known to the people of the world; as Alija Izetbegovic stated, "The so-called safe area has become the most unsafe place in the world."[64] Later Clinton would appear to back away from this policy.

The Clinton administration's flip-flop in policy was obvious to foreign policy observers. In the post–Cold War era, the United States no longer knew how to lead, and Europe was not sure that it wanted to follow. The president continued to insist that there was no change in policy by his administration, even though it was noticeable to everyone else. At a news conference with foreign journalists, a reporter stated:

> Mr. President ... You advocated lifting the arms embargo on the Muslims and striking and striking at some Serbian positions. And then you appeared to back away from that. Then you moved to a compromise for setting up safe havens. Now, that's a concept which you, yourself, described as a shooting gallery.[65]

President Clinton was also chided by the Republican opposition for his ever-changing Bosnian policy. Senator Dole, the Senate minority leader noted:

> after deciding on a course of action to address the war in Bosnia-Hercegovina nearly 3 weeks ago, the Clinton administration, instead of moving forward, now seemed to be drifting, or even backing away.
>
> At his press conference last week, the President claimed not to have changed his mind about the next steps, namely the so-called lift and strike options—steps which I strongly support. But, the newspapers and journals are filled with reports that the President is now

> abandoning his effort to build support among our allies for his decision and is deferring to them.
>
> Yesterday, in testimony to the House, Secretary Christopher added to that speculation by suggesting that rather than trying to end the fighting in Bosnia, the Clinton administration is attempting to contain the conflict.
>
> Indecision. Lack of clarity. Waffling. Shifting. These words and phrases have been used in recent days to describe President Clinton's Bosnia policy. Some even ask whether there is a Bosnia policy.[66]

The president seemed confused and unsure of what his next move should be.

In hindsight, the reasons for President Clinton's uncertainty were obvious. He was the first bona fide post–Cold War president. President Bush I had presided over the collapse of the Soviet Union, but Clinton was the first president who held office when there was no Soviet Union during the entire course of his term. Therefore, there was no precedent as to how to proceed, there was no longer a common foe to hold the Western alliance together, and there was less of an incentive for the United States' European partners to follow in her footsteps. The Gulf War had given a false impression of what the New World Order was to be. The actions of Saddam Hussein threatened the world economy. That made it easier for the Western alliance to take action. But the actions of Milosevic, Karadzic, and Mladic, while revolting, did not pose a direct challenge to the United States and Europe, or their way of life. Also, European unity was on the rise. The nagging question for Clinton was how to lead.

Clinton's fundamental failure, one that he was later to correct, was not knowing how to operate the presidency. After being on the job for a few months, Clinton had not yet mastered it. He realized the limitations of his office, but not its strengths, and he was yet to realize that what he initially considered to be a source of weakness in the presidency was actually its strength. President Clinton noted:

> Well, one of my great predecessors, Harry Truman, who was President, as you know, right after World War II, said that he discovered after he became President that his job largely consisted of trying to talk other people into doing what they ought to do anyway. Sometimes I feel that way, that I don't have as much power as I thought I would have.[67]

However, as Richard Neustadt has noted in *Presidential Power*, the greatest power that the president possesses is the power to persuade. This is an enormous power that has been utilized by the most successful presidents. Clinton's problem was that he did not make a compelling case to the American people that it was necessary for the United States to intervene in Bosnia to stop genocide.

Somalia also acted to restrain President Clinton's actions in Bosnia. The United States had committed peacekeeping troops to Somalia during the Bush I administration. Congress was beginning to question the effectiveness of the mission, then disaster struck on October 3, 1993. A U.S. helicopter was shot down and television cameras captured the gruesome scene of the body of a U.S. serviceman being dragged through the streets of Mogadishu. That helped to tie the president's hands temporarily. His every move came under the close scrutiny of Congress.

Bill Clinton may have been inconsistent about what he said he would do in Bosnia, but he was consistent about what he said he would not do—send combat troops to Bosnia. That was the consistent message of his administration throughout the war. Although he did promise that up to 25,000 U.S. peacekeepers could be deployed after a peace agreement was secured in Bosnia, he did not want U.S. troops to be placed in a hostile environment. Clinton may not have served in Vietnam, but he was a veteran of its legacy nevertheless.

Bosnia went from being a catastrophe for the Clinton administration to being nothing more than a public relations problem. By November 1993, Clinton administration officials were congratulating themselves because news of Bosnia was fading from the headlines.[68] It became an inconvenient issue to be managed just like any other insignificant issue. Administration officials soon learnt that there were some things that were beyond their control.

Ultimately, President Clinton was to learn an important lesson in leadership. As President Truman put it, "a successful administration is one of strong presidential leadership. Weak leadership—or no leadership—produces failure and often disaster."[69] Disaster struck in Sarajevo on February 5, 1994. A mortar killed sixty-nine people and wounded 200 others. It was obvious that Clinton's failure to lead had caused this disaster. President Clinton had two options. He could continue with a failed policy or he could adopt a bolder approach. The president opted for the latter. As a result, on March 1, 1994, the Washington Agreement was announced. It set up a framework for a Muslim-Croat federation to be established in Bosnia. It brought the fighting between the two groups to a halt and enabled them to shift their focus to their common enemy, the Serbs. Once Clinton decided to exert strong leadership, the crisis in Bosnia began to come to an end.

Clinton was now emboldened. He now sought a way to get around the United States' allies who were opposed to lifting the arms embargo on the former Yugoslavia and a Congress that favored lifting the embargo. On May 15, 1994, the Associated Press reported that Iran had shipped arms to the Bosnian Muslims despite the ban on such shipments by the United Nations. The report proved to be true. The arms could only have been transported to the beleaguered Bosnian government through Croatia. In April 1994, Franjo Tudjman, the president of Croatia, asked if the United States objected to Iranian arms flowing to the Bosnian government. The Clinton administration informed Peter Galbraith, the U.S. ambassador to Croatia, to tell President Tudjman that he had "no instructions" on the topic.[70] The Clinton administration gave its tacit consent to those shipments so that the Bosnian government could defend itself. And, in the process, President Clinton was able to avoid a battle with his European allies by maintaining the embargo, and he was able to accomplish the goals of Congress by allowing the Bosnian government to receive arms.

This was a bold step for the Clinton administration, but this change in policy caused confusion in the State Department, where officials admitted that there was a shift in U.S. policy toward Bosnia, but many of them did not know what the new policy was. It was reported:

> As confusion and controversy swirled around the Clinton administration's line on Bosnia at the start of this week, the U.S. Embassy in Sarajevo phoned Washington. The embassy wanted to know exactly what the U.S. policy on Bosnia was.[71]

The Clinton administration's new bold policy helped change the course of the war. The Croatian army launched an offensive in the Krajina region with the Clinton administration's backing. This offensive, combined with surprising victories by the Bosnian army and the NATO bombing of Bosnian Serb targets, helped bring an end to the war. However, there were limits to the risk that President Clinton was willing to take. He was still haunted by the angst of his generation, and refused to commit combat troops to the conflict in Bosnia for fear it would turn into another Vietnam.

Srebrenica will forever stand as a monument to the failure of the United States and the European Union to keep their promises. Genocide is an offense against humanity. The United States and its allies failed to come to the aid of the city—which had been designated as a UN safe haven—when it was under siege by Radko Mladac, whose presence in the area was a tip-off to the massacre that would follow. After the fall of Srebrenica, 8,000 men and boys were slaughtered. This happened because no one was willing to take action to prevent it. Bill Clinton is an intelligent and talented politician, yet he did not use his many gifts to explain the situation in Bosnia to the American people to bring genocide to an end.

Finally, enough was enough, and Richard Holbrooke, the assistant secretary of state for European and Canadian affairs, came up with an endgame strategy. Under the Dayton Agreement, Bosnia was to be partitioned into two sectors, a Muslim-Croat federation and a Serb sector. The Muslim-Croat sector was to consist of 51 percent of the territory, and the Serb sector was to constitute the other 49 percent. A federal government was also created. The fighting came to an end, but Bosnia would never be the same. It is ironic that people in Bosnia from various cultural backgrounds coexisted in peace for many years, but myths about ancient hatreds between them prevented the United States and its allies from intervening. The West hesitated just long enough for genocide to take place. The war in Bosnia showed that the Convention on the Prevention and Punishment of the Crime of Genocide has become a worthless document. There is no place for the weak or the helpless in the New World Order. After all, big fish eat little fish, don't they? This is considered to be in accordance with the laws of nature.

The Congress and President Clinton

The consensus in Congress to lift the arms embargo against Bosnia when President Bush I was in office did not disappear when Bill Clinton became the president. It intensified. Congress thought that it had a partner in Bill Clinton with respect to Bosnia, more so than with President Bush I, but to the disappointment and consternation of many in Congress during the early days of his administration, Bill Clinton began to resemble George Bush I with respect to his Bosnia policy. Congress acted as a motivating force that moved Clinton to adopt a bolder policy though some members of Congress were motivated by partisan purposes.

During the 1992 presidential campaign, Bill Clinton spoke out in favor of "lift and strike." Senator Joseph Lieberman (Democrat-Connecticut) defended his position in the Senate. Senator Lieberman stated:

> On Monday, the President's press secretary, Marlin Fitzwater, criticized Gov. Bill Clinton's very sensible, humane, and measured proposal for dealing with the crisis in Bosnia, calling them reckless. Governor Clinton

> simply, and correctly, in my view, called on the President to seek U.N. authorization of selective air strikes against those who are attacking the international relief effort. He did not call for all-out war. He did not call for the introduction of ground combat forces. He called for U.S. naval forces to participate in an international effort to protect relief supplies.
>
> This is a proposal that has been echoed by members of both parties in this Chamber, and indeed, may I say, as recently as yesterday by the Secretary of Defense himself. It is not a reckless proposal. In fact, to call Governor Clinton's proposal reckless is itself reckless, because it breaks a bipartisan consensus on how to deal with the tragedy in this region of the world that has formed in this Chamber.[72]

Initially Clinton was in sync with Congress, until Secretary of State Christopher's failed European trip.

After Clinton failed to convince the United States' European allies to lift the arms embargo, problems with Congress began. President Clinton backed away from "lift and strike" to maintain harmony with European leaders. He argued that the arms embargo should not be lifted unilaterally, because of objections from European countries with peacekeepers on the ground in Bosnia. They believed that their troops would be endangered if the arms embargo was lifted. Congress, on the other hand, felt that it was important to get weapons to the beleaguered Bosnian government for defending itself and its people who faced genocide. Congress felt an urgency to act, while President Clinton just seemed trapped. This set in motion a struggle between the president and Congress over Bosnia.

Some of the most powerful members of the U. S. Senate were in favor of lifting the arms embargo against Bosnia. Support for this measure cut across party lines. The senators Dole (Republican-Kansas), Pell (Democrat–Rhode Island), DeConcini (Republican–New Mexico), Lieberman (Democrat-Connecticut), Mitchell (Democrat-Maine), Bumpers (Democrat-Arkansas), and others wanted the embargo lifted. Initially, Senator Dole led a bipartisan effort to lift the embargo. Dole noted:

> Despite President Clinton's claimed preference for lifting the embargo against Bosnia and Hercegovina, the United States is not lobbying other Security Council members to gain their support for this measure.
>
> The administration has decided not to play a leading role in the Security Council, rather it has decided to play follow the leader, and the leaders in this case are the British, French and Russians—whose policies, diplomatic initiatives and involvement in Bosnia and Hercegovina to date have not brought Bosnia any closer to peace than it was 15 months ago when the war started.[73]

Many in the Senate felt the same as Dole.

This bipartisan group tried to influence the course of the United States' policy in Bosnia. On June 10, 1993, the senators Dole, Biden (Democrat-Delaware), DeConcini (Republican–New Mexico), D'Amato (Republican–New York), and Lieberman (Democrat-Connecticut) submitted Senate Resolution 116 to the Committee on Foreign Relations. It stated that the United States would not undermine the sovereignty of Bosnia, or recognize its incorporation into any other state. The measure did not make it to the floor of the Senate, but it served notice to the Clinton administration that the prevailing view in Congress was that a more forceful policy needed to be implemented. This was just a precursor of things to come.

The next year, the situation between the president and Congress did not improve. It grew more intense. The prevailing view was still that the embargo needed to be lifted, and that the United States should do so unilaterally, even if Europe was not willing to act in unison with it. On January 29, 1994, the Senate passed a nonbinding resolution to unilaterally lift the arms embargo against Bosnia by a vote of 87–9. The President was attempting to balance his policy between Congress and the United States' European allies, but the Senate believed that Clinton's policy was too weak.

This battle raged on. Senator Dole introduced legislation to end the arms embargo against Bosnia. Initially, Dole had bipartisan support for this measure. In February 1994, Dole and Senator Lieberman worked together to obtain the signature of forty-nine other senators, and sent a letter to President Clinton urging him to exercise leadership and to unilaterally lift the Bosnian arms embargo. It stated that the United States' European allies would follow his lead if the embargo were lifted, but there was no clear-cut evidence that they would do this.

Two months later, a major clash took place between the president and Congress. In April 1994, both Houses of Congress passed the Foreign Relations Authorization Act. President Clinton signed it into law on April 30, 1994. The bill contained the nonbinding sense of Congress that the arms embargo against Bosnia should be lifted. It was similar to the one that the Senate had passed in January. The battle between the Congress and the president was on.

The bipartisan effort to lift the arms embargo grew even more intense in the months that followed. Senator Dole introduced legislation that went beyond the previous Senate resolutions. It would have required the president to lift the arms embargo; however, a fissure developed in the bipartisan effort. Congressional elections were approaching. It would have been an embarrassment to the

Democrats if Congress chose to override Clinton's judgment on a major foreign policy issue during an election year, yet something needed to be done. Therefore, Senator Mitchell (Democrat-Maine), the Senate majority leader, introduced legislation similar to Dole's, but it would not have required the president to lift the arms embargo against Bosnia unilaterally. He could only do so after a resolution to lift the embargo had failed in the Security Council and Clinton had consulted with Congress about lifting the embargo unilaterally. The Mitchell Amendment was less restrictive than Dole's measure and did not usurp the president's authority like the Dole Amendment. Ironically, both bills were passed in May 1994. The net effect was to add confusion and to leave the embargo intact.

Once more, Senator Dole attempted to whittle together a bipartisan coalition to lift the arms embargo. On June 24, 1994, he introduced the Bosnia Self-Defense Act that was cosponsored by the senators DeConcini (Republican–New Mexico), D'Amato (Republican–New York), Levin (Democrat-Michigan), Hutchinson (Republican-Texas), Feingold (Democrat-Wisconsin), Jeffords (Republican-Vermont), Wallop (Republican-Wyoming), Luger (Republican-Indiana), McConnell (Republican-Kentucky), Brown (Republican-Colorado), Murkowski (Republican-Alaska), Helms (Republican–North Carolina), Gordon (Republican-Washington), and Moynihan (Democrat–New York). It sought to lift the embargo so Bosnia could exercise the right to self-defense in accordance with Article 51 of the UN Charter. This effort to lift the embargo failed.

Senator Dole's bipartisan effort to lift the arms embargo against Bosnia turned partisan. His presidential ambitions got the better of him. On the one hand, he evoked images of weakness and impotence when discussing the Clinton administration's handling of Bosnia, yet Dole sought to restrict the action of the Clinton administration to deploy troops in Bosnia. Senator Dole insisted that if the Clinton administration sent troops to Bosnia, they could only be used to assist the withdrawal of UN peacekeepers.[74] Moreover, Dole's decision to aggressively pursue the arms embargo issue after 1994 also calls his motives into question. On June 24, 1994, Senator John McCain (Republican-Arizona) placed an article from the *Washington Times* in the *Congressional Record*. The article "Iranian Weapons Sent Via-Croatia-Aid to Moslems Gets U.S. Wink" by Bill Gertz revealed that Iranian arms were making their way to the Bosnian government. The Clinton administration had reached an agreement with the Congress on November 10, 1994, that it would no longer use resources to enforce the arms embargo. This was a de facto lifting of the arms embargo. Moreover, Dole indicated that he knew that arms were being sent to the Bosnian government. On June 7, 1995, Dole stated, "Iran is a key supplier of arms to the Bosnians."[75] He knew that the Bosnian government now had a supply of arms, but he continued to use the arms embargo as an issue to criticize Clinton.

President Clinton did not have an easier time with the House of Representatives regarding the arms embargo against Bosnia. A bipartisan coalition in the House also sought to overturn the arms embargo as well. In July 1995, the Republican-controlled House and Senate voted overwhelmingly to lift the arms embargo against Bosnia. The measure did not hold in the face of a veto by President Clinton. In his statement to Congress after vetoing the measure, President Clinton stated:

> Events in the past few weeks have opened new possibilities for negotiations. We will test these new realities and we are now engaged without allies and others in using these opportunities to settle this terrible war by agreement. This is not the time for the United States to pull the plug on the UN mission.[76]

There was now no need to lift the embargo. President Clinton had found a way to get around his European allies and Congress to secure arms for the Bosnian government and everyone knew it.

The International Community

The term "international community" is a misnomer. A community implies a close social setting where there are cultural norms and a close association among the members of society. This is true for the United States and its western European allies, but not for the rest of the world. In fact, the international system resembled more of a community during the Cold War than it does today. Today, the international system resembles more of a metropolis than a community. In a metropolis an individual has few friends and weak associations and affinity with members of the greater society. This is why genocide in Bosnia was allowed to continue for three years with a weak response from the international community.

The Cold War and Devolution

The international system was more akin to an international community during the Cold War than it is now. During the Cold War, the two ideological camps were led by hegemons, the United States and the Soviet Union. The Cold War was based on a zero-sum game. The two superpowers had core areas and key allies they defended. The United States' key allies were located in Western Europe. The Soviet Union's allies were in Eastern Europe. This post–World War II arrangement was solidified in the Helsinki Final Act of 1975. Third World countries constituted a gray area. A Third World country would be extended protection by a superpower (such as the United States) if it had some compelling interest in that country and was threatened by a rival.

Now, in the post–Cold War era, things have changed. The lack of a common enemy means that there is less cohesion among the United States and its allies. The Gulf War created a false impression that collective security could be used against an aggressor; however, European countries no longer have an incentive to follow the lead of the United States. Moreover, ties among Western European countries increased with the emergence of the European Union and its development of a single currency, the Euro.

As a result, the international system has devolved to a degree. In the absence of a direct threat to its security, Europe is less likely to rely on the United States for leadership. This makes it more difficult to form coalitions for quick action. Gray areas that were not part of the superpower blocs, such as Yugoslavia, lost their value at the end of the Cold War; therefore the problems of the former Yugoslavia were ignored by the United States and its allies for too long. This influenced their perception of the conflict and the solutions offered to end it.

THE UNITED STATES AND EUROPE: THE LOST AND THE LEADERLESS

Bosnia was thrust into the lap of Europe because the Bush I administration believed that it did not have a dog in that fight. Initially, Europe seemed to grasp the problem and proposed a workable solution. The Carrington Plan had the potential to prevent war in Bosnia. It went to the heart of the problem. Unlike the other plans that would be proposed, it guaranteed the individual the right to maintain his nationality. It allowed the six republics of the former Yugoslavia as much sovereignty as they wanted. The Memoranda on the Convention at the Hague was passed on November 4, 1991; it called for a new relationship between the republics based on:

(a) the sovereignty and independence of the republics with internationally recognized character and status for those who wish it;

(b) the free association of republics with internationally recognized character and status (borders) ...
(c) comprehensive arrangements that include a mechanism for the supervision and protection of human rights and the special protection of particular groups and regions;
(d) a common state consisting of republics with equal rights for those republics which wish to remain within a common state;
(e) the involvement of European institutions where this seems appropriate;
(f) the recognition of the independence of those republics which wish it, within their present frontiers.

The plan sought to restore the right to a cultural identity to citizens throughout the former Yugoslavia, as was the case during Tito's rule. Citizens of the various republics would be on an equal social footing regardless of their nationality.

Unfortunately, the Carrington Plan was never implemented. Under the Carrington Plan, the Krajina Serbs and the Bosnian Serbs would have been granted autonomy, but Serbia would have stayed the same size. The plan would have thwarted Milosevic's territorial ambitions, therefore Milosovic vetoed it. It would have implemented democracy throughout the former Yugoslavia.

The international community acted mildly when Milosevic rejected the Carrington Plan. There was no attempt at arm-twisting. Extreme sanctions might have helped to pressure Milosevic to accept the plan. Thus, the Carrington Plan, the best peace plan that was put forth for Bosnia, was allowed to die. As late as 1993, the Clinton administration was attempting to get the United Nations to enact sanctions to prevent Yugoslavia from importing nonessential food—caviar, beer, wine, and microwave popcorn—but was rebuffed by the UN Sanctions Committee.[77]

The subsequent peace plans that followed the Carrington Plan called for the implementation of apartheid in Bosnia. The peace plans from the Vance-Owens Plan to the Dayton Peace Accords called for Bosnia to be carved up according to nationality. In the end, the plans rewarded the aggressors who initiated ethnic cleansing and abandoned the principles of democracy. The international community failed to grasp what was at stake in Bosnia and the rest of the former Yugoslavia. It was a case of democratis interruptus. Social and cultural guarantees needed to be added to the new government institutions to make democracy work in the Balkans, instead the international community viewed the conflict as pathological and thought that the best way to handle the conflict was to divide the combatants. They helped to impose a plan on Bosnia that they never would have accepted themselves because it was an insult to the principles of democracy. In the end, the international community grew tired of the Bosnia problem and just wanted it to go away.

However, Alija Izetbegovic, the president of Bosnia, would not allow it to go away. He sought to establish Bosnia-Herzegovina as an undivided democratic entity. Izetbegovic fought against the establishment of apartheid in Bosnia; yet, he found his efforts foiled by the West. The United States and the European Union sought to undermine Izetbegovic. When the Invincible Plan[78] was being negotiated, the United States brought Fikret Abdic, Izetbegovic's political rival, into the negotiations. This was done to reduce the stature of Izetbegovic from a statesman to the leader of a Muslim faction. Izetbegovic was browbeaten and humiliated by the West until he finally gave in to the ethnic division of his country and signed the Dayton Accords.

The behavior of the international community during the war in Bosnia sent a negative message to the budding democracies of the world. In effect, it was a signal to them that if they came under attack there would be no help unless they were perceived to be of some economic value to the West. As the former president Nixon stated:

> As the post–Cold War era in Europe begins, the crisis in Yugoslavia has set a profoundly dangerous precedent: While communism has collapsed around the world, the West has mounted a comically tepid response to attempts by Serbian hard-line communists to dismember the democratic government of Croatia.
>
> A neutral Western position appeases the aggressors in Serbia and the Serbian dominated federal army. It will give a green light to aggressors world-wide and send a discouraging signal to the world's struggling democrats, not only in the former Soviet Union but even in China.[79]

The West often criticizes Muslim countries for their lack of democracy. In Bosnia, Muslims were fighting in defense of democracy but the West turned its back on them.

It is ironic that during the days of the Cold War, the West emphasized Basket III of the Helsinki Final Act of 1975. Basket III deals with human rights guarantees. The United States and its European allies used to criticize the Soviet Union for violating the human rights embodied in Basket III; yet, in the face of massive human rights violations in the former Yugoslavia, the United States and Western Europe no longer seemed committed to defending human rights. The defense of human rights was what was needed to secure the rights of the minorities in the various republics in Yugoslavia. The protection of human rights would have dampened the need for rebellion.

There was also a notable pattern of prejudice among the western European UN workers and peacekeepers. They had an anti-Muslim bias that ultimately worked in favor of the Serbs, who always got the benefit of the doubt; the Muslims never did.

> General Lewis MacKenzie had first given credence to the idea that the Bosnian government, as part of a strategy to bring the international community into the war on its side, had taken to bombing its own people.[80]

There was no proof to substantiate such an outrageous accusation. Cognitive dissonance was a factor in how the UN workers and peacekeepers perceived events. The Serbs were viewed as rational, and the Bosnian Muslims were viewed as irrational. The Serbs' power garnered respect for them, while the weak position of the Bosnian Muslims reinforced existing biases and disrespect. The anti-Muslim bias hit its lowest point after the fall of Srebrenica in July 1995. Dutch UN peacekeepers helped the Serb victors load Bosnian Muslim civilians onto buses that took them to be executed.[81]

Letting the people of Bosnia-Herzegovina die was a value judgment. The West did not view the victims as worthy of the price that would have had to be paid to stop the genocide. They let people die and still tried to maintain their image as the defenders of justice. All could clearly see that the emperor had no clothes.

Media Coverage

The media played a vital role by informing the world about the events that were unfolding in Bosnia. The media also exerted a strong influence on the U.S. Congress. During debate, members of Congress frequently had newspaper articles about Bosnia placed in the *Congressional Record*, as previously noted in this chapter. The problem with the media coverage of the war in Bosnia was how the war was covered. Instead of portraying the war as a fight to institute democracy and its related principles, the war was portrayed as a tribal conflict. This helped to confuse the American public. They played a minimum role in determining the policy the United States adopted in Bosnia.

Reports by Roy Gutman of *Newsday*, the *Guardian*, and the Associated Press played a vital role by keeping the world informed about the horrible events that were unfolding in Bosnia. Moreover, newspapers such as *The New York Times* took a strong stand against the aggression in Bosnia initiated by Slobodan Milosevic. In the early days of the war an article in *The New York Times* stated:

> It is not too late to send a formal message through diplomatic ultimatums, backed by the threat of armed intervention. Mr. Milosevic recognizes only one language, military force; the rest of the world may soon have to speak of it.[82]

The conservative media icon George F. Will also took a strong stance in support of human rights in Bosnia. When defenders of the Bosnian arms embargo, such as Lord Owens, charged that lifting the embargo would only "level the killing field," Will retorted:

> Today defenders of the embargo say it economizes violence because lifting it would prolong the fighting. This argument is especially unpleasant when used by the British, who today might be obeying German traffic laws if Lend-Lease had not prolonged the fighting.[83]

The press did an adequate job—but the coverage could have been better. The press should have taken more time to explain the conflict to the American people, whom it was empowered to serve. In the United States, many newspapers and television stations do not have foreign correspondents; instead they rely on the wire services for their information. However, the Associated Press often portrayed the war in Bosnia as a tribal conflict between Muslims and Serbs. The government of Bosnia-Herzegovina was democratic and tried to foster multiculturalism. The government of Bosnia-Herzegovina and its forces were often simply referred to as "Muslims." As noted above, after winning the election in Bosnia, Izetbegovic shared power with the other nationalities. Moreover, one of the heroes of the Bosnian army was Colonel Petrovic, a Serb, yet the term "Muslim" was often used to describe all organs of the Bosnian government. What this did was to delegitimize the Bosnian government, its institutions, and its army in the eyes of many of the people who read these press reports.

A brief survey of Associated Press reports shows repeated references to the Bosnian government and army as "Muslims." In 1992 there were ten such references, and as the war escalated the number of references increased. By 1993 there were fifteen such references, and sixteen in 1994. As the war began to wind down, there were five such references in 1995. The wire services have an enormous impact since many news services around the country depend on them for news from abroad. Such wording can affect one's perception. Thus many Americans viewed the Bosnian war as an ancient tribal conflict. Hence, it was viewed as pathological and something beyond the control of the United States, and, thus, the American public was not aroused in the midst of genocide.

Moreover, there was scant mention of Croats during the Bosnian war. Croatian troops often crossed the border into Bosnia, and Croatia was a major factor in bringing the war to an end, yet war coverage often was centered on Sarajevo, Bosnia's capital. The rural areas of Bosnia suffered more damage and loss of life than Sarajevo, but these events were not always covered.

The reports of the war in Bosnia were flawed but they were vital, nevertheless, and proved the importance of a free press. The press was able to document the genocide and the massive crimes against humanity that occurred in Bosnia. Many are still being punished for these crimes today. The U.S. press provided a vital service in Bosnia by serving as the eyes of the world.

CONCLUSION

Reality seldom changes. What was true seventy years ago is still true today. Appeasement does not work. Neville Chamberlain had an excuse—he did not know the consequences of his actions—but we have had seventy years to ponder the consequences of appeasement. Yet, during the war in Bosnia the same mistakes were made with similar consequences. Genocide, the unthinkable, has happened in our lifetime, and we have no one except ourselves to blame.

In the end, the mass destruction of human life could have been prevented if the United States had stood up for the principles it claims to adhere to. It failed to live up to these principles because it was haunted by the ghost of a past war—Vietnam.

The United States must pick and choose its battles carefully, but it cannot run away from its responsibilities. When faced with genocide it must act and act decisively. In many ways, the United States has become a paper tiger. It has lost its way. Some situations require muscle, some diplomacy, and others both. The United States must take the necessary actions when required. Every situation is not another Vietnam waiting to happen.

Eventually, a young president found his courage and his voice and was able to put an end to the nightmare in Bosnia; however, he would soon forget the lessons he learned in Bosnia and would pay a price for it three years later in Kosovo.

As the Cold War has faded, regionalism has grown. If a real international community is to emerge, human rights must be defended and international law must be enforced. Otherwise, there will be more shock and horror to come in the future, and we will still not be able to understand why.

CHAPTER 6

THE WAR IN KOSOVO

History has surely taught us that when you defer the tough decisions, when you let butchers continue and the tyrants and dictators continue, it gets worse. And it has gotten worse with Milosevic.

—Senator Chuck Hagel, May 3, 1999

INTRODUCTION

The war in Kosovo was the most divisive foreign policy issue of the post–Cold War era. It was the second time that the United States had intervened to stop genocide committed by Slobodan Milosevic, the "Butcher of the Balkans". Kosovo was more than a debate about whether the United States and its NATO allies should intervene in the affairs of a sovereign state to halt genocide. Kosovo demonstrated how myths and prejudices can be manipulated to inflame racial and ethnic hatred. The war in Kosovo was also about the legacy of the Cold War. Was the Cold War fought to defend a balance of power, or was it fought in defense of freedom and human rights, the same values that were defended during World War II? The war in Kosovo also determined how U.S. foreign policy would be defined during the post–Cold War era. Some felt that since the Cold War was over, there was no longer a need for extensive U.S. involvement overseas, while others felt that the United States needed to remain involved in international affairs to protect human rights and to help shape the post–Cold War world. The political alignments on this issue often did not correspond to a party affiliation or ideology.

The war in Kosovo was notable for its international implications as well. During the war in Bosnia, the Clinton administration had belatedly included European Muslims in international society by defending their human rights. During the war in Kosovo, that decision was up for review by NATO and members of Congress. Many members of Congress wanted to revoke those rights and expunge the Albanians of Kosovo (Kosovars) from the rolls of international society.

THE HISTORICAL TRUTH ABOUT ALBANIANS AND SERBS IN KOSOVO

The story of the Balkans is not easy to understand or simple to decipher. However, what is apparent is that the entire region is engulfed in myths. Kosovo is often called the cradle of Serbian culture and the Serbian Jerusalem. It is said to be the area where the Patriarchate of the Serbian Orthodox Church originated. The fact that Albanians have become the dominant group in Kosovo is an irritant to many Serbs today because they do not want to see an area that they hold so dear in the hands of a people whom many of them despise (Kosovar Albanians).

A specter haunts the Balkans. It is the specter of violence, but that specter is really a phantom. Scholars who have studied various regions of the Balkans, such as Kosovo, note the cooperation, appreciation, and collaboration among the people of that region. They have lived in relative peace with each other for approximately 900 years, unlike the image of the Balkans portrayed by Robert D. Kaplan in his book *Balkan Ghost*.[1] The animosity between Serbs and Albanians is a relatively recent historical occurrence. The Battle of Kosovo Polje (the Field of Blackbirds), which occurred in 1389, is often cited as the source of animosity between them. According to Serbian folklore, despite the gallant and heroic efforts of the Serbs on the field, this battle led to the downfall of the Serbian Empire and their victimization and exploitation by the invading Ottomans (Muslims). The story goes that the Serbs survived this period of humiliation and liberated themselves from Ottoman rule in 1878. Myths are often romantic, seductive, and inaccurate. The truth is often bland and lacks the lure of myths. The myths surrounding Kosovo developed during the late nineteenth century when nationalism was growing in the Balkans. The Enlightenment challenged the role of religion and sought to empower the individual. This naturally affected how people perceived themselves. As a result, religion was weakened and people began to identify themselves more by language, customs, and a shared history.

This led to the growth of nationalism among the Serbs. By the late nineteenth century, myths that did not reflect the reality about the Battle of Kosovo became part of the political socialization of Serbs.

THE TRUTH ABOUT KOSOVO

Kosovo is not the cradle of Serbian culture. The origins of the Serbian Empire and the Serbian Patriarchate can be traced to Rascia (Sandzak), which is northwest of Kosovo. The Serbs settled in the area in the early seventh century and began to expand into outlying areas. By the 1160s, the Serbian Nemanjid dynasty was established. The Serbian Empire extended out from Rascia to Nis (northeast Serbia), Montenegro, northern Albania, Kosovo, and northern Macedonia. The Serbian Orthodox Church was established in 1219 in Rascia, the seat of the Serbian Empire. Hence, the Patriarchate was established in Rascia and not in Kosovo. In the latter part of the thirteenth century, when the church in Rascia burned down, the Patriarchate moved to Pec in Kosovo.

The Serbian Empire reached its heights under the reign of Dusan (1331–1355). After his reign, the Serbian Empire began to disintegrate. Here we see the flaw in the Serbian myth regarding the Battle of Kosovo. The Serbian Empire had begun to decline prior to the Battle of Kosovo. The Serbs suffered a major defeat at the hands of the Ottoman Empire during the Battle of Marica in Bulgaria on September 26, 1371. This is when the Ottoman invasion of Serbian-held areas began.

Moreover, the myths about the Battle of Kosovo lead one to believe that the defeat of the Serbs on the battlefield of Kosovo Polje in 1389 led to the destruction of the Serbian state. This is not true. While the Serbs, under the leadership of Prince Lazar, were defeated, the Serbian state continued to exist. Under the leadership of Prince Lazar's son Stefan Lazarevic, Serbia became a vassal of the Ottoman Empire; therefore, Serbia contributed soldiers to the Sultan's army in return for autonomy. The Serbian state continued to exist for another seventy years. In fact, "the cultural history of the Serbian people [after the Battle of Kosovo] was something of a golden age."[2] Serbian literature and art flourished. The defeat of the Serbs at Kosovo Polje neither destroyed Serbian culture nor the Serbian state.

The Balkans are often viewed as a cauldron of ethnic hatred. The animosity between Serbs and Albanians in Kosovo is cited as a prime example of hatred among ethnic groups in the region; however, history tells us a different story. What is often forgotten is that Albanians fought on the side of the Serbs during the Battle of Kosovo Polje in 1389. One of the heroes of the Battle of Kosovo, Milos Kobilic, may have been an Albanian.[3] In addition, the Albanians and Serbs of Kosovo were allies during the Ottoman-Hapsburg War (1683–1699); they both fought on the side of the Hapsburgs (Austrians) against the Ottomans. They also fought together on the side of the Austrians against the Ottomans in 1737.

Religious conflicts in the Balkans are also cited as having deep-seated historical roots. The Ottoman rulers of the Balkans viewed Catholicism with skepticism. Catholics were perceived as the Pope's foreign agents. There was more tolerance for the Orthodox since many of the Orthodox churches were autocephalous (independent) and lay within the borders of the Ottoman Empire. When the relationships between people of different religions in Kosovo are examined, history reveals some conflicts among them, but these conflicts do not have ancient roots. They are of recent origin. There has been a long history of religious tolerance, cooperation, and accommodation in Kosovo. In the parts of the Balkans under Ottoman rule, one could reduce one's tax burden, and sometimes avoid military service, by converting to Islam. Many Albanians and Serbs in Kosovo converted to Islam to lighten their tax burden and to avoid military service in the Janissary corps. Nevertheless, many of them continued to practice Christianity despite their conversion to Islam. This was the phenomenon know as crypto-Christianity.[4] Outside of their homes, they were Muslims. At home, they continued to practice Christianity and their wives continued to practice Christianity as well. Syncretism became a common practice in Kosovo. Muslims often had their children baptized in Christian churches, and Catholics would often designate Muslims as the godparents of their children.[5] Christians and Muslims also respected each other's houses of worship.

The roots of the current conflict between Albanians and Serbs in Kosovo can be traced back to 1878. In 1877 Russia declared war on the Ottoman Empire. Serbia, which had gained autonomy within the Ottoman Empire, took advantage of the situation, teamed up with Montenegro, and invaded Kosovo, which was still under Ottoman rule. This was an opportunity for Serbia to gain its independence and to create a Greater Serbia by expanding its borders. These events occurred when nationalism was sweeping the Balkans. The Serbs were able to gain independence, but the Treaty of Berlin (1878) returned Kosovo to the Ottoman Empire. However, Serbia's attempt to annex Kosovo created animosity between Serbia and the Albanians of Kosovo. At the time of the Serbian invasion, the Kosovar

Albanians were trying to gain more autonomy within the Ottoman Empire. Serbia was a threat to that effort and emerged as an adversary that wanted to conquer their homeland. Albanian nationalism was blossoming. Consequently, the Kosovars formed the League of Prizren to protect the area from foreign (non-Ottoman) domination.

Another major blow to Albanian-Serb relations occurred a few years later. In October 1912, Serbia, Montenegro, Bulgaria, and Greece launched an attack to dismember the decaying Ottoman Empire. This war was notable for its brutality. Acts of genocide and mayhem were committed during the war. Civilians were massacred and people's lips and noses were severed.[6] Thus, the relationship between Serbs and Kosovar Albanians began to spiral downward. From this battle, the Serbs gained control of Kosovo, their "mythic land" of origin.

The Kosovar Albanians were denied the opportunity to become part of the autonomous Albanian state that was created in 1912. Kosovo was now ruled by a new group of invaders, the Serbs. The Serbian overlords treated the Serbs of Kosovo as brothers and the Albanians as a conquered people. Freedom of expression and assembly were not allowed. For the Albanians of Kosovo, their province became a police state. The Serbian administrators prohibited the Kosovar Albanians from crossing the border into Albania. This denied them access to the markets, friends, and family they had prior to the Serbian takeover of Kosovo.

During World War I, Serbia fought on the side of the Triple Entente against the Central Powers. Kosovar Albanians were exempt from military service in Serbia's army. Nevertheless, 50,000 Kosovar Albanians enlisted in the Serbian army.[7] When the Austrian and Bulgarian armies invaded Serbia, the Serbian army was forced to retreat through Kosovo. Subsequently, Austria-Hungary and Bulgaria occupied the area. During the occupation, some Albanian Kosovars volunteered for service in the Austrian military. The Kosovars and the Austrians saw the relationship as being mutually beneficial, since they shared a common enemy—the Serbs. The Austrians also allowed the Kosovars to set up local governments and Albanian language schools, something the Serbs had not allowed them to do. If one is to have an occupier, it is better to have a benign one than a harsh one.

By November 1918, the tide in the war turned in favor of the Entente, and Serbian troops returned to Kosovo. They proceeded to take revenge on all Albanians, armed or unarmed, civilian, or military-related. In the areas in and around Pec and Gjakova, women and children were massacred, villages destroyed, and lives crushed.[8]

THE SUPPRESSION AND ABUSE OF ALBANIANS IN THE FOUR YUGOSLAVIAS

After World War I, Serbia, and hence Kosovo, was incorporated into a new state, the Kingdom of the Serbs, Croats, and Slovenes. There was irony in the creation of this state. The Conference of Versailles was supposed to address the issue of self-determination for the various nationalities in Europe, yet the Kosovar Albanians were denied self-determination. Once more, they were placed under foreign rule, this time in the newly created, Serb-dominated kingdom, instead of being allowed to unite with Albania. The Kingdom of the Serbs, Croats, and Slovenes was not created to fulfill the national aspirations of the people within its borders. It was created to maintain the post–World War I balance of power. It was feared that if the various nationalities of the Balkans were given their own small states, they might fall prey to larger states with territorial ambitions. Italy and Bulgaria laid claims to various parts of this newly created country.[9] Various nationalities were "wrapped together" in many of the Balkan states, and therefore denied self-determination as a means to thwart attacks by larger countries. This was the fate of the Kosovar Albanians. In this new state, renamed the Kingdom of Yugoslavia (the Kingdom of the South Slavs), they once more fell under Serbian domination. Miranda Vickers characterized this period as a time of oppression for the Kosovars by the Serbs. She wrote that, "Throughout … 1918–1941, the Albanians had no specifically guaranteed minority rights and lived under virtual Serb domination."[10] Albanians were not allowed to open schools in their native language; the schools in the area taught students in Serbo-Croat. The Kosovar Albanians were also not allowed to print newspapers in Albanian. However, German, Hungarian, Czech, Turkish, and Russian minorities were allowed to have newspapers in their own language. According to Noel Malcolm, the official justification for this was that most Albanians were illiterate, and qualified teachers could not be found who knew the language. Yet, "seventy-five per cent of the population of Montenegro had been illiterate in 1918, but that had not stopped the development of education and publications there."[11] Problems with illiteracy among the Albanians could easily have been dealt with by recruiting schoolteachers from Albania, which shared a common border with the Kingdom of Yugoslavia.

In 1918, the Serbian-dominated Yugoslav government also began to send Serbian settlers into Kosovo to colonize it. Kosovo had become overwhelmingly Albanian. As a means to "take back Kosovo," which was now wrongly viewed as the cradle of Serb civilization, the government sent Serbian settlers into the area to alter the demographic balance. This increased tensions and created social unrest between Albanians and Serbs. Kosovar Albanians felt that they were not full-fledged citizens of Yugoslavia.

During World War II, Yugoslavia was attacked and occupied by the Nazis. Many Albanians saw this as an opportunity to strike back at their Serbian oppressors. Some Kosovars took advantage of the situation and attacked their Serbian neighbors, and some also volunteered to fight for the Nazis. Other Kosovars took advantage of this period to organize politically in the hope of gaining independence in the future.

THE SECOND YUGOSLAVIA 1945–1980

The second phase in Yugoslavia's history occurred under the leadership of Josip Broz (Tito), the leader of the Partisan Movement. The Partisans were Communists who had liberated Yugoslavia from the Nazis; however, the Partisans failed to attract a following among Kosovar Albanians. They viewed it as a Slavic organization. In fact, the Partisans crushed the Kosovars' resistance in Kosovo. During this phase of Kosovo's incorporation into Yugoslavia, the Kosovars saw their fortunes rise to near equality with the other national groups in Yugoslavia.

Initially, the Kosovar Albanians did not see their fortunes improve in Tito's Yugoslavia, despite the various provisions of the 1946 Constitution of Yugoslavia that guaranteed equality to all citizens. For example, Chapter I of Article 1 stated:

> The Federal Peoples Republic of Yugoslavia is a federal people's state republic in form, a community of peoples equal in rights who, on the basis of the right of self-determination, including the right of separation, have expressed their will to live together in a federative state.[12]

Chapter I of Article 2 stated:

> The Federal People's Republic of Yugoslavia is composed of the People's Republic of Serbia, the People's Republic of Croatia, the People's Republic of Slovenia, the People's Republic of Bosnia and Herzegovina, the People's Republic of Macedonia and the People's Republic of Montenegro. The People's Republic of Serbia includes the Autonomous Province of Vojvodina and the Autonomous Kosovo-Metohijan Region.[13]

The Kosovar Albanians were finally granted social and political equality, self-government, equality before the law regardless of race and creed, and freedom of religion. They had been denied these rights by the Kingdom of Yugoslavia.

As noted above, Kosovo and Vojvodina were recognized as part of Serbia but were granted self-government. However, the constitution made a distinction between the two areas. Chapter I of Article 2 stated that Vojvodina was an autonomous province while Kosovo was an autonomous region. The differences between the two can be found by examining Chapter XI and Chapter XII of the 1946 Constitution of Yugoslavia. Article 105 of Chapter XI states: "The highest organ of state authority of the autonomous province is the people's assembly of the autonomous province." On the other hand, Article 106 of Chapter XI states: "The highest organ of the state authority of an autonomous region is the regional people's committee." A more extensive reading of the constitution helps to further clarify matters. Chapter XII makes a distinction between a people's assembly that governs an autonomous province and a people's committee that governs in an autonomous region. Article 107 of Chapter XII stated that people's committees are the organs of localities (villages and small towns), town wards, towns, departments, and regions. In other words, a people's assembly was a legislature that governed an entire province, while a people's committee was a local organ of government and only governed part of a province. In addition, it has been pointed out that as an autonomous province, Vojvodina also had a supreme court while Kosovo did not.[14]

Despite the legal equality granted to the Kosovar Albanians, they were treated like criminals for two reasons. First, the Kosovars collaborated with the Nazis during World War II. Second, hostility developed between Yugoslavia and Albania as a result of Tito's break with Moscow and subsequent expulsion from the Communist Information Bureau (Cominform).[15] Enver Hoxha, the Communist leader of Albania, broke his close friendship with Tito and joined Moscow's allies in provoking border clashes with Yugoslavia. Tito viewed the Kosovars as potential supporters of Albania. Hoxha began to champion their cause and engaged in polemics about the abuse of Kosovar Albanians by Tito, who had virtually declared Kosovar Albanians an enemy of the people. Their homes were raided for weapons and searched for Cominformist (Hoxha supporters). Restrictions were also placed on the practice of Islam—the religion of most Kosovar Albanians. Muslims were no longer allowed to teach their children in mosques. Tito sought to rid himself of a portion of the "Albanian menace" by allowing them to register as Turks in the census. This allowed Kosovars to immigrate to Turkey.

A de facto colonization of Kosovo had taken place under Tito. Though legally equal, in reality, the Kosovars were second-class citizens whom the government distrusted and wanted to get rid of. For the average Kosovar, his life was that of a colonized man. He lived a life of domination. Serbs and Montenegrins dominated industry, education, administration, and security, even though their combined total made up only about one-fourth of the population of Kosovo.

Repression did not work; it only helped to spur nationalism among the Kosovars, thus undermining the Yugoslav government's campaign of "Brotherhood and Unity." Therefore, in 1966, Aleksandar Rankovic, the vice president of Yugoslavia and the minister of the interior, who relished the persecution of Kosovars, was sacked at the League of Communists' Fourth Plenum at Brioni. Tito could not beat the Kosovars into submission; therefore, he allowed them to join Yugoslavia as full-fledged citizens. In December 1968, Yugoslavia's constitution was amended to provide Kosovo with its own assembly, Supreme Court, and representation in Yugoslavia's parliament. The following year, Kosovo was provided with its own constitution and autonomous university (the University of Prishtina), where classes would be available in Albanian. In 1974, Yugoslavia adopted a new constitution that provided Kosovo and Vojvodina with seats on the Yugoslav presidency. Kosovo and Vojvodina became de facto republics. The only thing they could not do that a republic could was to secede from Yugoslavia. In addition to the changes mentioned above, an affirmative action program was also enacted for Kosovars. This meant that they now had greater representation in government, the local affiliate of the League of Communists, industry, and administration. For many Serbs in Kosovo, this was too much. From a psychological perspective, they were taken out of their comfort zone. They had been taught that Albanians were an inferior people with an inferior culture. Now, they had to deal with Albanians in positions of authority and social equals. Many Serbs chose to leave Kosovo rather than to make the necessary psychological adjustments that would allow them to perceive of Albanians as equals. Many Serbs also left Kosovo because of the lack of jobs. Kosovo was the poorest region in Yugoslavia. Competition for jobs was often a source of conflict between Serbs and Kosovar Albanians.

Nevertheless, the changes in the structure of the Yugoslav government did not satisfy the Kosovars. They had rising expectations.

The 1974 constitution designated them as a nationality, rather than as a nation. While the Kosovars had a de facto republic, they did not have a legal republic with the right to secede like the other republics. This distinction was subtle but important. Most Kosovars did not want to secede to merge with Albania. Myths about "mother Albania" had been shattered. Many Kosovar Albanians had gone to Albania for visits and were aghast at the grinding poverty in Hoxha's Albania. Moreover, Hoxha was the ultimate Stalinist. What the Kosovars wanted was to join the other nations of Yugoslavia on an equal footing. For this to happen, they had to be designated as a nation of Yugoslavia instead of as a nationality. Their request for a de jure Kosovo republic was denied. The Kosovars believed that being designated as a nationality resigned them to an inferior social status. There were more Kosovars than Macedonians or Montenegrins, yet these groups had their own republics and the Kosovars did not; therefore, nationalism and unrest grew among the Kosovars.

The Serbs of Kosovo and Serbia proper were puzzled by the growing militancy of the Kosovar Albanians. Serbs had a paternalistic attitude toward Kosovars. They felt that they had "given" the Kosovar Albanians their rights; therefore, they had nothing against which they could protest. If one group is in a position to "give" freedom to another, then real equality does not exist. A Serb man living in Kosovo stated, "The demonstrations [in Kosovo] were caused by [Albanians] having too many rights."[16]

A wider rift had now opened between Serbs and Kosovars. One of the reasons for the rift was that the Kosovars failed to communicate effectively with a wider audience. The Serbs felt that the only reason why the Kosovar Albanians wanted their own republic was to secede from Yugoslavia and become part of Albania. A Serb woman who lived in Kosovo stated: "They [Kosovar] [Albanians] were asking for the republic in order to separate, and that cannot happen."[17] The Kosovars failed to let others know that they wanted a republic because they wanted to join Yugoslavia as first-class citizens.

From 1974 onward until the 1980s, Kosovo became a hotbed of social unrest. Freedom of expression increased, but the largest percentage of political prisoners in Yugoslavia was in Kosovo.[18] There were massive student protests in 1974 and 1981.

THE THIRD YUGOSLAVIA 1980–1991

In 1980 Josip Broz Tito, the man who had initially brutalized the Kosovars and tried to cleanse Kosovo of them and who had finally reconciled with them, died. In the wake of his death, Kosovo became the center of politics in Yugoslavia.

In 1981, demonstrations that started at the University of Prishtina over living conditions and the quality of food quickly turned into riots throughout the province. Construction workers, metal workers, mine workers, high school students, administrators, teachers, and others joined the protest. The protests were an outpouring of nationalism and frustration.

Kosovo was the poorest region in Yugoslavia. Noel Malcolm noted:

> The unemployment level in Kosovo was the highest in the whole country: officially 67,000 people were registered as unemployed, but observers estimated the actual figure at 250,000. Out of a population of 1.5 million only 178,000 had jobs in all forms of state-run enterprises (civil service, schools, hospitals, factories, and so on); and a significant ethnic imbalance was still in place, with the Serbs and Montenegrins, who formed 15 per cent of the population holding 30 per cent of these jobs.[19]

The Yugoslav federal authorities responded by sending in 35,000 troops to crack down on Kosovo. This cost Yugoslavia $67,000 a day. They engaged in this action despite the fact that they were $20 billion in debt to the West.[20] In addition, the League of Communists of Kosovo and the University of Prishtina were purged of suspected sympathizers of Kosovar nationalism. Textbooks from Albania were banned and cultural exchanges with Albania canceled. From 1981–1989, 584,323 Kosovar Albanians, half of the adults, were arrested and interrogated.[21] It was as if Aleksandar Rankovic had risen from the grave and been reinstalled as the head of the security forces.

The backlash among the Serbs and Montenegrins in Kosovo was immediate. Many decided to leave. Some of them left because of the miserable economic conditions in Kosovo, while others left because they said that they were pressured and harassed. This was noted in Serbia proper. The release of the draft of the memorandum of the Serbian Academy of Science and Arts in 1986, which was discussed in Chapter 5, added to the ongoing controversy by stipulating that the autonomous provinces of Kosovo and Vojvodina had been created to weaken Serbia. Kosovo was now at the heart of politics in Serbia. The door was now open for the situation to be exploited by politicians.

Amidst complaints that Serbs were being mistreated in Kosovo, Ivan Stambolic, the president of Serbia, sent his deputy, Slobodan Milosevic, to Kosovo to deal with the matter. On April 20, 1987, Milosevic met with Communist officials. Miroslav Solevic, a Serb activist in Kosovo, asked Milosevic to come back to Kosovo. Milosevic agreed to return in four days. On April 24, 1987, Milosevic returned to Kosovo. He was to speak at the House of Culture in Kosovo Polje, but there was a disturbance outside the building. Serb protestors were battling the Kosovar Albanian–dominated police force. The protestors had previously arranged for a truck full of stones to be parked outside the building so they could be thrown at the police.[22] Milosevic stepped outside the building and stepped into Serbian folklore when he told the crowd: "No one should dare to beat you." Those words were captured on video and shown repeatedly on television in Belgrade. Kosovo was a symbol of Serb identity. Realizing this, Milosevic took advantage of the political situation afforded him. This would eventually make Milosevic a Serbian hero. Inside the House of Culture, Milosevic told the crowd:

> You should stay here. This is your house. Your meadows and gardens. Your memories. You shouldn't abandon your land just because it is difficult to live, because you are pressured by injustice and degradation. It was never a part of the Serbian and Montenegrin character to give up in the face of obstacles, to demobilize when it is time to fight ... You should stay here for the sake of your ancestors and descendants. Otherwise your ancestors will be defiled and descendants disappointed. But I don't suggest that you stay, endure, and tolerate a situation that you're not satisfied with. On the contrary, you should change it with the rest of the progressive people here, in Serbia and Yugoslavia.[23]

Like a sly politician, Slobodan Milosevic talked out of both sides of his mouth about Kosovo. A few weeks later, on June 4, 1987, before a gathering of secret police, Milosevic denounced the memorandum of the Serbian Academy of the Sciences and the Arts, which supported the cause of Serbian nationalism—the cause he had spoken in behalf of in Kosovo a few weeks earlier.[24] Milosevic was hedging his bets to see which direction the Serbian political wind would blow. It blew in favor of Serbian nationalism; therefore, Milosevic championed its cause. In September 1987, Milosevic ousted his friend and mentor, Ivan Stambolic, as the president of Serbia.

Once he was firmly in charge of Serbia, Milosevic proceeded to strip Kosovo and Vojvodina of their autonomy. First, he purged the leadership of the League of Communists of Kosovo, Vojvodina, and

Montenegro in 1988. Then in 1989, Milosevic proceeded to strip Kosovo and Vojvodina of their autonomy. Now, Milosevic controlled four of the eight seats on the rotating Yugoslav presidency. On June 28, 1989, Milosevic spoke before one million Serbs gathered in Kosovo Polje to commemorate the 600th anniversary of the Battle of Kosovo Polje. He ended his speech on an ominous note. He said: "Six centuries later, again we are in battles and quarrels. They are not armed battles, though such things should not be excluded yet."[25] It was as if he was calling one million Serbs to arms for another Battle of Kosovo.

Milosevic instituted a plan to recolonize Kosovo. In 1990 measures were enacted that nullified the sale of property to Albanians by departing Serbs. Funds were provided to Serbs who moved to Kosovo for building new houses. The management of companies in Kosovo was Serbianized, and they were forced to hire a Serb for every Albanian worker hired. Kosovars were also dismissed from their jobs for participating in strikes and required to sign loyalty oaths to Serbia, and its ruling party, the instrument that was used to disenfranchise them and dehumanize them.

The response of the Kosovar Albanians to these repressive measures was rather surprising. The jobs of thousands of Kosovars were placed on the line. Given the large size of many Albanian families, one would have expected capitulation rather than resistance, but this was not the case. The Kosovars overwhelmingly refused to submit to this colonial policy. On July 2, 1990, the Kosovo assembly voted to make Kosovo an independent republic within Yugoslavia; therefore, they acted to delegitimize Serbian authority by ignoring it and forming their own parallel society. Taxes and contributions from abroad were collected that allowed the Kosovars to set up their own schools and health and social services.

The Kosovars also set up their own parallel political institutions. In 1991 the Kosovars held a referendum, and they voted for Kosovo to become a sovereign republic. The Democratic League of Kosovo (LDK) became the dominant party among the Kosovars. Dr. Ibrahim Rugova, the head of LDK, was elected the president of Kosovo in 1992, an assembly was elected, and a shadow government was formed. Rugova was a professor of Albanian literature. He was also a pacifist. Serbs and other groups in Yugoslavia often stereotyped Albanians as violent and as rapists, yet the Kosovar Albanians chose the path of nonviolent resistance. Overwhelmingly Muslim, the Kosovars were also aware of the portrayal of Muslims in Western societies as terrorists; therefore, they contemplated converting to Catholicism, the religion of their ancestors, en masse.[26]

The events leading to the breakup of Yugoslavia were discussed in Chapter 5. Kosovo played a crucial role in Yugoslavia's breakup. The events that transpired in Kosovo served as a warning to various republics of Yugoslavia that they would be subject to domination by Milosevic and to Serbian chauvinism if they remained a part of Yugoslavia.

THE FOURTH YUGOSLAVIA 1991–2006

The fourth Yugoslavia was all that remained of Yugoslavia, Serbia, and Montenegro (the rump Yugoslavia), through four Balkan wars (Slovenia, Croatia, Bosnia, and eventually Kosovo). It was during this period, when global attention began to focus on the war in Bosnia, that a new word was added to the international vernacular: ethnic cleansing. It would later be used with respect to the oncoming war in Kosovo as well.

Ethnic cleansing is a form of genocide that is defined by the Convention on the Prevention and Punishment for the Crime of Genocide as the forced removal of a group from a community. The forced removal can be by terror, murder, or physical force. Its ultimate goal is the elimination of a targeted group.

Ominous signs regarding Kosovo's future were beginning to appear at the beginning of this era. Despite the global attention drawn to the region by the Balkan wars during the reign of Milosevic, Rugova's movement failed to gain the respect of the West. The Kosovars were treated in a paternalistic manner by western governments. For example,

> In April 1992, at a meeting in London called to discuss impending war in Bosnia, the Rugova delegation came but members were treated as observers. The group was not allowed to participate in deliberations and had to be satisfied to watch the discussion on a television monitor in a separate room.[27]

The United States displayed the same attitude toward Rugova during the peace talks at Dayton, Ohio, in 1995. Kosovo was left off the agenda completely. Peaceful Muslims who were trying to gain the attention and assistance of the West were ignored. This sent a negative message to the Muslim world that only violence would get the West's attention and respect.

During the early 1990s, the only attention that Kosovo received from the West came in the form of the so-called Christmas warning that—as some U.S. politicians would later claim—deterred Milosevic from attacking Kosovo. President Bush I issued the Christmas warning on December 24, 1992, when the war in Bosnia was being fought. Secretary of State Lawrence Eagleburger sent a cable to Milosevic that stated: "In the event of conflict in Kosovo caused by Serbian action, the U.S. will be prepared to employ military force against Serbians in Kosovo and Serbia proper."[28] Bush had previously failed to deter Milosevic, who was now engaged in his second Balkan war. Bush now hoped to contain the damage. It is doubtful that the Christmas warning had any impact at all. Bush did not even mention it in *A World Transformed*, the presidential memoirs he coauthored with his national security advisor, Brent Scowcroft. As Julie Mertus has pointed out, Milosevic had ongoing wars in Bosnia and Croatia, and had Kosovo firmly under his control. Therefore, he did not need to start another Balkan war in Kosovo at this time to maintain control over it. As a result, the Christmas warning had no deterrent effect because there was no possibility of Kosovo being attacked when it was issued. This was like someone telling a city dweller to snap his fingers to protect himself from lions in an area where lions are not present. When no lion appears one should not assume that the finger-snapping worked. It obviously did not. It was not until the end of the third Balkan war of the 1990s (Bosnia) that Milosevic turned his sights on Kosovo, to cleanse it of Albanians.

PRELUDE TO WAR AND GENOCIDE

The war in Kosovo was a war that should not have occurred, but it occurred due to the indifference of the United States and its Western European allies. It occurred because the leaders of the western alliance were not willing to back up their brave words with deeds. They had dealt with Slobodan Milosevic, the "Butcher of the Balkans", before and the results had been deadly; now they found themselves facing the same situation they had faced in Bosnia. If the United States and its European allies had been willing to take quick and decisive action, the war in Kosovo would not have happened. Milosevic had always probed to see how far he could go, and had always backed down when he was met with resistance.

Words must be matched by deeds, otherwise, one's credibility is lost. Initially, the United States and its allies were not willing to make a firm commitment to deter an attack against Kosovo, but once the West made a firm commitment to Kosovo, Milosevic was finally convinced that he could not succeed. But, by then, Kosovo was desecrated and its people devastated. Genocide ended, but the actions of the West raised more questions than it answered.

When the United States and its European allies finally became involved, it was to preserve their credibility more than to defend human rights in Kosovo. The war in Kosovo also exposed a wide gap in humanity. It exposed man's inability to relate to his fellow man. This revealed the possibility of genocide occurring in the future.

THE WAR IN KOSOVO AND THE MYTH OF HISTORY

Many are quick to cite the defeat of the Serbs at Kosovo Polje as the root cause of war in Kosovo. It is true that the Serbs view Kosovo as the cradle of their civilization, and the defeat of the Serbs by the Ottoman Turks in 1389 holds a solemn place in Serbian history, but this was not the reason for the war in Kosovo in 1999.

The war in Kosovo occurred because Slobodan Milosevic sought to divert the attention of the people of Serbia away from his failed policies in the rump Yugoslavia. After the death of Tito, Kosovo, along with Vojvodina, was awarded a seat on the Yugoslav presidency. As mentioned previously, Milosevic stripped Kosovo and Vojvodina of their autonomy and their seats on the Yugoslav presidency. This allowed him to consolidate his control of the rump Yugoslavia by fanning the flames of Serbian nationalism.

The War

The war in Kosovo began because the Albanian majority was stripped of their autonomy. As a result, the Serbian minority that had suffered at the hands of the Albanian majority now turned the tables and exploited the Albanian majority and denied them equal rights. Previously, efforts had been made to rectify the problem peacefully. Ibrahim Rugova led the Kosovar Albanian nonviolent independence movement. Rugova even prevailed in elections for independence set up by the Kosovar Albanians; nevertheless, the results were not recognized by the rump Yugoslavia or by any other country. As a result, Albanians continued to be an oppressed majority in Kosovo. Therefore, the Kosovo Liberation Army (KLA) that advocated independence from Serbia through the use of violence gained a substantial following.

The actions of the KLA provoked harsh responses from the Serbian-controlled federal government. In 1997, the KLA began to attack and kill the police in Kosovo. Things came to a climax in

March 1997 when 30,000 Kosovar Albanians, who were protesting the deaths of their compatriots, clashed with the police.

Slobodan Milosevic had ulterior motives for exploiting the conflict in Kosovo. In 1997 Milosevic's protégé Zoran Lilic failed to capture a majority of the votes in his quest for the presidency of Serbia and was forced into a runoff. In December 1997, the Organization for Security and Cooperation in Europe (OSCE) reported that there was widespread fraud in the presidential election won by Milosevic's Socialist Party. Given the political turmoil in Serbia, Kosovo represented an opportunity for Milosevic to consolidate his power in the rump Yugoslavia by diverting the country's attention away from its problems.

Milosevic took advantage of unrest in Kosovo to fan the flames of Serbian nationalism. Kosovo holds a sacred place in Serbian history. The Serbs regard it as the cradle of their civilization. By portraying himself as the defender of the cradle of Serbian culture, Milosevic sought to bolster his standing, using the Field of Blackbirds as a convenient means to divert the public attention away from economic misery. Milosevic sought to escalate the crisis in Kosovo rather than to resolve it. In July 1998, 25,000 Albanian Kosovars fled the city of Orahovac as fighting erupted between the Serbs and the KLA.

As the violence escalated, it became obvious to Milosevic that his policy was paying dividends. He could consolidate his support in the rump Yugoslavia by exploiting the situation in Kosovo, and did not have to worry about direct intervention from the West. After all, the West had stalled and resisted direct intervention in the war in Bosnia; they were initially content to sit and watch as events unfolded.

By October 1998, Milosevic agreed to a cease-fire in Kosovo. By this time, NATO was threatening to use air strikes. This tactic was typical of Milosevic. He always pushed a situation to its limits to obtain the maximum gains; then, when it appeared that the West had formed a consensus, Milosevic would back down. He always probed to find out how much room he had to maneuver.

When the United States and its allies appeared to weaken their commitment to Kosovo by only sending lightly armed observers, instead of combat troops, to defend Kosovo, Milosevic took this as a sign of weakness. As a result, Milosevic ended the cease-fire in Kosovo in November 1998. To him, the lack of a firm commitment to Kosovo meant that the West was bluffing and was trying to avoid a confrontation. This was reinforced by the constant message coming from the United States that ground troops would not be deployed in Kosovo; therefore, Milosevic took measures to ensure that Kosovo would remain a part of Serbia.

Milosevic's tactics were the same as those he had used while trying to prevent the various republics of Yugoslavia from seceding. He employed extreme brutal force. Milosevic and his band of terrorists sought to hold on to Kosovo by driving the Kosovar Albanians out of Kosovo. In other words, they adopted a policy of genocide. The international community had adopted a firm policy against genocide. The Convention on the Prevention and Punishment of the Crime of Genocide was adopted by the United Nations General Assembly in 1948 as a guarantee that the atrocities of Hitler would not be repeated. In Article II of the Convention, genocide is defined as:

(a) Killing members of the group;
(b) Causing serious bodily or mental harm to members of the group;
(c) Deliberately inflicting on the group conditions of life calculated to bring about its physical destruction in whole or in part;
(d) imposing measures intended to prevent births within the group.[29]

All of these things happened at Milosevic's directive; therefore, Milosevic's tactics constituted genocide.

Milosevic gambled on the indifference of western countries. He gambled that they would show the same indifference toward Kosovo that they had initially shown toward Bosnia. Milosevic gambled that Western Europe and the United States would define their national interest in narrow, materialistic terms. He gambled that the United States and its European allies would merely try to bluff their way out of a tense situation. Milosevic believed this because the West only seemed committed to talk, not to action.

From October 1998 until NATO began its air strikes in March 1999, Kosovar Albanians were displaced from their homes. By the time the NATO bombing commenced, 450,000 people had been "ethnically cleansed" from their respective communities. The military conflict ended on June 10, 1999. Over one million people had been displaced from their homes before the shameful nightmare caused by the megalomania of Milosevic and the indifference of the West finally ended.

The U.S. Response

In the realm of foreign policy, U.S. politicians face a dilemma between doing what is popular and doing what is right. The two choices do not always coincide. There was a need for firm action to let Milosevic know that genocide would not be tolerated. If action was to be taken against Milosevic, Europe could not act alone. It needed the support of the United States. The United States' European allies lacked the necessary weapons required to deliver the type of air strikes necessary to liberate Kosovo from Milosevic's henchmen.[30] Therefore, if action was to be taken, the United States would have to lead.

In addition, U.S. politicians faced a potential political crisis if they opted for military action. The Vietnam syndrome and memories of Somalia still loomed large. As a result, the American public, politicians, and the media eschewed long-term military commitments and were reluctant to use ground forces. This reluctance was reflected in public opinion polls that showed that the American public was strongly opposed to the deployment of ground forces in Kosovo.[31] Air strikes seemed like a more viable option because they minimized the risk of U.S. casualties.

The NATO bombing campaign in Serbia brought genocide to an end in the Balkans, but the war in Kosovo also exposed many weaknesses in U.S. foreign policy. The United States was not poised to act quickly to prevent or stop genocide. The war showed how indifferent the American people could be to foreign affairs, even when fundamental principles of human decency were violated. It also showed how narrowly defined U.S. foreign policy had become in the post–Cold War era. In essence, it revealed that the United States was still not prepared for the post–Cold War world. Those who were willing to commit genocide in nonstrategic areas had little to fear from the United States, its European allies, or the United Nations. Unfortunately, the end of the war in Kosovo was not the end of modern genocide, but an indicator of what was to happen in the future.

The Congress

Serbs cite the Battle of Kosovo in 1389 as the crucial event that determined the future of the Serbian nation. Similarly, a U.S. battle of Kosovo was waged in Congress from 1998–1999 to determine the future of U.S. foreign policy. At times, the Congressional debate about Kosovo was contentious, scholarly, foolish, and surreal.

The House of Representatives was the most partisan chamber of Congress. In January 1998, the Monica Lewinsky scandal erupted and calls for Clinton's impeachment reverberated throughout the Republican-controlled chamber. To that end, the House of Representatives began to draw up articles of impeachment and impeached Clinton on December 19, 1998. It was against this political backdrop that the political situation in Kosovo began to escalate.

It was apparent that it would not be easy for Bill Clinton to gain support for his foreign policy from the Republicans in the House who were trying to remove him from office. On March 18, 1998, House Concurrent Resolution 227 (H. Con. Res. 227) was brought to the floor for a vote. The resolution directed the president to remove troops from Bosnia pursuant to Section 5(c) of the War Powers Resolution. Section 5(c) of the War Powers Resolution allows Congress to withdraw U.S. troops from an area by passing a concurrent resolution.[32] The resolution was defeated—225 nays to 193 yeas. Just as the situation in the Balkans was escalating, some members of the House wanted to withdraw from the region. This showed that the United States' commitment to the Balkans was weakening. This probably strengthened Milosevic's resolve to fight the KLA, because it appeared that the United States would soon be leaving the region; therefore, the Kosovars would be at his mercy.

In a similar vein, an attempt was being made in the U.S. Senate to withdraw U.S. troops from Bosnia. On March 23, 1998, Senator Kay Bailey Hutchinson (Republican-Texas) introduced Amendment 2083 to the 1998 Emergency Supplemental Appropriations Act. This amendment sought the withdrawal of U.S. peacekeeping forces from Bosnia by January 1, 1999. This amendment, and the subsequent amendments adopted by Senator Hutchinson to withdraw U.S. troops from Bosnia, was not based on military necessity, and the withdrawal dates were arbitrary. Hutchinson's amendment was tabled. Benchmarks had already been established by the U. S. military for reduction of U.S. soldiers in the Bosnian peacekeeping mission (SFOR).[33] Hutchinson ignored this and turned the withdrawal of U.S. forces from Bosnia into a recurring political battle with the Clinton administration. Earlier, on March 13, she had published an article in the *Wall Street Journal* titled "One Balkan Quagmire is Enough."

Some members of the Senate, such as Senator Judd Gregg (Republican–New Hampshire), argued that there were no definable U.S. interests in Kosovo. Gregg stated:

> Is there any definable American interest? In many instances this could be international interest which impact us significantly, such as the Gulf War, where European oil was at risk.[34]

Gregg, like others, defined the national interest in material/economic terms. He did not consider halting genocide and saving the lives of Kosovar Albanians to be in the national interest. In *Shake Hands With the Devil*, Romeo Dallaire wrote that a U.S. officer informed him that the lives of 800,000 Rwandans were not worth the lives of ten U.S. soldiers.[35] Apparently Gregg had engaged in a similar calculation and come to the same conclusion about the Kosovars. When the U.S. Senate is in session, the Pledge of Allegiance is recited on a daily basis. It pledges liberty and justice for all. For many, this has become nothing more than a hollow exercise.

Senator Joseph Biden (Democrat-Delaware) displayed scholarly knowledge as he spoke about the events leading up to the clash between Milosevic and the KLA and the mishandling of the situation by the United States and its allies. Biden noted:

> One would hope that the West has learned something from its pathetic temporization in Bosnia earlier this decade.
>
> ... it was only the use of American airpower for 3 weeks in the fall of 1995 that brought Milosevic and his Bosnian Serb puppets to the bargaining table.[36]

Overall, the debate in both houses of Congress seemed split into two distinct coalitions. One coalition consisted of liberals and realists. On the one hand, these liberals were committed "peaceniks" who wanted to focus on domestic issues. This included members of the House of Representatives such as Dennis Kucinich. He is a member of the Serbian Caucus; however, this did not appear to be the main reason why he opposed the bombing of Serbia. Kucinich had consistently displayed a domestic social policy orientation and opposition to war. Standing side by side with these liberals were realists. They felt that since there was no direct threat to the United States, the security interest of the United States did not warrant intervention in Kosovo. This was the position of Kay Bailey Hutchinson in the Senate.

On the other hand, there were foreign policy liberals who stressed the need to defend human rights to stop genocide, when possible. This was the position of Representative Tom Lantos (Democrat-California), the only Holocaust survivor in Congress, and Mary Landrieu (Democrat-Louisiana) in the Senate. They were joined by foreign policy moderates, such as Senator Chuck Hagel (Republican-Nebraska). Hagel noted the need to adapt to a changing world when he said:

> The United States of America must lead the world in the 21st century. We are the only dominant power in the world today, which provides us with immense opportunity ... America must not be intimidated by the unprecedented rate of change and uncertainty in the world.[37]

The moderates believed that the United States and NATO had to adapt to the post–Cold War changes in the world, or both risked becoming irrelevant. In the House, the peacenik-realist coalition prevailed, while in the Senate, the human rights–moderate coalition prevailed.

This division within Congress became even more pronounced in 1999. It was the year of Bill Clinton's impeachment trial. It was also the year that the Serbian government commenced with Operation Horse Shoe, a full-scale effort to cleanse Kosovo of all 1.8 million of its Albanian inhabitants; hence, it was a period of determining what should be the appropriate U.S. response to this action. Would the citizenship that Bill Clinton granted to European Muslims for inclusion in international society, which entitled them to human rights, be revoked?

The impeachment trial of William Jefferson Clinton, the 42nd president of the United States, commenced on January 14, 1999. On February 12, 1999, Clinton was acquitted by the Senate, but partisanship was still prevalent in both houses of Congress. The partisanship in the House of Representatives came to the forefront on March 11, 1999, during the debate on House Resolution 103. This was a resolution to allow the House to vote on another resolution (House Concurrent Resolution 42 or H. Con. Res. 42) to allow U.S. troops to be used as part of a peacekeeping operation in Kosovo. H. Con. Res. 42 was authored by Representative Benjamin Gilman (Republican–New York) who spoke out about the atrocities in Kosovo, yet he was opposed to the deployment of ground troops in Kosovo. This resolution was being debated prior to the reconvening of the peace talks between the Kosovar Albanians and Serbia in Paris. Some members of the House, such as Representative Eliot Engel (Democrat–New York), believed that the resolution was unwarranted interference in the ongoing peace talks. Engel said:

> Senator Dole was quite eloquent yesterday. He said, quite simply, first we get an agreement. Then and then we take it before Congress to ratify the agreement. We do not do it the other way around.[38]

Representative Tillie Fowler (Republican-Florida) also introduced an amendment to prohibit ground troops from being deployed in Kosovo. H. Con. Res. 42 passed by a vote of 219 to 191; nevertheless the resolution had no effect, since it was a concurrent resolution—only bills and joint resolutions can be enacted into law. This was an attempt to embarrass Clinton by showing a lack of Congressional support for his peace initiative in Kosovo.

The differences in the prevailing mood of each house of Congress could be witnessed by the way they responded to Operation Allied Force (NATO's bombing mission against Serbia). On March 23, 1999, the U.S. Senate approved Senate Concurrent Resolution 21, a concurrent resolution sponsored by Senators Biden (Democrat-Delaware), Warner (Democrat-Virginia), Levin (Democrat-Michigan), Byrd (Democrat–West Virginia), and McConnell (Republican-Kentucky). It authorized the president to conduct air and missile strikes against Yugoslavia, in conjunction with NATO. Previously, amendments to a spending bill to prevent the use of ground forces in Yugoslavia had been withdrawn. This same measure failed to pass in the House on April 28, 1999, by a vote of 213–213.

The House of Representatives remained perplexed and disengaged throughout the bombing campaign against Yugoslavia. On April 28, 1999, the House voted for House Resolution 1569 that restricted the use of U.S. ground troops in Kosovo; it passed 249 to 180. Yet House Resolution 82, directing the president to withdraw U.S. forces from military operations in Yugoslavia, failed to pass with 130 supporting the measure and 290 in opposition. The House conveyed a message of ambiguity when U.S. forces were under hostile fire.

The U.S. Congress was also a chamber of indifference and misinformation. Some members of Congress were indifferent to the genocide occurring in Kosovo and tried to rationalize it. For instance, Senator James Inhofe (Republican-Oklahoma) pointed out that in recent years millions had died in Rwanda, Sudan, Ethiopia, Algeria, and in other areas; therefore, he questioned why Kosovo warranted special attention. Moreover, Inhofe also said, "Are there any good guys in the fight that stretches back over 500 years?"[39] It was nothing more than an excuse to let genocide continue. Some members of Congress, such as Representative Tom Campbell (Republican-California), believed that the United States did not have the right to attack Serbia, a sovereign state, since Serbia had not attacked the United States. He subscribed to a Hobbesian concept of sovereignty. In *The Leviathan*, Thomas Hobbes wrote:

> The sovereign's action cannot be justly accused by the subject . . . every particular man is author of all the sovereign doth; and consequently he that complaineth of injury from the sovereign, complaineth of that whereof he himself is author; and ought not to accuse any man but himself.[40]

This was an ancient notion that a sovereign state was an independent entity, and its rulers were free to treat its citizens and subjects as they pleased. This concept of sovereignty no longer applied. The Principles of the Nuremberg Tribunal (1950) altered the concept of state sovereignty. Principle III stated:

> The fact that a person who committed an act which constitutes a crime under international law acted as Head of State or responsible Government official does not relieve him from responsibility under international law.[41]

Principle VI notes that crimes against humanity are punishable under international law. They are defined as:

> Murder, extermination, enslavement, deportation, and other inhuman acts done against any civilian population, or persecutions on political, racial or religious grounds, when such acts are done or such persecutions are carried on in execution of or in connection with any crime against peace or any war crime.[42]

Sovereignty can no longer be used to shield human rights violations.

After the bombing stopped on June 10, 1999, and NATO proved victorious, Clinton's political enemies continued to seethe with bitterness. Representative John Duncan (Republican-Tennessee) and Senator Larry Craig (Republican-Idaho) denied that the war had accomplished anything. Nevertheless, the successful outcome of the war in Kosovo meant that European Muslims had not been expunged from the rolls of international society. They were still entitled to human rights.

Clinton's Dilemma

Bill Clinton had dealt with Slobodan Milosevic before. Clinton should have been familiar with Milosevic's tendency to lie, frustrate, and stall. Clinton also knew firsthand of Milosevic's disrespect for human life that was witnessed as events unfolded in Bosnia. He also knew that to make Milosevic heel, he could not mince his words. Strong words would have to be backed by strong deeds. Therefore, it is bewildering why Clinton, as the leader of the western alliance, did not take decisive action by moving combat troops into the Balkans, instead of observers, to deter Milosevic at the onset of the crisis. Because Clinton failed to take immediate action, Milosevic stalled and bided his time.

As genocide was being committed in Kosovo, President Clinton faced many obstacles. It did not appear that the American public would support the use of ground troops, but it seemed that the use of air strikes would be possible; however, air strikes would require sustained action. The use of ground troops would have required President Clinton to go against the existing political culture that prevailed in the United States. Perhaps it would have required him to commit political suicide; however, he was unlikely to do this. Once elected, a political figure does everything he can to remain in office. Engaging in actions that pose a risk to one's perpetuation in office are usually avoided; hence, Clinton only had two viable options—do nothing or use air strikes. Doing nothing would have made Clinton vulnerable to charges of complicity in the face of genocide. Using air strikes allowed Clinton to take action while minimizing the risk of U.S. casualties. Clinton opted for the latter.

Bill Clinton had major objectives he wanted to accomplish in Kosovo. He made it known:

> From the outset, we had three objectives in Kosovo: first to end the violence that threatens the fragile stability of the Balkans; second to prevent a humanitarian crisis from becoming a catastrophe by stopping the repression of Kosovar Albanians; and third to put Kosovo back in the hands of its people by giving them self-government again.[43]

The war in Kosovo finally ended when President Clinton realized that Serbia itself had to pay a price for its aggression; therefore, power lines, bridges, and fuel supplies were attacked by the United States and its NATO allies. This brought the war in Kosovo to an abrupt end.

The Media

Slobodan Milosevic might have gotten away with genocide if it had not been for the U.S. media. The Associated Press and *The New York Times* undertook the most extensive coverage of events in Kosovo by U.S. news outlets. By 1998 Steve Erlanger, Alan Cowell, Craig Whitney, and Chris Hedges became familiar names to readers of *The New York Times* who followed news about Kosovo. The U.S. news media did nothing extraordinary, but just doing their job proved adequate enough. Most newspapers did not advocate U.S. intervention on behalf of the Kosovar Albanians. The exceptions were *The Philadelphia Inquirer* and *The Washington Times.*

The old proverb that a picture is worth a thousand words proved to be true regarding news coverage of Kosovo. On television screens and in newspaper pictures, America and the world saw the faces of innocence. These were not people who had firebombed police stations or manned machine guns. These were innocent people who were forced to take their belongings and live in the forest and mountains with their children. There were over one million of them. If it had not been for the extreme cruelty of Slobodan Milosevic, Americans might have been content to read and watch stories about the death of Sonny Bono, Mary Kay Laterneau and her underaged lover, and the retirement of Michael Jordan. If the faces of the innocent had not been shown, the war in Kosovo might have come to an end before NATO achieved its objectives.

The United Nations

The United Nations was ineffective at preventing or stopping genocide in Kosovo. It was hampered by its structure, cultural factors, and geopolitics. The structure of the United Nations hampered the search for a solution to the conflict in Kosovo. Russia is one of the five permanent members of the Security Council that wields veto power. Serbia is Russia's traditional ally. This made using the United Nations as an agency for collective security against Serbia impossible since Russia could veto any Security Council resolution authorizing military action against Serbia.

Culture also undermined the efforts of the United Nations. The Russian public felt an affinity with the Serbs; both are Slavs and Orthodox. Therefore, this placed restraints on the options available to Boris Yeltsin, the president of the Russian Federation. On the other hand, cultural dissimilarity between the Kosovar Albanians and the permanent members of the Security Council hurt their cause. The Kosovars are predominantly Muslim. No Muslim country is a permanent member of the Security Council. European Muslims were the newest members of international society and therefore had little clout.

Geopolitics also played a role in constricting the United Nations. Serbia is located in central Europe. This area has traditionally been within Russia's sphere of influence. Russia was not going to authorize the use of force in this area; therefore, it was necessary to go outside of the United Nations and rely instead on NATO to stop the genocide in Kosovo.

The Nature of Democracy

At first glance, it would seem that the democratic process was a hindrance to the United States' response to the crises in the Balkans.

This would explain why President Bush I and President Clinton were slow to act, although Clinton acted much more decisively. Democracy, especially in the United States, is based on Burkean incrementalism. Change takes place in small increments, and the change that does come forth is usually based on consensus. In the absence of consensus, nothing is usually done. This makes the governing process in the United States unwieldy, cumbersome, and slow.

Similar observations were made by John F. Kennedy in *Why England Slept*. Kennedy observed, "given the conditions of democratic government, a free press, public elections, ... given rule by the majority, it is unreasonable to blame the entire situation on one man or group."[44] Both the Bush I administration and the Clinton administration were slow to respond to the post–Cold War crises that they faced. The very nature of the democratic process gives us some insight into their slow response; however, it does not give a complete explanation.

There is more to America sleeping, while genocide was being committed at the dawn of the twenty-first century, than the failure of U.S. democracy. U.S. leaders were not the only ones who were slow to respond to the crises. The American people also failed to respond to the crises as well. In *Why England Slept*, John F. Kennedy also observed that "leaders are only responsible for their failures only in the governing sector and cannot be held responsible for the failure of the nation as a whole." Despite the fact that news about the genocide that was taking place in the Balkans and Africa reached the American people, they did not demand that their government take decisive action. Simply pointing to the nature of U.S. democracy masks the real problem. In other words, the average American was not able to conceive of his country's national interest in human terms when it came to the people of Rwanda and the Balkans. Between the call and response of the president, Congress, and the American people, something was missing. There was a failure to empathize with these people during their most desperate hour of need. This is something that is culturally based.

When a disaster in a foreign country is caused by the forces of nature, the American people are often among the first to respond and are often among the most generous. This is a great sign of sympathy for the less fortunate; however, empathy is different. It entails seeing yourself, when you see others, and often requires greater sacrifice. When genocide began in the Balkans, Rwanda, and Kosovo, the American people did not demand that their government take military action to stop it. There was a lack of consensus over what to do.

Simply put, the American people felt sorry for the victims, but did not feel that they were worth dying for. A culturally based barrier separates Americans from many of the peoples of the world. Under these circumstances, it appears that President Clinton did the best that he could do to protect the Kosovar Albanians when they were under attack. Aspects of American culture that affect the United States' foreign policy will be discussed in the following chapters.

Chapter 7

The War in Darfur: Genocide on Our Watch

Sudan has become today's world capital of human pain, suffering and agony. There, one part of the population has been—and still is—subjected by another part, the dominating part, to humiliation, hunger and death. For a while, the so-called civilized world knew about it and preferred to look away. Now, people know. And so they have no excuse for their passivity bordering on indifference.

—*Elie Wiesel*, "On the Atrocities in Sudan," *New York, NY, July 14, 2004*[1]

Introduction

Genocide has happened on our watch in Darfur. This cannot be denied. To the casual observer, it appears to be a clear case of the Arab minority regime in Khartoum committing acts of genocide against Africans in the western province of Sudan, Darfur. In reality it is more complex than this. Sudan has only had ten years of peace since it gained independence in 1956 and has not moved beyond its colonial legacy. The government has failed to deal effectively with its economic, social, and political problems. Therefore, it uses a segment of its population as scapegoats. The regime in Sudan does this by using a racial paradigm to disguise the fact that it is a failed state.[2] Its predecessors used similar tactics. The government of Sudan has lost legitimacy. Therefore, it resorts to *chronic Arabism/Islamism* to garner support among Arabs in Sudan and in the other countries. "Them against us."

This has been an effective strategy that has allowed the regime of Omar al-Bashir to cling to power. But it has also disguised the real motive behind the regime's policy of genocide.

Knowing the real policy and motives of the regime also demonstrates that the racialized policies and tactics used in Darfur are not new. These same policies and practices were used during the civil war in southern Sudan as well. As the war in the south drew to a close, racialized terror simply shifted to Darfur. Moreover, these same tactics most likely will be used again in another arena in Sudan if the genocide in Darfur is brought to an end. This is the only way that the Khartoum clique can cling to power.

Creating the Paradigm of Race, Culture, and Ethnicity in Sudan

Sudan's political, social, and cultural divisions lie deep within its history. If we pry it open, we will find that the root causes of these cleavages are the Arab slave trade, colonialism, and the postcolonial failed state. The history of Sudan is well known. History has been used in Sudan to create the prism of the racialized state that the regime in Khartoum uses to sustain itself in power. The Sudanese are selective in their use of history. The selective parts of history that are used involve events that transpired from the sixth to the twentieth centuries. This history is vital if one is to understand the policy and events that are currently taking place in Sudan.

In the sixth century, there were three Christian Nubian kingdoms in Sudan, Nobatia, Makuria, and Alodia. The Arabs referred to the area as *bilad al-Sudan* (land of the Blacks). They mainly farmed, engaged in pastoral activities, and traded with outlying areas. However, things were to change by the middle of the seventh century, when Khalid ibn al-Walid conquered Egypt. This resulted in the dual process of the Islamization and Arabization of North Africa. It also placed Egypt on a collision course with the Nubian kingdoms of Sudan. Egypt tried, but it could not conquer its Nubian neighbors. Therefore, a nonaggression pact/trade agreement (*Baqt* treaty) was signed between the Nubian kingdoms and Egypt in 652 A.D. The pact called for peace between Egypt and the three kingdoms. The trade portion of the agreement called for the Nubians to provide Egypt with 400 slaves a year. In return, Egypt was to provide the Nubian kingdoms with food and clothing. This agreement was to remain in effect for almost 700 years. After the decline of the three Nubian kingdoms, the Funj, or the Arabized/Islamized southern Nubians, established a sultanate (the Black Sultanate) at Sennar. It fostered the Arabization and Islamization of the people of Sudan. This sultanate lasted from 1501 to 1821.

In 1821, Muhammad Ali, the pasha of Egypt, invaded Sudan in search of slaves for his army, ivory, and gold. The forces of Muhammad Ali annexed the northern part of Sudan. Southern Sudan was continuously raided for slaves. Subsequently, southern Sudan was also captured by Egypt. Sudan became an Egyptian colony. Egyptian imperialism spawned resentment among many people in Sudan. Muhammad Ahmad, a Dervish religious leader, believed that Egypt had a corrupting influence on Sudan. Therefore, he proclaimed himself the *Mahdi* (the messiah) in 1881, and led a revolt against Egyptian authority in Sudan. Muhammad Ahmad sought to restore the core Islamic values entrenched in the *Koran, Hadith,* and *Sunna*. The Mahdist revolt against Egypt was successful, and the Mahdist state ruled Sudan from 1883 to 1898. During this period, Egypt remained a constant threat to the Mahdist state, especially after Egypt became a British protectorate in 1882.[3]

The rationale for the British invasion and occupation of Egypt was that the Egyptian pasha Ismail (the grandson of Muhammad Ali) had incurred enormous debt that he was unable to repay to European financiers. This obtuse excuse masked the real motives of the British. In reality, the British invaded Egypt because of its strategic location. Control of Egypt, in turn, provided them with the means to gain control over Sudan.

> Britain sought control over the Sudan for imperial strategic reasons that were largely related to preventing other European powers from seizing the source of the Nile and gaining a foothold along the Red Sea from which they could threaten the sea route to India.[4]

In 1899 Great Britain and Egypt conquered Sudan. In 1916 the independent sultanate of Darfur was annexed and became part of Sudan. Egypt and Great Britain formed a partnership (the Anglo-Egyptian Condominium) to rule Sudan jointly. In reality, Great Britain was the senior partner, given that Egypt was a protectorate of Great Britain.

It was during this colonial period that the foundation of the historical myths were laid that were to haunt Sudan and lead to genocide in Darfur. For it was under the colonial administration of the British that one saw an emphasis placed on the Arabism of the indigenous people of Sudan. Ignorant of the histories of the various indigenous groups in Sudan, the British perceived the Arabs to be more intelligent, advanced, and civilized than the other groups in Sudan. The British therefore categorized the people of Sudan as either "Arab" or "African"; neither category was anthropologically accurate, as Ann Mosely Lesch stated: "most Arabs in the Sudan are really Arabized Nubians, Dinka, Nuba, Shilluk, Fur, of Beja."[5] Being Arab meant being privileged and being African meant being despised. Hence, it became important to try to link one's genealogy to an Arab ancestor if one could or to make one up. Colonialism helped to blur the vision of truth that many of the groups in Sudan were related and were not purely "Arab" or "African." People were encouraged to reject their indigenous African roots. In the eighteenth century, *awlad al-Bahar*—the so-called riverine Arabs—came to Durbar and settled in the Nile Valley. They became the most privileged group in Sudan. Being Arab in this colonial power structure meant that one had access to an education and could work as a civil servant, gain access to government contracts and property, and engage in business endeavors. Being African in this colonial setup meant that one could still be enslaved: "[The British] believed that sudden abolition would lead to moral decay and to social problems such as vagrancy and prostitution."[6] The British perpetuated slavery in Sudan even though they had participated earlier in the Berlin Conference of 1884–85 that was held to end the Arab slave trade. Here the true motives of the British became obvious. They perpetuated a policy of "divide and conquer." Colonial authorities did not allow travel among the different regions of Sudan by its inhabitants. The British also instituted Lord Lugard's policy of indirect rule. The rationale was to avoid conflict among the various ethnic groups. However, the end result was social division and separation among the various people of Sudan. In other words, the real motive was to prevent the people of Sudan from uniting against the imperial power. Therefore, some were given privileges while others were denied them. The denial of privileges to the "Africans" of southern Sudan can be witnessed in the fact that the British used Syrians, Armenians, Greeks, and northerners as merchants to facilitate commerce instead of the indigenous people of the south. Ali Mazrui has referred to this tactic as the use of a buffer race to act as a liaison between the indigenous people and the colonial authorities. It also prevented the rise of an African merchant class in southern Sudan. The British used similar policies in other colonies such as Ghana and Uganda.

Culture became the essential dividing line in Sudan. It has been pointed out by observers of Sudanese affairs that the terms "African" and "Arab" are based on culture rather than strictly on physical features or skin color.[7] Gerard Prunier has stated, "In terms of skin colour everybody [in Sudan] is black."[8] During the precolonial period there was certainly a cultural dividing line as well. Arab/ Muslim Sudanese enslaved African Muslims, African Christians, and animists. Africans also enslaved others who did not belong to their ethnic group to comply with the Baqt treaty. Nevertheless, the cultural dividing lines were not drawn as sharply as they were during the colonial era.

> Though Islam eventually became the religion of the Sudanic kings, the kings themselves continued to claim customary rights and powers which were not based on Islamic precepts.[9]

What became apparent during the colonial era was that a regime could remain in power if it fostered social, political, and economic divisions among its inhabitants. In many ways, the colonial policy of the British in Sudan paralleled that of the Belgians in Rwanda (see Chapter 4). The colonial authorities were successful in creating social divisions and ethnic cleavages among the people of Sudan that acted as a barrier, thereby preventing them from presenting a united front against the occupiers. If the "Arabs" had embraced their African roots, perhaps the various groups could have united against the European encroachers. "Arab" and "African" were politically driven identities. The colonial regime was successful in getting the people of Sudan to think in terms of race, to think that they were different from each other by rewarding one group and punishing the other. This was the lesson that was learned from colonialism, and it has sustained the various regimes that have ruled Sudan since its independence in 1956; it continues to sustain the regime in Khartoum today and is responsible for genocide in Darfur.

Lack of National Identity

Sudan lacks a national identity and the state lacks legitimacy. This is what has prevented its people from going beyond their primordial (social/cultural) identity and assuming a broader Sudanese supranational identity that crosses cultural boundaries. During the colonial era, the various groups were segregated and a racial hierarchy was established. Moreover, Sudan never developed a broad-based nationalist movement like many other colonies. Since the movement of the various people of Sudan was limited by the British authorities through the Pass Port and Permit Ordinance, there was little interaction among them. Colonialism created and reinforced ethnic identities and stereotypes. As a result, the northern sector of Sudan was unified while the south was Balkanized. Furthermore, the British quickly acquiesced to independence for Sudan to head off the growing influence of Egypt among the Sudanese elite and to counter the efforts of the Egyptian crown to regain control of Sudan.

The British selected the southerners who were to take part in negotiations for independence. Representatives from southern Sudan asked for a federal system to safeguard their rights but they were denied that. Instead, a unitary system was chosen. Moreover, they were only allocated 14 percent of the seats in the legislature. Arabic was to be the official language. The Sudanese commission appointed no southerners as governors, not even in the South. As a result, Sudan began to take on an Arab identity. People in southern Sudan began to fear domination by the Arab north. Such fears tipped off an incident that was to launch Sudan into civil war. In 1955, prior to independence, a mutiny broke out in the southern province of Equitoria. Southern soldiers had been ordered to go north to Khartoum for an independence celebration. Fearing for their lives, they refused to go. Violent demonstrations broke out in the South, and northerners were attacked. A civil war began that was to last from 1955 to 1972.

During this period, the features of the Sudanese political system were revealed; features that are still prevalent today and are a major factor in the war in Darfur. When the political system in Sudan is subjected to stress, it breaks down and the government resorts to a policy of *chronic Arabism*. This policy of "them versus us" emphasizes aspects of Arab culture as a means to regain the support of its Arab population. After independence, it became obvious that bonds of national unity had not been formed among Africans and Arabs. It was also obvious that strong political bonds did not exist among the ruling Arab elite. Their common identity was based on cultural, religious, and social traits. There was no common political culture, consensus on policy, political identity, or desire to work together due to factionalism. Political power was divided among various Sufi orders, the Mahdiyya, the Mirghaniyya, the Islamic Movement of Liberation, and the al-Ashiqqa Party. The word Sudanese had no meaning to them. Rather, they defined themselves in terms of their Arab identity and Islam.

As David Easton, Karl Deutsch, Gabriel Almond, and others have noted, demands are communicated within a political system.[10] These demands are processed and result in policy outputs that help to sustain the system, which is thus able to learn and adapt to its ever changing political environment. In Sudan, this has not occurred. Neither learning nor policy adjustments have taken place. So, whenever the system has been subjected to strong demands, communication within the government has broken down, resulting in lack of policy outputs and government paralysis. Sudan's political factions have not been willing to engage in the compromise that will produce a policy for enabling the state to sustain itself and maintain legitimacy among its citizens. This lack of flexibility has become a hallmark of all Sudanese governments since independence and has been a major factor in their collapse. It is also one of the main reasons why Sudan has only been at peace for ten years since its independence in 1956. Sudan is a failed state. Hence, the resort to *chronic Arabism* to shore up support for the regime. In 1958, after the Federal Party of the south swept the elections in the southern districts and gained allies in the eastern and western regions, the government collapsed. The Federal Party was poised to push its agenda for a federal system of government and equal rights for southerners and their culture. Additionally, the price of cotton on the international market collapsed. Instead of dealing with these problems, Prime Minister Khalil handed over power to General Ibrahim Abbud, who tried to assimilate the south through a policy based on conversion to Islam, the expulsion of Christian missionaries and the taking over of their schools, the mandatory use of Arabic, and scorched-earth military tactics in the south. This policy did not work. It only stressed the system more. The heavy military spending and the decline in the price of cotton on the international market meant that money was not available for social services in Khartoum and other outlying areas.

The stress on the political system led to the downfall of the Abbud regime and the resumption of civilian government in October 1964 (the October Revolution). During this period, the pattern of paralysis and collapse followed by the installation of a military government was seen once more. In 1966 Sadiq al-Mahdi became the prime minister of Sudan. Al-Mahdi was the Oxford-educated great-grandson of the Mahdi. Al-Mahdi believed that the state should personify Arab culture and that southerners should be converted to Islam; he supported a constitution based on *Shari'a* (Islamic law). The political establishment in Khartoum was apprehensive about the political gains made by the Islamic Charter Front (Muslim Brothers) headed by Hasan al-Turabi. The Arabs were trying to "out-Arab" each other. As a result, repression in the south increased and the civilian government fell once again and was taken over by a military coup. This has become a familiar story now.

The military coup of Jaafar Numeri was led by secular junior officers like himself. Despite this fact and Numeri's rhetoric about finding a nonmilitary solution to the Southern Problem, the war continued for the next two years. In 1972, the war ended. The south was granted a degree of home rule and Numeri became popular in southern Sudan. Nevertheless, the war was to resume when the Sudanese political system was placed under stress. Sudan faced mounting debt due to a decline in agricultural output. Therefore, Numeri sought assistance from the International Monetary Fund (IMF) that demanded the implementation of an austerity (structural adjustment) program.

> The annual balance of payments deficit rose from £S 30.5 million in 1973–74 to £S 310.6 million in 1981–82. The Sudan's outstanding external debt at the end of 1982 was $6 billion.[11]

As economic conditions worsened and people took to the streets in protest against the high prices of bread, fuel, and other basic necessities, Numeri, the erstwhile secularist who had come to power with the support of Communists, invited his political opponents to return to Sudan and instituted *Shari'a* (Islamic law) in September 1983 (the September laws). Therefore, *chronic Arabism* was used to prop up a regime that had lost legitimacy. As a result, civil war erupted again in southern Sudan due to the implementation of the policy of *chronic Arabism*. Numeri was overthrown in April 1985.[12]

From the ashes of Numeri's dictatorship rose the second civilian government of Sadiq al-Mahdi in 1986. G. Norman Anderson who served as the U.S. ambassador to Sudan from 1986 to 1989 noted a recurring pattern of behavior among both the civilian and military governments of Sudan. He observed that Sudan's political leaders were not able to work effectively to solve the country's problems.[13] During the early days of his administration, Sadiq was inflexible in his position with respect to southern Sudan. He pursued a policy of Arabization and Islamization. He also proved unable to deal effectively with Sudan's economic problems.

Sadiq's Umma Party was not able to work with its coalition partner, the Democratic Unionist Party (DUP). Due to the resulting paralysis, the government could not even formulate a coherent foreign policy.

> During the first two years, for example, the DUP foreign minister tried to improve relations with Egypt, Iraq, and the United States, whereas the Prime Minister al-Mahdi courted Libya, Iraq, and the USSR and criticized the IMF.[14]

In addition, there were severe economic problems that were not dealt with effectively by the government. The infrastructure was falling apart, and bread, sugar, tea, gasoline, electricity, and water were in short supply. Furthermore, Sudan also faced demands for structural adjustment from the IMF. Al-Mahdi's government was not able to cope with the strain. Nevertheless, to al-Mahdi's credit, his government was on the verge of abandoning the policy of *chronic Arabism*. During a peace conference between the north and south, he had agreed to accept the DUP–Sudanese People's Liberation Army/Movement (SPLA/M) agreement that called for the suspension of *Shari'a,* a cease-fire, national unity, and an end to military pacts. This is why the National Islamic Front (NIF) overthrew Sadiq al-Mahdi's government in 1989.

The National Islamic Front of Hasan al-Turabi overthrew al-Mahdi's government to prevent it from making accommodation with the SPLA/M rebel forces of the south headed by John Garang. Peace would have deprived the NIF of the means to come to power. However, once in power, the NIF (now the National Congress Party) made accommodation with John Garang's SPLA/M rebel forces. This does not mean that the policy of *chronic Arabism* was abandoned; however, it merely shifted location from southern Sudan to Darfur in western Sudan. Bringing the war in the south to an end allowed the regime in Khartoum to reap profits from oil in that region. However, the regime continued its policy of *chronic Arabism* to garner support in the Arab community of Sudan and other countries.

THE WAR IN DARFUR

There is an inherent link between the war in southern Sudan and the war in Darfur. The war in Darfur began in 2003 when the war in southern Sudan was winding down. It intensified as the war in southern Sudan came to an end in 2005. Darfurians, who were once viewed as northerners by the people of southern Sudan, now became the victims of the same scorched-earth tactics of bombing, raiding, rape, pillage, and enslavement used in the south. In many ways the war had just shifted locations, and the policy of *chronic Arabism* continued as a means to prop up a failed regime.

Most westerners were at a loss to explain the conflict in Darfur. The conflict between northern Sudan and southern Sudan was inaccurately viewed through the prism of the Muslim north versus the Christian south. Clearly, this paradigm did not fit Darfur where the battle pitted Muslims against Muslims. Moreover, many of the groups fighting against the government in Darfur, such as the Berti, Birgid, Beigo, Mima, and Gimir, all speak Arabic though they do not consider themselves to be Arabs.[15]

Drought is also sometimes cited as the cause of the conflict in Darfur. In this scenario, drought conditions have pitted African farmers against Arab nomads. What is often overlooked is that the two groups have a history of cooperation. The Arabs in Darfur had a history of cooperation with the various non-Muslim groups in the outlying areas. Douglass H. Johnson has stated:

> many Muslim pastoralists such as the [Arab] Baqqara in Darfur ... frequently sought protection from the demands of the state by fleeing to or allying with non-Muslim people.[16]

There was also an informal land use system whereby the "African" farmers of Darfur would share their land with the "Arab" nomads.

> In the past, the [Arab] nomads would graze their goats and cattle in the North of Darfur during the rainy season, then move to the greener south during the dry season. After the rains, when the [African] farmers had gathered in their crops, the nomads would tend their herds in the farmers' empty fields.[17]

Traditional leaders also worked together to ameliorate land disputes. However, in the 1970s and 1980s, Darfur experienced drought. This resulting desertification of the land compelled many of the nomadic Arabs to head to the southern portion of Darfur in search of more lush land for their livestock. This put them in conflict with the sedentary African farmers. The traditional means that had been used to settle disputes over land usage was no longer functional since it had been usurped by the Numeri regime that supplanted traditional leaders with pro-Arab administrators. This pitted African groups such as the Fur, Birgid, and Daju against *dar*-less (landless) Arab groups such as the Misiriya, Huttiya, Ta'alba, Tarjam, Sa'ada, Mahariya, and Bani Mansur.[18] On the other hand, Arabs with dar (land), such as the Habbaniya, Beni, and Ta'aisha in southern Darfur and the Beni Hussein in northern Darfur, remained neutral.[19] Since the 1970s, this conflict has resulted in the slaughter and enslavement of various African groups, much like the conflict in southern Sudan.

Most political observers cite the drought mentioned above as the cause of the genocide in Darfur. However, the reasons for these heinous acts being committed run much deeper. Genocide in Darfur is the direct result of a deliberate policy perpetuated by Omar al-Bashir, the president of Sudan. Darfur, like the other outlying regions of Khartoum, has long been neglected, though drought has been occurring there since the 1970s. The regional government has been denied funds to upgrade the water system. In the 1980s,

> More boreholes were needed and few had been dug over the previous twenty years ... Funds earmarked for water projects had been stolen, miles of piping imported for Darfur had been lying for years in Port Sudan with nobody bothering to collect it.[20]

The regime in Khartoum has not adequately provided for the needs of its people, especially in the area outside of the capital. Ironically, David Hoile has stated that the rebellion in Darfur was not justified because Darfur was not neglected by the current central government. He has stated:

> with regard to development in Darfur since the present government came to power in 1989. The government has stated that before 1989, there were only 16 high schools in Darfur: there are presently 250 schools: [they] increased from 241 in 1986 to 786 in 2003 ... The number of hospitals in Darfur has increased under this government from three in 1988 to 23 hospitals in 2001.[21]

Nevertheless, when viewed from a broader perspective, things look quite different from the rosy picture that Hoile paints. Richard Lobban as well as others have pointed out that only about 20 percent of Sudan's population lives in Khartoum; yet 50 percent of its doctors reside there, 70 percent of its electricity is consumed there, and 70 percent of its industry is located there as well.[22] Furthermore, Hoile missed the point that the rebellion is not about infrastructure. The Sudanese Liberation Army/Movement (SLA/M) has stated that it is not fighting for more infrastructure in Darfur. It is fighting for justice.[23]

Both the African and Arab populations of Darfur have been neglected, because the administration in Khartoum views Darfur as a backwater area. Yet, it tries to maintain "Arab solidarity" with the nomadic herders even though the two groups, more often than not, have nothing in common. Most of the nomads are illiterate while the Khartoum clique is well-educated. Many of the Arabs of Darfur have a history of a migratory lifestyle while the Arabs of Khartoum are sedentary. The Khartoum clique has once more implemented the policy of *chronic Arabism* by pretending to be the "brothers" of the Arabs of Darfur and arming them with the means to engage in a massive land grab after years of failing to provide for their needs. The regime in Khartoum, whom the Janjaweed and the other Arab groups view as their brothers, are in fact their oppressors. The Arabs of Darfur have suffered from the effects of drought and neglect just like the Africans. The government policy of *chronic Arabism* has also worked in getting Africans to view the political events through the racial lens that Khartoum has provided. Thus, by getting both the victim and the victimizer to see through this racial paradigm, the regime in Khartoum is able to cover its tracks as a failed state. It tries to deceive people into believing that the events transpiring in Darfur are cases of ethnic warfare rather than what they are—genocide. As Albert Meimi stated in *The Colonizer and the Colonized*,

> [The usurper] endeavors to falsify history, he rewrites laws, he would extinguish memories. Anything to transform his usurpation into legitimacy.[24]

Regarding the colonized, he wrote:

> The most serious blow suffered by the colonized is being removed from history and from the community. Colonization usurps any free role in either war or peace, every decision contributing to his destiny and that of the world, and all cultural and social responsibility.[25]

The use of *chronic Arabism* has been used not only to obtain support for the Khartoum regime within Sudan but also among Arab states as well. In 2006 the Arab League held its summit in Khartoum, and since that time the Arab League has refused to denounce al-Bashir or the genocide in Darfur. Despite the indictment of Omar al-Bashir by the International Criminal Court (ICC) in 2008 and the issuing of a warrant for his arrest by the ICC, on March 4, 2009, Arab countries and the Arab League have rallied around him. He was welcomed in Egypt on March 25, 2009, by Hosni Mubarak, even though a terrorist group operating out of Sudan had tried to assassinate Mubarak in 1995. Subsequently, he was also embraced warmly at the Arab League Summit in Qatar. But there can be no doubt that genocide has been committed in Darfur.

REFLECTIONS ON DARFUR

The Convention on the Prevention and Punishment of the Crime of Genocide is dead. What other conclusion can be drawn after reading the "Report of the International Commission of Inquiry on Darfur to the United Nations Secretary-General?"[26] The report indicated that crimes against humanity occurred in Darfur. But it stopped short of calling the crimes genocide. Nevertheless, acts of genocide did occur in Darfur. The report was carefully worded to absolve the permanent members of the Security Council of any responsibility for the heinous acts that transpired there. But the blood of the victims cannot be completely wiped from their hands.

The crisis in Darfur also demonstrates many of the shortcomings of the international system. The term international community is a misnomer. The situation in Darfur readily points out that the world's nations have fallen short of forming a community. Neighbors look out for each other's well-being in a community. Conversely, in a society neighbors merely coexist with one another.

The crisis in Darfur also shows that international law has become unenforceable, because those entrusted to enforce it are often the biggest violators of international law. In other words, how can international law be enforced when the sheriff is an outlaw?

DARFUR AND GENOCIDE

The events that occurred in Darfur are not imaginary. The government of Sudan and its surrogates, the Janjaweed, attacked the civilian population in Darfur. As a result, 2.71 million civilians have been displaced and over 400,000 people killed. These facts alone do not seem to indicate that genocide occurred in Darfur. However, when one examines how events unfolded in Darfur, it becomes obvious that genocide did indeed occur in that region of Sudan.

Genocide is defined in the Convention on the Prevention and Punishment for the Crime of Genocide. The Convention defines genocide as the following:

> (a) Killing members of the group;
> (b) Causing serious bodily or mental harm to members of the group;
> (c) Deliberately inflicting on the group conditions of life calculated to bring about its physical destruction in whole or in part;
> (d) Imposing measures intended to prevent births within the group;
> (e) Forcibly transferring children of the group to another group.[27]

Without a doubt, genocide occurred in Darfur as one of the main aims of genocide is to eliminate a group. The "Report of the International Commission of Inquiry on Darfur to the United Nations Secretary-General" indicates that the acts of violence were not random. They targeted particular groups. For example, the Sudanese government and their Janjaweed agents targeted members of the Zaghwa, Fur, and Masaalit. The government of Sudan is run by people who are predominantly Arab like their Janjaweed surrogates.[28] Members of the Zaghawa, Fur, and Masaalit ethnic groups have been designated as "Africans." This is not a racial grouping per se but a designated cultural group, nevertheless. The attacks were obviously targeted against these groups to provide *dar* (land) to the landless Arabs. The attacks took place against more than 2,000 villages that were predominantly African.[29] Moreover, during the attack against the African villagers, the Arab-based Janjaweed made the following statements leaving no doubt that the attacks were racially motivated.

> When asked why they believed they were attacked some witnesses stated "because they want our land and cattle" or "they want to eliminate us from the area." Other witnesses referred to statements made by their aggressors during some of the attacks, such as "you are Tora Bora, the SLA are your families," "the Fur are slaves, we will kill them," "we are here to eradicate blacks (nuba)," "we will drive you to poverty," "this is not your land," or "you are not from here."[30]

From the comments above, it is apparent that Africans were victims of racially motivated attacks by Arabs, and the goal was to cleanse the land of their presence. This constitutes genocide.

Other forms of genocide were also used against the African population of Darfur. According to the Convention on the Prevention and Punishment of the Crime of Genocide, "causing serious bodily or mental harm to members of the group" also constitutes genocide. In Darfur, rape was used as a weapon of warfare. Sudanese soldiers and their Janjaweed agents used rape to physically injure and humiliate the indigenous women and girls of Darfur. According to the "Report of the International Commission of Inquiry on Darfur to the United Nations Secretary-General,"

> Various sources reported widespread rape and other serious forms of violence committed against women and girls in all three states of Darfur. According to these sources, the rape of individual victims was multiple, carried out by more than one man and accompanied by other severe forms of violence, including beating and whipping. In some cases, women were raped in public, and in some incidences, the women were further berated and called "slaves or Tora Bora [black dust]."[31]

The following has also been reported:

> First, deliberate aggression against women and girls, including gang rapes, occurred during the attacks on the villages. Second, women and girls were abducted, held in confinement for several days and repeatedly raped during that time. Third, rape and other forms of sexual violence caused during the flight and further displacement including when women left towns and IDP sites to collect wood or water. In certain areas, rape also occurred inside towns. Some women and girls became pregnant as a result of rape.[32]

These acts of violence against women were not random acts of violence by individuals. They were coordinated with the intent to humiliate and inflict physical and psychological harm on the victims. Furthermore, if the rape victims became pregnant, they would have to endure the physical pain of childbirth and the psychological pain of social ostracism for having given birth to the children of the enemy. The rape victims were often branded on the hand and forced to live with the memories of the violent acts committed against them and the possibility of being shunned by their families and communities.

The evidence also indicates that genocide occurred in Darfur due to the nature of the attacks against the indigenous people of Darfur. Sudanese troops and the Janjaweed militias leveled villages in Darfur. Crops, cattle, livestock, huts, and personal possessions were destroyed with the intent of driving out the indigenous people by making it impossible for them to sustain themselves in the region. Frequently, many of the indigenous Africans refused to return to their villages for fear of further attacks. In some cases, Arabs from other regions of Sudan moved into the area. These acts constitute genocide. According to the Convention, "deliberately inflicting on the group conditions of life calculated to bring about its physical destruction in whole or in part" also constitutes an act of genocide. The attacks were planned to drive people away from their villages. It was genocide.

The government of Sudan and its Janjaweed surrogates also undertook measures that negatively affected the fertility rate of the peoples of Darfur. Civilian men and boys were murdered en masse by the Sudanese government and the Janjaweed forces.[33] Such attacks undoubtedly had an adverse impact on the fertility rate of the targeted African population of Darfur. Fewer males affect the group's ability to reproduce itself, thereby negatively affecting its population. The Convention defines this as genocide. It states that genocide is "imposing measures intended to prevent Births within the group." Genocide is the policy of the government of Sudan and the Janjaweed.

Genocide in Darfur has not been a priority issue for the permanent members of the Security Council, which consists of countries that are supposed to uphold international law but failed to do so in Darfur. The Security Council has been slow to respond to the crisis. In fact, Russia and China have aggravated the situation. Their actions have led to more deaths and destruction in Darfur.

RUSSIA AND CHINA: OUTLAW SHERIFFS

The law becomes unenforceable when those who are supposed to uphold it willingly violate it. In other words, the law becomes unenforceable when the sheriff is an outlaw. This is currently the situation with respect to Darfur. Russia and China, two permanent members of the UN Security Council who are supposed to uphold international law, have contributed to the genocide that has taken place in Darfur. First, the Security Council enacted a weak arms embargo against Darfur. It excluded the Sudanese government that has used the arms it has imported to arm its Janjaweed ally. Second, the United Nations failed to take action when it received reports about violations of the arms embargo from the UN Panel of Experts.[34] Russia and China are guilty of complicity in genocide because they have empowered the government of Sudan and the Janjaweed with the means to commit genocide.

> Sudan had imported $24 million worth of arms and ammunition from the People's Republic of China, as well as nearly $57 million worth of parts and aircraft equipment and $2 million worth of parts of helicopters and aeroplanes from China, according to data from Sudan for 2005, the last available trade figures.[35]

During the period January–March 2007, Chinese A-5 Fanton jet fighters were transferred to Nyala airport in Darfur.[36] These aircraft were used to bomb civilian villages in Darfur.[37] Russia has also been a party to genocide in Darfur. In October 2004, Russian-made Mi-8 helicopters were used to attack villages in Darfur.[38] It has also been reported:

> In 2005, the Russian Federation exported to Sudan $21 million worth of aircraft and associated equipment including spare parts and $137 million of helicopters, adding to its substantial arms deliveries in previous years ... Russian Mi-24 helicopter gunships acquired by the Sudanese Air Force [was used] to launch attacks in Darfur.[39]

Despite theses violations, neither Russia nor China have been ostracized by their fellow Security Council members.

The United States is also indirectly guilty of complicity in the genocide that occurred in Darfur. It has not examined this issue with the same sense of urgency it has other issues, such as the war in Iraq or the acquisition of nuclear weapons by North Korea and Iran. The United States has also not pressed the issue of Russia's and China's roles in aiding genocide in Sudan. It wants China's cooperation in its battle to keep nuclear weapons out of North Korea's hands. The United States is also borrowing Chinese money to finance its massive deficit. Therefore, the United States is not going to rock the boat with China over the issue of genocide in Darfur. Also, the United States had sought Russia's cooperation to settle the issue of independence for Kosovo. Russia was used as a conduit to Serbia, whose cooperation the United States had sought to work out an agreement. In essence, the United States did not consider the people of Darfur to be worth the effort needed to pressure Russia and China to stop aiding genocide. Politics got in the way of stopping genocide.

The net effect of this negligence is that those who have been trusted to uphold international law have in effect chosen to violate it. What do you do when the sheriff is an outlaw? The law becomes unenforceable. The low priority given to Darfur can be witnessed by the fact that it took three years to get a UN peacekeeping force on the ground in Darfur. Furthermore, the Sudanese government has shown a blatant disrespect for the UN peacekeeping force by attacking it with gunfire on several occasions.[40] The Security Council has not taken retaliatory action against Sudan. Because of incidents like these and the outlaw sheriffs on the Security Council, the United Nations has been ineffective in stopping genocide in Darfur. The reason why genocide still occurs and is tolerated is because the international community exists in name only. In other words, there is no international civil society.

THE AMERICAN PUBLIC

Unlike the other episodes of genocide that transpired in the 1990s, the American public was aware of what was going on in Darfur and tried to stop it. "Save Darfur" became a rallying cry. Nevertheless, despite public involvement, genocide in Darfur continued unabated. It is important to understand the paradox of why the greater involvement of the American public in such a major issue did not result in genocide being brought to an end in Darfur.

Initially, due to sparse media coverage, the American public did not demonstrate a great deal of concern regarding the events that were unfolding in Darfur. However, as media coverage grew, so did the concern of the American people. There were a number of reasons for this. First, the government of Sudan had developed a nefarious reputation among conservative Christians in the United States. They viewed the Sudanese civil war as a battle between the "Muslim north" and the "Christian south." The conservative Christian community was appalled at the scorched-earth tactics used by the government-backed militias in southern Sudan. They recoiled in horror after learning about the rape and enslavement of thousands of women and children in southern Sudan. Many American Christians became involved in various redemption programs to purchase the freedom of southern Sudanese slaves. When news of Darfur reached the conservative American Christian community, they were equally dismayed that the same tactics, policies, and practices that they had fought against in southern Sudan were now being deployed in western Sudan. They demanded that their Republican allies in Congress and the president take bold action to alleviate the situation in Darfur.

The crisis in Darfur is notable for the involvement of American youth. During the episodes of genocide in Rwanda, Bosnia, and Kosovo, America's youth had slept just like the rest of the American public. By 2004 they were out in the forefront of the struggle to "Save Darfur." There are a number of reasons for this turnaround. First, the ten-year anniversary of the Rwandan genocide was observed in 2004. Second, this coincided with the release of the movie "Hotel Rwanda." This helped to heighten the awareness about genocide being committed in Darfur. What is also important in understanding the involvement of American youth is how the message of genocide reached them. The movie "Hotel Rwanda" was a part of American pop culture. Likewise, news regarding Darfur spread across the Internet. These are modes of information and communication utilized by American youth on a routine basis. College campuses became a staging point for organizing rallies and protests demanding that colleges, universities, and other institutions divest funds from companies doing business with the government of Sudan. American youth also demanded that the government take action to bring the genocide in Darfur to an end. Apathetic American youth had finally woken up. Thus, a broad-based coalition of conservative Christians, American youth, Jews, and Armenians was formed. It seemed absurd to think that such a broad-based coalition could be denied. In 2005, when asked, 66 percent of Americans supported the United States' contributing troops to a UN mission to stop the genocide. Justice for Darfur seemed to be on the way. The American people did not surrender to genocide but their government did.

CONGRESS

Republican members of the House of Representatives and the Senate initially championed Darfur's cause. Like the Sudanese Civil War, this was their issue. With the exception of Representative Donald Payne (Democrat–New Jersey), who also took a leadership role, Democrats in both chambers acquiesced to Republican leadership on the issue.

Initially, in the House, Republicans such as Frank Wolf of Virginia spoke out against the atrocities in Darfur and labeled them as genocide. Wolf held the government of Sudan in contempt and wanted his colleagues to know of the atrocities it had committed during the Sudanese Civil War. Therefore, in 2002 he placed the findings of the International Eminent Persons Group that was created to investigate reports of slavery and abduction before the House. The report noted:

> Many of those who were abducted and enslaved remain with their abductors in the area of South Darfur or West Kordofan; some people escape or are returned; and others are sold or transferred to third parties.[41]

A few months later, Congress passed the Sudanese Peace Act. The bill was sponsored in the House of Representatives by Thomas Tancredo (Republican-Colorado) and thirteen bipartisan cosponsors (eight Republicans and five Democrats, including Representative Wolf). It then went to the Senate where it was approved unanimously. President Bush II signed the bill on October 21, 2002. It included the following findings:

- The Government of Sudan['s] … prosecution of the war … cost more than 2,000,000 lives … and displaces 4,000,000 people.
- Continued leadership of the United State is crucial. Through manipulation of traditional rivalries among peoples in areas outside of full control, the government of Sudan has used divide-and-conquer techniques effectively to subjugate the population.
- The Government of Sudan utilizes and organizes militias, Popular Defense Forces and other irregular units for enslaving parties …
- The acts of the government of Sudan … constitute genocide.[42]

The Act also condemned the government of Sudan for slavery and other human rights abuses. It authorized the president to provide $100 million annually in assistance to the areas outside of the government's control for the fiscal years 2003, 2004, and 2005.

The president was also to report to Congress every six months as to whether the parties embroiled in the conflict in southern Sudan were negotiating in good faith and whether the government of Sudan had interfered in humanitarian efforts. If it was determined that the government of Sudan was not cooperating in the peace effort, then the U.S. secretary of treasury was to instruct directors of international financial institutions to vote against extending loans, credit, or guarantees to the government of Sudan. On September 24, 2003, Wolf condemned the government of Sudan for slavery and sex trafficking. On April 2, 2004, Wolf took to the floor of the House of Representatives once more. This time, he called attention to what was transpiring in Darfur. Wolf stated:

> As the world waits and watches, the people of Darfur region in Sudan are being wiped out. This crisis began in February 2003 when the rebel groups in Darfur state began to fight government security forces. In early February 2004, the government launched a major military offensive against the rebel forces. The result has been brutal attacks by ground and air forces against innocent civilians and undefended villages. Thousands have been killed. Millions more remain beyond the reach of aid.[43]

Wolf then proceeded to speak on behalf of House Concurrent Resolution 403 that condemned the government of Sudan for its attacks on civilians and asked the United Nations to determine whether crimes against humanity had been committed.

Representative Wolf adopted this cause as his own. He would often take time to point out articles about the mass murder, rape, and pillaging taking place in Darfur that were reported in the *New York Times*. He also raised questions regarding the delay of aid to civilians in Darfur. The government of Sudan was engaged in a sadistic game with aid workers so they could not distribute aid to civilians. Gerard Prunier stated:

> travel permits for Darfur would be issued to NGO workers but made valid only for three days; then the beneficiaries were told that they had to give seventy-two hours pre-flight notice before going, meaning that their permits would have expired by the time they were to be used.[44]

In the Senate the cause for Darfur was taken up by members such as Senators Brownback (Republican-Kansas), Feingold (Democrat-Wisconsin), Durbin (Democrat-Illinois), and McCain (Republican-Arizona). McCain railed against the tactics used by the government of Sudan in Darfur. McCain pointed out that:

> The government of Sudan is actually using Russian-made Antonov bombers and MiG fighters to kill the civilian population. They are not simply attacking military targets but are focusing on civilian targets such as water wells, granaries, houses and crops.[45]

Four days later, on May 10, 2004, the Senate passed a concurrent resolution sponsored by Senator Brownback to condemn the government of Sudan for attacks against innocent civilians. The measure was sponsored by Representative Wolf in the House and passed on May 17, 2004.

The effort to save Darfur did not end with resolutions passed by both houses of Congress. Representative Wolf kept up the pressure and sent a letter to Kofi Annan, the secretary-general of the United Nations. It was signed by Wolf and a bipartisan coalition consisting of forty-four other members of the House of Representatives. The letter asked Annan to go to Darfur to end the genocide. The letter stated:

> We are extremely concerned that the crisis in Darfur, Sudan had not received the international attention or response that is needed to save the lives of hundreds of thousands of innocent civilians.[46]

It went on to make the following point:

> The international community must act swiftly. Failure to act will bring certain death to the thousands languishing in camps. The world will wake up 10 years from now and wonder why more was not done to protect humanity.[47]

Senator Richard Durbin also placed an article from the *Los Angeles Times* in the *Congressional Record* about how the murder and rape conducted by the Janjaweed was contributing to the spread of HIV, Ebola, West Nile Virus, and other diseases.[48] However, Representative Chris Van Hollen (Democrat-Maryland) was beginning to see the futility of the Congressional effort. On June 25, 2004, he noted that the Convention on the Prevention and Punishment of the Crime of Genocide calls for prevention—not just punishment after the fact. Congressional action did not end the genocide.

Wolf continued to act as the House's point man on Darfur. He often called his colleague's attention to articles from a variety of sources, ranging from the BBC to *The New York Times*. However, by July 2004, a new critic with a stronger voice emerged in the Senate, Joe Biden of Delaware. Biden not only condemned the atrocities of the government of Sudan, but also condemned the policies of the

Bush II administration for not taking bolder action to bring the horrors in Darfur to an end. Biden pointed out the futility of the policy that the Bush II administration was pursuing at the United Nations:

> The administration is circulating a draft United Nations Security Council resolution which puts sanctions on the janjaweed. I do not think pursuing a resolution which would impose an arms and travel embargo on the janjaweed will improve the security situation in Darfur. I am sure there must be a strategy behind this resolution, but on its face, it is hard to see. The janjaweed is not a state actor. It is not even an independent actor. It certainly is not accepting arms shipments from foreign governments. The janjaweed is armed and supplied by the Government of Sudan. And last I heard the only place the janjaweed has traveled is across the border into Chad to further harass the victims.[49]

Biden's criticism was significant. Previously, the actions of the government of Sudan were condemned. However, Biden also became a critic of the Bush II administration's policy in Darfur.

In the House of Representatives, the tone remained cordial with the president. Nevertheless, on July 21, 2004, the House passed a concurrent resolution (House Concurrent Resolution 467), declaring that genocide had occurred in Darfur. The resolution stated:

> The violence in Darfur appears to be particularly directed at a specific group based on their ethnic identity and appears to be systemized ... Resolved by the House of Representatives (the Senate concurring), That Congress—... declares the atrocities unfolding in Darfur, Sudan, are genocide ... and calls upon the United Nations and the Secretary General to assert leadership by calling the atrocities being committed in Darfur by their rightful name: "genocide."[50]

During debate on the resolution, Representative Wolf stated, "we have a responsibility and duty to the people of Darfur to try to stop [genocide] in its tracks." However, he did not say how this was to be done. The Democrats in the House were beginning to find their voice—more of them began to speak out against the genocide taking place in Darfur. In the Senate, the measure had bipartisan sponsorship. Senator Corzine (Democrat–New Jersey) and Senator Brownback (Republican-Kansas) sponsored the resolution in the Senate that was notable for what it did and for what it did not do. The resolution placed a great deal of the burden of action on the United Nations. Using the word genocide meant invoking the Convention on the

Prevention and Punishment of the Crime of Genocide. To enforce the treaty, the United Nations would need the strong backing of the five permanent members of the Security Council, especially the United States. As Senator Biden pointed out, the administration of George W. Bush had not made such a commitment. The resolution was also notable because it commended the administration's actions in seeking a peaceful resolution of the conflict. This indicated that neither the Republican-led House nor the Republican-controlled Senate were willing to break ranks with the president. Gradually, more Democrats began to step forward to champion the cause of Darfur.

Representative Wolf continued to speak out passionately against the atrocities in Darfur. However, Wolf, his fellow Republicans in the House, in the Senate, as well as the Democrats in both bodies did not call upon the president to intervene militarily in Darfur against the genocide. In fact, at one point, Wolf thanked the Bush II administration for documenting the atrocities, and made an appeal to the international community to take action.[51] Senator Bill Frist (Republican-Tennessee), a physician, was the majority leader in the Senate. Frist made annual trips to the Darfur region to spend time with refugees. However, his main focus, like Bush's, was on humanitarian aid. Criticism of the international community and the United Nations became routine. Appeals were often made to the United Nations to take action as if it had a standing army that could be deployed in a crisis situation. Appeals were also made to the international community as if it could act in the absence of U.S. involvement and leadership. At this point, no one except Biden seemed willing to take on Bush. And even his criticism at this point did not emphasize military intervention.

On September 9, 2004, when testifying before the Senate Foreign Relations Committee, Secretary of State Colin Powell said that genocide had been committed in Darfur. The Bush II administration now appeared to be on the same page as Congress. The Clinton administration had played word games and refused to call the mass killings in Rwanda genocide for fear of invoking the Convention on the Prevention and Punishment of the Crime of Genocide. Now that the Bush II administration had found the courage to call the killings in Darfur genocide, hope was raised that something would be done to stop it. But that hope was soon lost.

To Charles B. Rangel (Democrat–New York), the long-serving Congressman from New York, the gap between U.S. rhetoric and action became intolerable. On November 17, 2004, Rangel took to the floor of the House of Representatives and demanded that the United States start using its muscle to back its morals. Rangel said:

> Despite widespread condemnation by the international community regarding the Darfur genocide, few in the West have been willing to offer troops or logistics to the peacekeeping effort. The African Union has attempted to fill the void through its seven hundred man observer force. However, the AU force is severely undermanned and underfunded.[52]

Rangel also made the point that:

> The AU will no doubt need assistance in such an endeavor, America, as the greatest military power in the world, should not allow this deficiency to continue. Indeed, the U.S. currently has a contingent of 2,500 troops in Djibouti, from which it can initially draw.[53]

Late in 2004, both houses of Congress passed the Comprehensive Peace in Sudan Act of 2004. The Act cited the genocide committed by the Sudanese government and its Janjaweed henchmen. It also stated that:

> the United States government and the international community should—provide all necessary assistance to deploy and sustain an African Union force to the Darfur region ... the President, acting through the Secretary of State and the Permanent Representative of the United States to the United Nations, should—condemn any failure on the part of the Government of Sudan to fulfill its obligations under United Nations Security Council Resolutions ... [the United States should] press the United Nations Security Council to pursue accountability of those individuals who are responsible for orchestrating and carrying out the atrocities in the Darfur region.[54]

The Comprehensive Peace in Sudan Act of 2004 was meaningless. It did not call for action to be taken to stop the genocide, nor did it encourage the president to do so. It provided funding for humanitarian relief. This amounted to doing nothing more than dealing with the effects of genocide rather than preventing it or stopping it. Moreover, the Act called for the president to pursue those who were responsible for the genocide in Darfur and to hold them accountable for their crimes. This was difficult to do since George W. Bush did not support the ICC. In 2005 Bush finally acquiesced and allowed the Security Council to refer the matter to the ICC. It was ironic that many Republicans who had criticized the United Nations over the years and denied it funding now looked to it to solve the crisis in Darfur rather than take the initiative themselves.

The year 2005 was something of a learning year for members of both houses of Congress. The effort to save Darfur that had once been led by Republicans had now become a bipartisan effort. Members of Congress also learned that their actions were limited without the support of the president. As the situation in Darfur worsened, members of Congress placed articles about the tragedy transpiring in Darfur in the *Congressional Record.* In 2005, the Darfur Accountability Act (Senate Resolution 495) was introduced. It was sponsored by Senator Corzine (Democrat–New Jersey) and cosponsored by Senators Brownback (Republican-Kansas), Dodd (Democrat-Connecticut), Feingold (Democrat-Wisconsin), Durbin (Democrat-Illinois), Lieberman (Democrat-Connecticut), Talent (Republican-Missouri), DeWine (Republican-Ohio), and Coburn (Republican-Oklahoma). It sought to go beyond talk and to stop the genocide in Darfur. The bill confirmed that genocide had taken place in Darfur, and called for a military no-fly zone in Darfur, reports on the progress of the African Union (AU) peacekeeping mission in Darfur, and stronger arms sanctions to be implemented against the government of Sudan. This was the first time that Congress had taken action to stop the genocide in Darfur. Unfortunately, for the measure to be effective, the president would have to take the initiative to implement the no-fly zone. Senator Durbin recalled that the president showed no such inclination. So, Durbin asked President Bush II:

> What are you going to do about Darfur? Sadly, the response was what I have heard over and over again from so many different sources: We are going to count on the African Union, a group of soldiers from Africa who are moving into the region. How many soldiers are moving into this region where helpless people are being killed? The best estimates are 3,000 soldiers. How big is this region? It is about the size of the state of Texas. How in the world can we expect to have an impact on this senseless killing?[55]

The measure did not pass in 2005 due to opposition from the Bush II administration. Also early in 2005, Representative Wolf turned his ire on the United Nations. Wolf stated, "The Security Council must take immediate, effective measures to stop the bloodshed."[56] In a letter to Secretary-General Kofi Annan, Wolf stated that if the Security Council did not take meaningful action regarding Darfur, Annan should resign.[57] Was this an act of desperation on the part of Representative

Wolf? Perhaps it was. By now it had become obvious to Washington observers that despite labeling the atrocities in Darfur as genocide, the Bush administration was not going to take action outside of the realm of humanitarian aid. Maybe this was the reason why Wolf and Republicans in the Senate appealed to Kofi Annan, the secretary-general of the United Nations, rather than to George W. Bush, the president of the United States and the leader of their political party, to stop the genocide in Darfur. The gap between the rhetoric and the actions of the Bush II administration also became apparent to Representative Blumenauer (Democrat-Oregon). Blumenauer noted that $50 million in the foreign appropriation bill that would have allowed the AU peacekeeping mission in Darfur to expand from 6,000 troops to 7,700 troops was dropped. This was done at the request of the Bush administration.[58] Congress was fighting an uphill battle. The words of the Bush II administration did not match its deeds. Congress was responding to the demands of its constituents but could not move the president. For George W. Bush, the War on Terrorism had priority over the War in Darfur.

In 2005 Representative Charles Rangel (Democrat–New York) noted a subtle shift in the temper and tone of the Bush II administration's policy regarding Darfur. Rangel observed:

> Despite the financial assistance, the Administration has been quiet on the political front recently. In fact, they have seemingly backed away from referring to the crisis in Darfur as genocide, and have downplayed the casualty count in the region. As the New York Times Op-Ed asserts, Sudan's recent cooperation with the United States on intelligence matters, may be placating the Administration's stance toward the regime regarding Darfur.[59]

In 2005 the cry to "Save Darfur" had diminished. Therefore, the Bush II administration backed away from using the term genocide.

In 2006 members of Congress searched more intensely to find a way to stop the genocide in Darfur. While railing against the Arab League for refusing to cancel the summit that was scheduled in Khartoum, Representative Pallone (Democrat–New Jersey) said that "we have a moral obligation to do all we can to stop genocide in all its forms." However, he offered no specifics about what should be done to stop the genocide. Though the effort to end genocide in Darfur was still bipartisan, by 2006, Democrats took the lead on the issue because the Republicans were unwilling to take on the president in an election year. On February 1, 2006, Senator Biden (Democrat-Delaware), along with the cosponsors Senators Brownback (Republican-Kansas), Obama (Democrat-Illinois), Lugar (Republican-Indiana), Feingold (Democrat-Wisconsin), and Dodd (Democrat-Connecticut) introduced Senate Resolution 383. This resolution was different from the others. It called for American muscles to back up its morals. The resolution called on the president to do the following:

> take steps immediately to help improve the security situation in Darfur, including by—
>
> (A) proposing that NATO—
>   (i) consider how to implement and enforce and enforce a declared no-fly zone in Dafur; and
>   (ii) deploy troops to Darfur to support the African Union Mission in Sudan (AMIS) until a United Nations peacekeeping mission is fully deployed in the region; and
>
> (B) requesting supplementary funding to support a NATO mission in Darfur and the African Union Mission in Sudan (AMIS); … calls upon NATO allies, led by the United States to support such a mission; and … calls upon NATO headquarters staff to begin planning in advance such a mission.

Now, members of Congress were demanding that the president, in his capacity as commander-in-chief, save Darfur. Foreign policy is still the realm of the president no matter how just the cause. The president did not implement the provisions called for in the Senate resolution. For Bush, this was a humanitarian effort and not one that required the United States' military muscle. After all, his administration had played a key role in getting the government of Sudan to negotiate an end to the civil war in southern Sudan. From Bush's perspective why would Darfur be different? What Bush did not understand was that the war in Darfur was in fact a continuation of the Sudanese civil war. It had merely shifted locations. As a result, the genocide continued in Darfur.

On March 7, 2006, after coming back from a trip to Darfur, Congressman Michael Capuano (Democrat-Massachusetts) published an article in the *Boston Herald*. In his article, Capuano wrote, "I urge the president to fully support a U.N. peacekeeping mission and put the full weight of the U.S. military behind it." Democrats had now formed a consensus among themselves that the use of force was now necessary to end the genocide in Darfur. The only questions that remained were whether their Republican colleagues would follow suit and whether they would be able to persuade the president. The answer was a resounding no. On March 15, 2006,

Congressman Capuano offered an amendment to increase funding for the beleaguered AU Mission in Sudan by $50 million. Congressman Kolbe (Republican-Arizona) rose in opposition. He stated that it was not necessary because the administration's request was fully funded by the military assistance bill currently before the House. Therefore, Capuano's amendment was not necessary. Nevertheless, Capuano's bill to provide the additional funding barely passed by 213 to 208 votes. The words were willing but the action was weak. The additional funding for the peacekeeping mission in Darfur was insufficient. Darfur is approximately the size of Texas. A peacekeeping mission of 7,700 troops is insufficient to patrol such a large area.

The low priority given to the crisis in Darfur by the Bush II administration could be witnessed in its attempt to exploit the bipartisan coalition for Darfur. Funding for the War in Iraq was linked to emergency funding for assisting victims of Hurricane Katrina and the victims of genocide in Darfur. Bush was trying to exploit the bipartisan support in Congress for Darfur to get approval for funding related to the unpopular war in Iraq.

Also notable was the passage of the Darfur Peace and Accountability Act (House of Representatives Resolution 3127) by the House of Representatives on April 5, 2006. This bill was a watered-down version of the Darfur Genocide Accountability Act (House of Representatives Resolution 1424) that was originally introduced by Representative Payne (Democrat–New Jersey). The bill had 138 cosponsors. In its original version, the bill would have authorized the president to use armed drones against the Janjaweed, Sudanese aircraft, and military installations.[60] "The bill also called for capital market sanctions preventing any entity engaged in any commercial activity in Sudan from raising capital or trading securities on U.S. capital markets."[61] Representative Henry Hyde (Republican-Illinois), the chairman of the House International Relations Committee, submitted the Darfur Peace and Accountability Act in its place. The new version did not call for the use of force against Sudanese targets, nor did it call for commercial sanctions. The Darfur Peace and Accountability Act of 2006 called for the expansion and reenforcement of the AU Mission in Darfur by the United Nations and NATO, the suspension of Sudan from the United Nations until it stopped attacks against civilians, and the appointment of a presidential envoy to Sudan. It also urged the U.S. secretary of state to label the Janjaweed as a terrorist organization and to block the assets of Sudan and its government officials. Senator Corzine (Democrat–New Jersey) introduced the original Senate version of the bill (Senate Resolution 495) in March 2005.

It also called for a military no-fly zone and for a Chapter VII mandate to allow the peacekeepers in Darfur to protect the civilians instead of merely being observers. It encountered the wrath of the Bush II administration. Bush simply wanted to treat Darfur as a "humanitarian effort," and did not want to alienate the Sudanese government. Later, a watered-down version of the bill was sponsored by Senator Brownback (Republican-Kansas). Under pressure, President Bush II signed it into law on October 13, 2006. However, this version did not include a no-fly zone or refer specifically to a Chapter VII mandate.

This became a practical lesson in constitutional politics. In the realm of foreign policy, the president has the upper hand. The president decides the content of foreign policy. The Congress, through its control of the purse, can decide whether or not that policy will continue or not, but the president decides the substance of the policy. The futility of the Bush II administration's policy was obvious. Democrats in both houses broke rank with their Republican colleagues, and called for military action to end the genocide in Darfur. On April 27, 2006, Representative Jerrold Nadler (Democrat–New York) commented:

> the threat of sanctions has done little to end the atrocities. This dire crisis requires a much more robust response.
>
> Our commitment to end the Darfur genocide must be judged by only one test: What are we doing that serves to end the killing and the suffering.
>
> The aim should be to end the genocide, disarm the Arab militias, guarantee humanitarian assistance, protect civilians, secure refugee camps, and provide safety to families returning to their villages.
>
> Military experts have estimated that these tasks will require 40,000 to 50,000 well-trained troops. We also have new and innovative technologies that could protect civilians.[62]

The genocide would not be stopped by the United States. Bush had abandoned Darfur. It took one genocide, Rwanda, to shame Bill Clinton into stopping another, Bosnia. George W. Bush would not get a second chance.

The Republican members of Congress continued to make the United Nations the object of their appeals to conscience and of their ire. They railed against the UN Human Rights Commission that included gross violators of human rights, such as Sudan, China, Cuba, Zimbabwe, Belarus, and Libya. They made no appeal for President Bush II to take unilateral action to stop the genocide. It was obvious that Bush had decided on his course of action—to provide humanitarian relief and to do nothing more.

The Democratic voices grew louder and more prominent. Senator Hillary Rodham Clinton (Democrat–New York) wrote a letter to President Bush II dated March 15, 2006. The letter made the following recommendations: convene a conference of world leaders to address the crisis in Darfur, appoint a special envoy to Sudan, establish a UN peacekeeping mission with a Chapter VII mandate, request NATO assistance for the AU Peacekeeping Mission, and ask for a military no-fly zone to be enforced in Darfur.[63] Providing the peacekeeping force with a Chapter VII mandate, NATO assistance, and the implementation of a no-fly zone were the minimum requirements for providing safety to civilians in Darfur. Yet, Bush rejected them.

The chorus calling for presidential action grew louder as 2006 drew to a close. House Resolution 992, sponsored by Representative Frank Wolf (Republican-Virginia), passed by a vote of 414 to 3. It called for the appointment of a special envoy to Sudan. In the Senate, Resolution 559, sponsored by Senator Biden (Democrat-Delaware), was passed by a unanimous vote. It called for the establishment of a no-fly zone in Darfur. Also, Tom Lantos (Democrat-California), the only Holocaust survivor ever elected to Congress, published an op-ed article in the *Financial Times* on September 27, 2006. In that article, Lantos stated the following: "History will regard the situation in Sudan, as an African holocaust if the international community fails to protect innocent lives." Lantos also hinted at the use of force:

> The international community must put actions behind its now myriad words and commit to civilian protection by supporting the transition of the AU mission to the U.N. NATO must also broaden its support to the AU through its perilous and crucial transition to a U.N. peacekeeping mission that should deploy with or without the consent of the Sudanese government.

Lantos finished his article with an explicit call for the use of force against the government of Sudan: "If Khartoum persists in pursuing genocide, I support military action to neutralize those military forces employed by Sudan to attack civilians or to inhibit peacekeepers from their deployment."

The political heat was turned up on George W. Bush. He responded by signing the Darfur Peace and Accountability Act on October 13, 2006 (see details above). Nevertheless, he was not going to change his policy.

In 2007 Congressional Democrats continued their verbal assault on the Bush II administration, because it was continuing to downplay acts of genocide in Darfur. On February 16, 2007, Senator Durbin (Democrat-Illinois) castigated the special envoy to Sudan. Durbin said, "Ambassador Andrew Natsios told a student audience that genocide was no longer taking place in Darfur."[64] Bush-speak now became Clinton-speak, as the Bush II administration deployed Clintonesque word games to deny that genocide was occurring in Darfur. When testifying before the Senate Foreign Relations Committee in April 2007, Ambassador Natsios was asked by Senator Menendez (Democrat–New Jersey) whether genocide was occurring in Darfur. Natsios did not answer yes. He resorted to semantics. Senator Dodd (Democrat-Connecticut) called for the deployment of a NATO force in Darfur with U.S. participation.

China's connection with the genocidal regime in Khartoum also became a target for members of both parties in the House and Senate. Congressional Republicans were also fed up with the inaction of the Bush II administration. Representative Wolf called attention to Mia and Ronan Farrow's *Wall Street Journal* editorial titled "The Genocide Olympics," which criticized China, the host country of the 2008 Olympics, for its support of Sudanese genocide. China was purchasing oil from Sudan that in turn allowed Sudan to buy weapons to engage in genocide against civilians in Darfur. In a sense, this was an indirect criticism of President Bush II as well. Bush had failed to pressure China on Darfur. Bush also planned to attend "the Genocide Olympics" in Beijing. Moreover, Senator Durbin (Democrat-Illinois) called into question President Bush II's credibility on Darfur. He noted, "The President, a few weeks ago, gave a speech in which he said we have to go beyond declarations to do something. Yet it has not happened."[65] Durbin also called attention to the failure of Berkshire Hathway, an investment firm, to divest from PetroChina, a subsidiary of the Chinese government firm China National Petroleum. PetroChina is the largest oil company in Sudan. Senator Feingold also stressed the connection between China and Sudan. Nothing seemed to work. George W. Bush would not abandon his policy of inaction. On May 16, 2007, Senator Menendez (Democrat–New Jersey) introduced the China Resolution (Senate Resolution 203). Representative Barbara Lee (Democrat-California) introduced a similar measure in the House on May 21, 2007. These measures called for China to use its influence with Sudan to end the genocide in Darfur. Both resolutions were passed in their respective bodies with unanimous consent. Finally, in 2007, the House and the Senate passed the Sudan

Accountability and Divestment Act (Senate Resolution 2271). It provided legal protection to state and local governments that divested from companies doing business with Sudan.

On January 28, 2008, Senator Biden (Democrat-Delaware) introduced a resolution urging the international community to provide helicopters to the AU-UN Peacekeeping Mission in Darfur. It passed by unanimous consent. However, no helicopters would be forthcoming. President Bush was opposed to military action in Darfur. Representative Wolf once more focused on China's connections with the genocidal regime in Khartoum and its disrespect for human rights. What Wolf did not do early in 2008 was to criticize the Bush II administration for its failure to stand up for human rights. That would come later. On December 10, 2008, with the elections over, Representative Wolf, frustrated and disappointed, blasted the human rights record of the Bush II administration. He said:

> I believe that history will show a legacy of missed opportunities on human rights for the administration—failure to consistently apply their rhetoric; failure to be a tireless advocate for the voiceless.[66]

In 2009, a new president, Barack Obama, took office. With a new president in office, Representative Wolf took to the floor of the House to challenge President Obama to do something about the genocide in Darfur. On February 11, 2009, he called on President Obama to appoint a special envoy to Sudan. On March 4, 2009, Wolf also called on President Obama to take action to stop the killing in Darfur. He made a direct appeal to President Obama to take action. This is something that he had not done with President Bush II. Perhaps he believes that President Obama—unlike the previous president—will do something about the genocide in Darfur. On March 18, 2009, President Obama appointed Major General Scott Gration as a special envoy to Sudan. Nevertheless, the killing in Darfur continues; so far, 400,000 have died. So far, the Obama administration has mainly focused on the economic recovery of the United States. Darfur has not been a priority.

Congress failed because it kept looking to the president to take action on Darfur. Waiting for Bush was like waiting for Godot. Contrary to his rhetoric, Bush never got on board with the issue. A consensus had formed among the Democrats in Congress that more had to be done to save lives in Darfur. Yet, they continued to wait for a bold move from the president as well. Some Republicans agreed with their Democratic colleagues and therefore relinquished the lead on Darfur to them. However, other Republican members of the House and Senate were reluctant to break with the president. What members of both parties failed to realize is that they could act without the president since Congress has the power of the purse. Applied in a creative manner, it can have a major impact on U.S. foreign policy. Congress brought forth the end of the Vietnam War, and, more recently, it brought down the apartheid regime in South Africa. As Representative Kendrick Meek pointed out, when President Reagan vetoed the Comprehensive Anti-Apartheid Act, the 99th Congress overrode his veto. The resolutions and the economic sanctions enacted by Congress were weak. Therefore, Congress could have and should have taken the lead like it had done with South Africa. Strong sanctions could have been enacted against Khartoum, because the Foreign Commerce Clause of the Constitution gives Congress the right to regulate foreign commerce. The Sudan Accountability and Divestment Act of 2007 only provided legal protection for divestment in companies that engaged in mineral extraction, oil-related activities, or the production of military equipment.[67] Congress could have passed more comprehensive legislation and could also have turned up the economic heat on companies and countries that do business with Sudan by denying them access to the U.S. market. Congress could have banned countries such as the notorious Darfur Four—China, Russia, Algeria, and Pakistan—that have investments in Sudan's oil industry from doing business in the United States. Instead, Congress waited for Bush.

THE PRESIDENT

George W. Bush did not commit genocide in Darfur. Nevertheless, to a degree, he was responsible for its continuation. Instead of engagement, Bush opted for a policy of appeasement with the genocidal regime in Khartoum and appeared comfortable with the path he had chosen. This undermined efforts to stop the genocide. Paul Kennedy, the historian, has defined appeasement in the following manner:

> the policy of settling international (or for that matter, domestic) quarrels by admitting and satisfying grievances through rational negotiation and compromise, thereby avoiding the resort to armed conflict which would be expensive, bloody, and possibly dangerous.[68]

Bush, who was so reckless in the Middle East, was overly cautious in Africa. His appeasement policy targeted Congress, the American people, and the regime in Sudan.

Sudan was on George W. Bush's agenda before the war in Darfur began. He had been pressured by conservative Christian constituents and by Republicans in the House and the Senate to do something to end the Sudanese Civil War. Conservative Christians viewed the conflict as an Islamic jihad by the Muslim North against the Christian South. Bush was well aware of the atrocities committed by Sudan against civilians. On May 14, 2001, Bush spoke out against the human rights abuses in Sudan. Bush noted:

> Some crimes are being committed today by the government of Sudan, which is waging war against the country's traditionalist and Christian peoples. Some 2 million Sudanese have lost their lives; 4 million people have lost their home. Hospitals, schools, churches, and international relief stations have been bombarded over 18 years of Sudan's civil war.[69]

On October 21, 2002, President Bush II signed the Sudan Peace Act (Public Law 107-245-Oct. 21, 2002). It condemned the government of Sudan for committing genocide and slavery in southern Sudan. It also called on the U.S. president to find a comprehensive solution to end the war in southern Sudan. In addition, the president was to certify every six months whether the peace process was progressing and whether humanitarian aid had been interfered with. Even though the government of Sudan periodically blocked humanitarian aid, the Bush II administration nevertheless sent certification to Congress that Sudan had not. Here we see the first inklings of the Bush II administration's appeasement policy toward Sudan and Congress. The president seemed more interested in keeping the peace talks going than in punishing Sudan. Bush would later do the same thing after the passage of the Comprehensive Peace in Sudan Act of 2004 that required certification from the president that the government of Sudan was not interfering with the human rights monitors or humanitarian aid. Bush wanted to keep the parties in the Sudanese Civil War in the south engaged in the peace process. However, by ignoring these violations, he sealed the fate of Darfur. He sent an implicit message to Khartoum that Darfur did not carry the same weight as the war in the South. Moreover, Bush's failure to include Darfur in the ongoing talks also reinforced that message.

It became apparent that for the Bush II administration, the preemptive war in Iraq and the War on Terrorism took priority over genocide and slavery in Sudan. In April 2005, the CIA flew the chief of Sudanese intelligence, Major General Saleh Gosh, one of the architects of genocide in Darfur, to Washington, DC, for a meeting on terrorism.[70]

> Contacts between the Sudan government and the CIA and FBI over Islamist terrorist networks began as early as May 2000, when Khartoum released some dated information on Usama bin Ladin, but held back more.[71]

Bush believed that Khartoum was too valuable an ally in the War on Terrorism to be dealt with severely.[72] George W. Bush failed to make a conceptual link between genocide and the War on Terrorism. Genocide is state-sponsored terrorism against a targeted people. Killing en masse requires the support of the state. No private group or nonstate entity has the resources to carry out such a plan. Genocide is the ultimate denial of a people's identity. It assigns them to the lowest ranks of humanity and designates them as insignificant. Those who commit these acts are guilty of crimes against humanity. But those who have it in their power to prevent or stop it and fail to do so are equally guilty, for they have entered into a tacit partnership with those who have committed genocide. Adolf Hitler once asked, "Who after all, speaks today of the annihilation of the Armenians?" Working with Sudan in the War on Terrorism is like working with Adolf Hitler in a war against racism. It is illogical.

The regime in Khartoum became keenly aware that the Bush II administration was not going to undertake a policy that would pose a direct threat to its existence. Khartoum learned that it could defy Bush without penalty. Bush virtually admitted this at a press conference. On May 29, 2007, he stated, "One day after I spoke [about Darfur], the [Sudanese] military bombed a meeting of rebel commanders designed to discuss a possible peace deal with the government."[73] Similarly, in 2008, in an interview with Matt Frei of the BBC, Bush said that he was comfortable with his decision not to intervene militarily in Darfur.[74] The use of force would have made Khartoum calculate whether going along with its current course of action was worth the damage that would have been inflicted. Why weren't power grids knocked out in Khartoum like they were knocked out in Kosovo so the city would have to sleep under the stars like the people in the refugee camps at Darfur? Without the use of force no thinking by Khartoum was required. George W. Bush never made Omar al-Bashir pay a price for committing genocide. Khartoum was allowed to act with impunity.

Instead of treating the situation in Darfur as a human rights issue and thinking that its people were in need of liberation, George W. Bush treated Darfur as a humanitarian problem. During the closing days of the Bush II administration, a White House factsheet stated:

> Under President Bush's leadership, the United States and its partners freed 25 million Iraqis from the rule of Saddam Hussein, a dictator who murdered his own people, invaded his neighbors, and repeatedly defied United Nations resolutions.[75]

What was said of Saddam Hussein could have been said of Omar al-Bashir. He had oppressed the forty-one million people of his country, invaded Chad, committed genocide, and defied UN resolutions on a regular basis. Why was Sudan not on the Bush agenda as a candidate for liberation? This was never explained. Bush chose to throw money at the problem instead of solving it. The various factsheets put out by the Bush II White House stressed the president's freedom agenda but when it came to Darfur, they emphasized how much was being spent on humanitarian relief. Treating Darfur as a humanitarian effort rather than as part of the freedom agenda allowed genocide to continue in Darfur.

George W. Bush's policy toward Darfur was one of deception. Unlike Bill Clinton who never used the word genocide during the crisis in Rwanda, Bush's administration used the term early on to describe the events going on in Darfur. As a result, many viewed him as being empathetic toward the victims in Darfur. He denounced the atrocities of the regime in Khartoum, and met with members of Congress about Darfur and with members of various organizations trying to save Darfur. President Bush II even went before the United Nations and called the atrocities in Darfur genocide. Nevertheless, Bush's deeds never matched his words. For example, he said that the AU Mission in Darfur should be doubled. However, his administration blocked efforts to include an additional $50 million that was targeted for the expansion of the AU Mission. Bush often implored the United Nations to take strong action to deal with the crisis in Darfur. Yet, as the single most powerful individual in the world, he knew that it could not take action without his own firm commitment. He was encouraged by members of both parties to implement a no-fly zone but refused to do so. Bush's neocon agenda of preemptive war and dealing with the axis of evil (Iran, Iraq, North Korea, and Syria) took precedence over everything else, including genocide. Therefore, when it came to Darfur the mission was not accomplished. President Obama backed a no-fly zone when he was a member of the Senate. As president, he will perhaps take a more forceful stand regarding Darfur than the previous president did.

THE UNITED NATIONS

The United Nations is a voluntary international organization that consists of 192 countries. Republicans, headed by George W. Bush, treated it as though it was a sovereign entity with a standing army. By invoking the term "genocide," George W. Bush sought to absolve himself of the responsibility of stopping the killing in Darfur and tried to make it the United Nations' responsibility. In other words, George W. Bush used the term genocide for the very reason that Bill Clinton refused to use it, so that his administration would not have to take action. Using the term genocide has ramifications. When it is used there is the expectation that something will be done to stop it. On September 9, 2004, Secretary of State Colin Powell said that genocide had been committed in Darfur. Gerard Prunier stated:

> Colin Powell had practically been ordered to use the term "genocide" during this high profile 9 September 2004 testimony to the Senate Committee on Foreign Relations but that he also advised to add in the same breath that this did not obligate the United States to undertake ... military intervention.[76]

By using the term genocide, the Bush II administration sought to invoke Article 8 of the Convention on the Prevention and Punishment of the Crime of Genocide. Article 8 states:

> Any Contracting Party may call upon the competent organs of the United Nations to take such action under the Charter of the United Nations as they consider appropriate for the prevention and suppression of acts of genocide or any of the acts enumerated in article III.[77]

By making appeals to the United Nations, Bush sought to make Darfur the United Nations' problem. On the other hand, Kofi Annan, the UN secretary-general, acted like Bill Clinton during the crisis in Rwanda and refused to use the term for fear that Darfur would become the United Nations' problem. The term genocide is noticeably absent from the "Report of the International Commission of Inquiry on Darfur to the United Nations Secretary General" of 2005. The report describes acts of genocide in Darfur but the term genocide is not used. Instead, the euphemism "crimes against humanity" is used. If the term genocide was used, the Bush II administration would have had more ammunition to invoke the Genocide Convention. However, Secretary-General Annan would not have had the means to enforce the Convention, given the Bush II administration's unwillingness to provide the financial support for the expansion of the AU Mission and the hostility that Bush and his neocon advisors had shown toward the United Nations. The Bush administration's ultimate contempt for the United Nations was demonstrated by the appointment of John Bolton as the U.S. ambassador to the United Nations. Bolton had an overbearing demeanor and was contemptuous toward the organization. He was ill-suited for such a sensitive diplomatic position. This is why Bush had to appoint him by making a recess appointment. Due to his cantankerous manner, Bolton was not confirmed by the Republican-controlled Senate. Given this scenario, Annan opted for Clinton-style word games and thereby refused to call the unfolding tragedy in Darfur genocide. He knew that the United Nations could not take action because he did not have the full support of the United States. The "g" word became a political hot potato; no one wanted to be responsible for invoking the Genocide Convention.

The United Nations is only as strong as its members, especially the five permanent members of the Security Council, allow it to be. The Bush administration, as detailed above, did not give the United Nations its full support. China did not want to see strong sanctions enacted against Sudan either, because it had helped to fuel Sudan's genocide machine. China imports 70 percent of Sudan's oil, supplies Sudan with weapons, and has built weapons factories in Sudan. Russia, like China, is also one of the Darfur Four and has ties to Sudan's oil industry and supplies the Sudanese government with weapons as well. This is a major reason why more progress has not been made in stopping the genocide in Darfur. In 2007 the Security Council passed Resolution 1796—this created a hybrid UN-AU Mission in Darfur with a Chapter VII mandate. There are currently 12,937 peacekeepers in Darfur, an insufficient number to be effective. In Bosnia there were eighteen peacekeepers per 1,000 people. In Kosovo, there were twenty peacekeepers per 1,000 people. In Darfur, there are two peacekeepers per 1,000 people. Refugees are still harassed when they leave the camps that are often surrounded by Janjaweed forces. People are still suffering because the permanent members of the Security Council do not perceive genocide as being more important than their economic interests. Therefore, empty resolutions gave way to others, followed by additional meaningless debate. As a result, the genocide continues and the United Nations has failed in its responsibility to take collective action against genocide. It should be noted why it failed. The United Nations failed to halt genocide in Darfur because the United States, China, and Russia put their interest above that of the people of Darfur. The United

Nations is only as strong as its members allow it to be. It has proven to be ineffective at stopping genocide in Darfur. It has become an appeaser.

Susan Rice, who was appointed the United States ambassador to the United Nations by President Obama, lobbied for the implementation of a no-fly zone in Darfur prior to taking office.[78] Perhaps she will be able to forge a coalition at the United Nations that will "ground Sudan's killers".

IMPLICATIONS FOR INTERNATIONAL SOCIETY

The failure of international society to halt genocide in Darfur demonstrates that Africans have not been granted citizenship in this society. Membership in international society carries an explicit guarantee that one's human rights will be protected. European Muslims were the last group to be included in international society, which came to their rescue in Bosnia and Kosovo while Africans in Rwanda and Darfur were left to die. Africans are not full-fledged members of this society. Their membership is still pending. The members of international society are still not willing to incur the risk and the commitment that it will take to bring genocide to an end in an African country. Darfur taught us that Rwanda was no fluke. A cultural/racial divide still exists between the Third World and the West that negates the mechanism for stopping genocide.

THE MEDIA

The media played a crucial role by keeping politicians and the public informed about the ongoing crisis in Darfur. Nevertheless, it was not the traditional media outlets but the segment of the media that caters to popular culture that helped to build support for the effort to stop the genocide in Darfur. More Americans utilize this segment of the media than any other. This is what allowed the movement to "Save Darfur" to grow.

When the war in Darfur began in 2003, there were few media reports. Most of the Western world had never heard of Darfur. The U.S. media tends to ignore Africa until a crisis erupts. The French wire service Agence France Presse was one of the few Western news outlets that carried information about the SLA/M uprising against Khartoum in 2003. There were a few stories by the BBC early in 2004, but the main source of information continued to be the Agence France Presse. However, as the crisis worsened, coverage by the U.S. media increased. On January 17, 2004, a story, "War in Western Sudan Overshadows Peace in South," by Somini Sengupta, appeared in *The New York Times.* It told about the atrocities that were taking place in Darfur. The article portrayed the conflict in racial terms—African versus Arab. On March 24, 2004, *The New York Times* published "Ethnic Cleansing Again" by Nicholas Kristof, who described the conflict in terms of Arab versus African and placed the blame for the atrocities on the government of Sudan. He also described how the Janjaweed raided villages and killed innocent civilians. Others, including Samantha Power, wrote articles about Darfur that appeared in *The New York Times*, but Kristof would become *The New York Times*' leading writer on Darfur. He wrote five out of the nine articles that appeared in *The New York Times* from March 24 to April 25, 2004. By mid-2004, when the crisis escalated, most of the leading newspapers in the United States, such as the *Washington Post* and the *Los Angeles Times*, were covering the genocide taking place in Darfur.

The stories were descriptive and often graphic. They described the conflict as one between the Arab government—and its Janjaweed henchmen—and the African farmers of Darfur. The articles described how the Janjaweed raided villages, murdered, raped, drove people from their homes, and destroyed their lives. A notable article was an op-ed—"Policy Adrift on Darfur"—that appeared in the *Washington Post.* It was written by Senators Brownback (Republican-Kansas) and Obama (Democrat-Illinois). The article called attention to the deteriorating situation in the refugee camps that was caused by a lack of security. An unusual article titled "Rescue Darfur Now" appeared in the *Washington Post* on September 10, 2006. It was written by Senator John McCain (Republican-Arizona) and former Senator Bob Dole (Republican-Kansas). It was unusual because it explicitly called for military intervention.

The most consistent and wide-ranging reporting on the crisis in Darfur was undertaken by a non-American news source called the *Sudan Tribune.* It operates out of Paris and posts its stories on the Internet. The *Sudan Tribune* focused on the regional, internal, and global politics of Sudan, and posted stories by writers such as Professor Eric Reeves of Smith College.

Most of the articles were informative, but most of them suffered from the same shortcomings. They were descriptive and not analytical. They failed to see the inherent relationship between the Sudanese Civil War in the south that was ending and the one in Darfur that was beginning. They failed to notice that Sudan has only had ten years of peace in its turbulent history. And, most importantly, they failed to ask why the same policies were always implemented in Sudan regardless of whether it had a civilian or military government. If they had asked these questions, it would have been obvious that Sudan is a failed nation-state. It seeks to crush its opponents regardless of race or ethnicity rather than to give them a voice. The *Sudan Tribune* was the only paper to give coverage to Arabs in Darfur who rose against the government in Khartoum in 2008 and cooperated with rebel African factions. Also, the *Sudan Tribune* was one of the few papers to note the arrest of erstwhile government leader Hasan al-Turabi, now the head of the Popular Congress Party opposition, in January 2009 for saying that Omar al-Bashir should surrender to the ICC.

The media also failed to examine the demands of the Sudan Liberation Movement/Army (SLA/M) and the Justice and Equality Movement, the two main rebel groups fighting the government of Sudan in Darfur. This would have been helpful in determining the scope of their demands. Were the rebels being unreasonable? Did their demands go beyond concessions granted to southern Sudan in the Comprehensive Peace Agreement that ended the twenty-five-year war in southern Sudan? The *Sudan Tribune* was the only newspaper that carried the mission statement of the SLA/M, which contains the following demands:

- A secular state
- Liberal Democracy based on equal representation
- Respect for all races, religions, and cultures
- Due process and equal protection under the law.[79]

In essence, the SLA/M was asking for a secular democratic state with civil liberties and civil rights. Were they asking for more than had been granted to the SPLA/M in southern Sudan? The media never asked nor attempted to answer this question. A brief analysis would have revealed that the demands of the SLA/M were modest in comparison to what was granted to the SPLA/M. The Comprehensive Peace Agreement signed between the government of Sudan and the SPLA/M contained the following provisions:

1. Armed Forces: The North and South are to maintain separate armed forces. There is to be the withdrawal of 91,000 government troops from the South within 2 and a half years. The SPLA has 8 months to withdraw its forces from the North. The Naivasha Protocol that forms part of the CPA outlined the

	details of integration: it allows for the integrated units of 21,000 soldiers (of which half will be government and half SPLA) to be formed during the 6 year interim period. They are to be deployed to sensitive areas such as the 3 disputed areas. These units will be commonly stationed but maintain separate command and control structures. If, after the interim period the South decides not to secede, both sides will unify into a 39,000 strong force.
2. Autonomy:	The South will have autonomy for 6 years to be followed by a referendum in 2011 regarding secession from the Sudan.
3. Oil Wealth:	To be shared on a 50:50 basis between the Khartoum government and the SPLA.
4. Economic:	Two separate currencies are to be used within a dual banking system. The North will retain the Sudanese Pound while the South will opt for the Sudanese Dinar. Essentially, the dual banking system means that banks will be commonly stationed with two different windows for service.
5. Administration:	Positions in the central, transitional government are to be split 70.30 in favor of the government, and 55:45 in favor of the government in contentious areas of Abyei, the Blue Nile State and the Nuba Mountains. Bashir's position as Head of State is entrenched and Garang is to serve as Vice-President.
6. Islamic Law:	A government of national unity is to be formed. Shari'a is to remain applicable in the North and parts of the constitution are to be rewritten so that Shari'a does not apply to any non-Muslims throughout Sudan. The status of Shari'a in Khartoum is to be decided by an elected assembly.
7. Other:	Each territory is to use its own flag. The North will maintain use of the current Sudanese flag and the South is to introduce its own flag.[80]

The media failed to explain that the rebels in Darfur were not asking for autonomy, independence, or for a share in Darfur's oil wealth. Theirs was a political agenda to gain inclusion in the national government. In fact, western media outlets often seemed perplexed in their explanation of the SLA/M and its activities. For example, an article about Darfur appeared in the *Los Angeles Times* on March 21, 2009. The writer made it seem that the rebel groups were just as culpable as the government of Sudan for the destruction and mayhem occurring in Darfur.

Despite the widespread coverage of Darfur by the mainstream U.S. media, this is not how most Americans found out about what was going on in Darfur. The genocide in Darfur became part of American pop culture; the American media and pop culture are intertwined. There is a symbiotic relationship, they feed off each other. Media that feature elements of pop culture were mainly responsible for the involvement of the American public in the effort to save Darfur. After winning gold and silver medals in the speed skating competition at the 2006 Winter Olympics, Joey Cheek donated his $40,000 in prize money to help children in refugee camps in Darfur. His actions resulted in an additional $300,000 in contributions from the American public. Celebrities such as Mia Farrow, George Clooney, and Oprah were all recruited to help save Darfur. MTV also became involved. This is what caught the attention of most Americans. People were hearing about Darfur from popular celebrities and through a medium they accessed on a regular basis. Most of them had never heard of Nicholas Kristof or Eric Reeves, nor had they read anything they wrote, but they watched Oprah and MTV. Both the mainstream media and the media that caters to pop culture informed the American people about genocide in Darfur. Rather than sleeping through the news about genocide as they had in the past, the American people tried to stop it. Neither the American media nor the American people abandoned Darfur; the American government did.

CONCLUSION

Sudan has become a cesspool of human misery and suffering. Unfortunately, it will remain that way as long as the current regime is in power and as long as equality, respect, and the rule of law are not granted to all of its citizens; moreover, it will remain that way so long as the international community fails to intervene on behalf of the millions of refugees in the region. *Chronic Arabism*, the paradigm of death and destruction, must be abandoned. To a great extent, this policy has been beneficial to Khartoum. It has been able to use it for shoring up support from without and within Sudan. The country has also been effective at getting most observers of the conflict in Darfur to view it through racial lenses. Because of the massive atrocities generated by the policy of *chronic Arabism* our attention has been diverted, and few have bothered to ask why Sudan is always in a state of turmoil and why the policies of the various civilian and military regimes bear such a striking resemblance. As a state, Sudan is an abysmal failure, and its policy of constant racial agitation is the only thing that allows Khartoum to maintain rule over a dispirited people.

The best hope for the emergence of a "new Sudan" was John Garang, the Sudanese Abraham Lincoln. Garang, like Lincoln, fought against regionalism and sought to build a national identity for his country that went beyond parochial values. Much of the hope for a new Sudan died with Garang during a helicopter crash on July 30, 2005. Like Lincoln, he was not able to see his dream to fruition. The dream is now endangered and may never be realized. Garang sought and garnered support among both Africans and Arabs. His vision of Sudan was an inclusive one. Unfortunately, most politicians in Sudan have fallen into the trap of factionalism and cannot see beyond their region or ethnic group. They lack Garang's vision.

In many ways, the crisis in Darfur resembled the ethnic cleansing in Kosovo. Civilians were attacked and murdered, their villages pillaged, and their personal property stolen. The only thing that brought those heinous acts to a halt was the use of force. The aggressors were forced to pay a price for their actions. However, this required courage. The Janjaweed is not a professional army, nor are they skilled in guerilla warfare. They are rebels without a cause. They fight for money and property—not for justice or an ideology. In the face of this ragtag army, George W. Bush put up a white flag and surrendered to genocide, the ultimate act of terrorism and injustice. He enabled the regime in Khartoum. Thus, Darfur has become his Rwanda.

There are some lessons that the American people should have learned from the crisis in Darfur. Despite their involvement and concern, the genocide in Darfur has continued for a number of reasons. First, one needs to be specific in making a request to Congress. One cannot leave it to others to fill in the blanks. To their credit, the American people wanted to save Darfur. But, it was never stated specifically how this was to be done. Would the peaceniks in the movement support the use of force in Darfur? We do not know. It was left to the politicians in Congress to fill in the blanks. They, in turn, looked to President Bush II who never got on board with the issue. The most important lesson that should have been learned by the American people is that they are the most powerful force in the U.S. political system. They cannot turn an issue over to politicians and expect them to solve it. They themselves must take direct action. If their demands are not met, they must take direct action by voting out of office those who stand in the way of justice. Furthermore, they must maintain vigilance to make sure that their voices are heard.

Finally, another important lesson that should have been learned is that all is not lost with American youth. Despite an inadequate education system, their interest can be stirred regarding the major issues of the day, if the message reaches them through a medium they access on a routine basis. American youth were at the heart of the movement to "Save Darfur."

In the attempt to save Darfur, the American people have forgotten their own history. TransAfrica played a leading role in bringing apartheid to an end in South Africa by galvanizing support within the African American community and lobbying Congress. Apartheid became a global issue. TransAfrica and the African American community were ignored by the "Save Darfur" movement. The effort on behalf of Darfur has mainly consisted of white Americans. More needs to be done to build a stronger global coalition.

As Bill Clinton proved in Bosnia and Kosovo, genocide can be stopped if we have the will to do so. To save Darfur, we must first save ourselves from the sea of helplessness and hopelessness that often surrounds us. It is ironic that just as the American people were experiencing social and moral growth, their own government failed to follow their example. Nevertheless, the American people have continued to grow. This has culminated in the election of Barack Obama as the president of the United States. If President Obama is able to bring the genocide in Darfur to an end and the killers in Khartoum are still in power, they will simply try to shift their shell game of death and racial terror, *chronic Arabism,* from Darfur to the Nuba Mountains in Southern Kordofan Province. *Chronic Arabism* is the weak policy that the regime in Khartoum stands on. Let us hope that President Obama will not get bamboozled like his predecessor.

Part III

Understanding the Problem

Chapter 8

How We Relate

[Theodore Roosevelt] believed "the people" were so ignorant about foreign affairs that they should not direct an informed president like himself.[1]

The first section of this book consisted of case studies that examined genocide at the dawn of the twenty-first century. This section will examine why genocide occurred during this period. It will give a general overview of the political socialization process in the United States, and the following chapters will examine aspects of the process in depth to determine how they affect the United States' ability to relate to the world.

American Political Socialization

Economic interdependency has grown rapidly since the end of World War II, yet most Americans do not think in global terms. Most are not concerned about what happens abroad and believe that foreign affairs has no impact on their lives. It is ironic that so many Americans feel this way at a time when the United States is the preeminent military and economic power in the world. Americans also have unparalleled access to information via the Internet and the news media; however, most do not utilize them to stay abreast of world events.

This insular mentality is an outgrowth of the United States' unique global situation. Geographically, the United States is separated from most of the world by an ocean on each coast. The United States also has friendly relations with the two countries on its borders, Canada and Mexico. In addition, the curriculum taught in American schools is inward-looking. Multiculturalism in the United States focuses on the contributions that people from various racial and ethnic groups have made to the United States. Knowledge of other countries, people, their history, and culture is not emphasized, and the media tends to focus on domestic events. Therefore, the average American has little knowledge about other countries and feels disconnected from the rest of the world. As a result, when a crisis happens, the American people are often stunned and have no knowledge about the people involved, their history, or their problems.

Cultural Narcissism

Due to the endogamous nature of the American socialization process, many Americans lack knowledge of events outside of the United States and see no viable connection between themselves and people in other countries. Thus, Americans are often unable to relate to people who do not look like them, or have a different language, religion, and culture than they do.

The standard for decency that one often uses is one's own culture. Kinship culture is the basis for normative judgment. It is based on shared history, language, religion, race, suffering, and values. Among western countries, this is particularly true of France and the United States. Americans often react negatively when they hear a language other than English spoken within their borders. France and the United States are guilty of cultural chauvinism to some degree, France more so than the United States. On the other hand, despite the election of Barack Obama as the president of the United States, race is still a dominant factor in Americans' ability to relate to each other. Consequently, it is also a major factor in Americans' ability to relate to the peoples of the world.

Race and culture are used as a yardstick of one's humanity. During World War II, the U.S. government printed and distributed a booklet called *A Pocket Guide to China*. It contained a section on how to tell a Japanese person from a Chinese person. According to the pamphlet, Japanese people were sneaky, dishonest, and untrustworthy; on the other hand, the booklet stated that Chinese people were hardworking, honest, and humble. Japan was the United States' enemy and China was its ally; therefore, the U.S. government attempted to close the cultural/racial gap by showing similar traits between Americans and Chinese. This was an attempt to get the American people to relate better to an ally—China. Since Japan was the enemy, Japanese people were portrayed in such a way that Americans would hold them in contempt. In a sense, those who are viewed as similar to oneself are seen as the most human, and those who are different are seen as less human. This affects one's perception of events, as well as one's ability to relate to others. Ultimately, it is the cultural and racial distance that exists between Americans and the victims of genocide that prevents Americans from demanding immediate action from their government when genocide occurs. They do not understand the issues in the conflict, nor do they feel a sense of kinship with the victims of genocide.

Because a cultural gap exists between the United States and the Third World, Americans often see no reason for their country to become involved when a crisis occurs that requires military action, unless the United States itself is attacked. As a result, the United States often either fails to act or is slow to act during a crisis; therefore, lives that could have been saved are lost. Despite the fact that the United States receives numerous reports that genocide is occurring in various parts of the world, it does not take action to stop it. In *A Problem from Hell,* Samantha Power argued that genocide reports were not viewed as credible because the survivors of genocide were not from the West; thus, they were often viewed as being less than truthful. However, the problem goes much deeper than this. The United States and its allies do not act when genocide is taking place, not because the credibility of the victims is in doubt, but because the West does not feel that saving the victims is worth the cost and the effort. The evidence was overwhelming that genocide had occurred in Bosnia, Rwanda, Kosovo, and Darfur. Yet the problem was one of will: the West was not willing to act forcefully because it could not connect with the victims on a personal level. If the victims of genocide had been Canadian, British, or French, there is no doubt that the cavalry would have arrived in short order. Most of Saddam Hussein's Kurdish victims of the Anfal—genocide against the Kurds—wore pantaloons rather than suits and look at what happened to them. Questioning the credibility of the victims was simply an excuse to do nothing while genocide was being committed.

Revitalization Movement

The existence of a cultural gap explains why the United States sometimes fails to act during a crisis. On the other hand, the concept of revitalization explains situations in which the United States is willing to take quick and decisive action. Revitalization movements occur when a country faces a direct threat from another country or culture.

In the presence of such a threat, the populace feels threatened and makes a retreat into its own culture. This is often seen in the form of patriotism. It creates the mentality of "us against them." Robert K. Merton viewed this as an in-group (*gemeinschaft*), out-group (*gesellschaft*) syndrome.[2] An example of this behavior was the aftermath of the attack on the United States on September 11, 2001. One saw a massive display of flags and a call for retaliation among the American people. As a result, the United States attacked Afghanistan and toppled the Taliban, which had given aid and support to al-Qaeda, the terrorist group responsible for the attack. A similar response was seen when the Japanese attacked Pearl Harbor.

When a direct attack occurs, the public demands a response for they feel a sense of loss. The loss goes beyond those who have died in such an attack. The people feel that their culture and the essence of their very being are at stake, and feel a need to exert themselves and their culture. This gives them a feeling of security, for it helps to unite them with their fellow citizens, and gives them a feeling of inclusion; however, the unity is only limited to one's fellow citizens and others abroad who share similar values.

Many Americans often feel that it is "us against the rest of the world." This prevents them from feeling that they are a part of the world and from relating to other people; therefore, Americans sometimes have a feeling of oneness with each other, but not with the rest of the world.

SHARED EXPERIENCE

Shared experiences help to bridge the cultural gap and bring people together from diverse backgrounds. Having a shared experience creates a bond of solidarity between individuals or groups who do not share a common culture. For example, during the war in Bosnia, the World Jewish Congress made passionate pleas for the United States to come to the aid of the beleaguered Bosnian Muslims. To some, it would seem strange that they would make this request, given the conflict between the Israelis and Palestinians in the Middle East. On the other hand, their position is logically based upon the concept of shared experience. Because the Jewish community was subjected to genocide during World War II, the World Jewish Congress wanted the United States to act quickly and forcefully to end genocide in the Balkans. These members of the Jewish community were able to relate to the Bosnian Muslims because both communities had been subjected to genocide; thus different cultural groups can relate to each other if there is a common bond between them that can act to unite them.

The Importance of Empathy

Empathy is what allows one to cross the cultural gap and to form a common humanity. It allows people who come from different racial, ethnic, and cultural backgrounds to relate to each other. Empathy occurs when people see themselves when they see others, despite superficial differences that may exist between them. When this occurs, people are able to relate to each other and are concerned about each other's well-being. This is the state that must be achieved if genocide is to be prevented in the future. Genocide must not just be the problem of the victims: it must become a problem for all.

International Civil Society Does Not Exist

International civil society does not exist. What other conclusion can be drawn from the occurrence of genocide in Rwanda and Darfur and the lack of an effective response? Since the late twentieth century and on into the twenty-first century, genocide has become routine. There has been no collective effort to prevent genocide or to stop it in Africa once it has occurred. Africans have been denied the rights, grants, and immunities bestowed on members of international society. African countries have seats in the United Nations, but Africans are not full-fledged members of international society—they have been denied human rights. Therefore, they remain among the most vulnerable to acts of genocide. After genocide has occurred, the culprits have gone before international tribunals. The tribunals are nothing more than a cathartic exercise where international society releases its collective grief for the victims, like at a funeral, and waits for the next act of genocide to occur.

Without a doubt, an international society exists but it is not civil. Civil society denotes a sphere in which political, social, and economic discourse takes place among people, governments, and organizations. Civil society is also based on the rule of law and respect for all. It is supposed to cope with the diversity of interests it serves.

The current international system is governed in an undemocratic manner. It is a plutocracy, run by the rich for the rich. Such a system is inherently class/caste-based; therefore, there is an unequal distribution of justice. The peoples of the Third World lack the guarantee of the human rights that are included in the United Nations' Universal

Declaration of Human Rights and the Convention on the Prevention and Punishment of the Crime of Genocide. Instead of an international civil society based on the rule of law, the current international system is based on an Orwellian civil code of conduct in which some people are more equal than others. As a result of the lack of enforcement of international law, a message has been sent to the tyrants of the world: "You can engage in genocide today and worry about the consequences tomorrow." This is why genocide still occurs in the twenty-first century and may occur in the near future.

Hence, international society is uncivil. The plutocrats who run it claim to be the guardians of human rights. Yet, their hypocrisy has been exposed by the events in Bosnia, Rwanda, Kosovo, and Darfur, because they have failed to enforce, and extend to others, the same human rights they claim to believe in and want others to adopt. As a result, their moral authority has been compromised, for they have failed to protect the weakest members of international society. In a civil society, the strong are just and all members of society are equal. Until this happens, genocide will continue to be part of the political landscape of the future.

The Anatomy of Genocide

Genocide is possible when there is no empathy. Genocide does not occur because ethnic or racial divisions exist within a country. The four case studies of this volume reveal patterns of behavior that have led to genocide.

The first precursor to genocide is the delegitimization of the state. The precipitating event could be economic, political, or both. During the Weimar Republic in Germany, the state lost legitimacy due to the harsh economic terms imposed on it by the Treaty of Versailles. A crisis involving the legitimacy of the state arose in Yugoslavia, due to the Organization of the Petroleum Exporting Countries' (OPEC's) decision to increase the price of oil and the harsh loan terms imposed upon it by the IMF. A crisis involving the legitimacy of the state occurred in Rwanda because of the weak state of the economy and the assassination of Juvenal Habyarimana.

The second precursor to genocide is the seizure of the state by a cadre of nondemocratic elements. They may obtain power by democratic or other means; however, their aims are not to form a democratic state. Scapegoating is used by these elements to gain legitimacy among the masses. Prior to scapegoating, a society need not be divided by significant social, racial, or ethnic cleavages. During periods of economic and social unrest, one's national identity is weakened, because the state has essentially failed to provide for the individual's basic needs. It is hard to feel patriotic and to relate to the broader community if one is starving. At such times, one's primordial loyalty may be stronger than one's broader national identity, even if cross-cultural bridges and relationships have been built. Those who were once viewed as friends and neighbors are now blamed for society's ills due to the rhetoric of the demagogue in power. As the demagogue continues to agitate, conflict develops beyond the point of ethnic or racial conflict. It moves from the point of wanting to punish the scapegoat to the point of eliminating the scapegoated group. This is what happened in Germany. German Jews were well-integrated into Germany society. However, when the Nazis came to power, they used Jews as scapegoats, which resulted in atrocities such as Kristallnacht (Crystal Night) and, ultimately, the Holocaust. In a similar vein, Sarajevo was a well-integrated city where citizens scoffed at the notion of a civil war coming to their area. Yet due to the scapegoating tactics of Milosevic and his allies, the memorandum of the Serbian Academy of the Sciences and the Arts made it seem as if the Serbs were the victims of economic and political discrimination in post–World War II Yugoslavia and as if the other ethnic groups had benefited at the Serbs' expense. Genocidal states were failed states. Rather than address the problems at hand, they had chosen to attack a segment of their population and blame them for the ongoing problems.

The third element that is necessary for genocide to take place is the lack of an effective international enforcement mechanism to deter or punish those who have engaged in genocidal actions. International law has rendered more protection to the perpetuators of genocide than to their victims because of sovereign immunity. Sovereign immunity shields a country from lawsuits in another country.

> The scope of the sovereign's immunity includes States, heads of State, and (since World War II) State government agencies that are conducting State Business (as opposed to private Enterprises). State practice has historically employed theory of sovereign immunity.[3]

Since World War II, those who have been punished for genocide have been punished after the fact. That is, they have been punished after they have left office or have been driven from power. This point is illustrated by the Nuremberg trials, which occurred after the culprits had been driven from power. One can also look at the

International Criminal Tribunal for the former Yugoslavia and the International Criminal Tribunal for Rwanda. Both courts punished those who were no longer in power; hence international law failed to deter genocide.

THE SIGNIFICANCE OF THE INDICTMENT OF OMAR AL-BASHIR

Laws and customs are subject to change over time. International law is currently undergoing changes that could result in genocide being deterred or interrupted. The International Criminal Court was created in 1998. Initially, it was hampered in its pursuit of justice by two facets of international law: functional immunity and personal immunity. Functional immunity shields a political leader from being prosecuted for life in foreign courts for acts carried out as part of his official duties. Personal immunity also shields government officials from being prosecuted in foreign courts for all acts while in office, "irrespective of the gravity."[4] Therefore, incumbent government leaders were free to engage in genocidal action without retribution. This has now changed.

On July 14, 2008, the International Criminal Court indicted Omar al-Bashir, the president of Sudan. This was the second time that a sitting head of government has been indicted for genocide, Slobodan Milosevic being the first. Within less than a year, the Court issued an arrest warrant for al-Bashir on March 3, 2009. These acts by the International Criminal Court mean that perpetuators of genocide can no longer hide behind claims of state sovereignty. An international community is finally forming that will hold national leaders accountable for their actions while in office. The taint of genocide is now upon Omar al-Bashir and Sudan. This is a taint that no political leader or state wants to bear, or be associated with. In *The Leviathan*, Thomas Hobbes stated:

> every particular man is author of all the sovereign doth: and consequently he that complaineth of that whereof he himself is author; and therefore ought not to accuse any man but himself.[5]

In other words, a citizen dare not accuse a ruler because he rules on behalf of the citizen; therefore, he can do no wrong to the said person. Now, the International Criminal Court has separated the accuser from the leaders holding them responsible for their action just like anyone else. International law now has meaning for both the living and the dead. It is about time. The International Criminal Court has planted the seeds for a hostile international society to grow into a legitimate international community. Other Sudanese government officials who need to be indicted by the International Criminal Court remain at large.[6] The work of the Court is getting underway.

Chapter 9

The Media

Introduction

In the previous chapters, the media was mentioned as one of the reasons why the United States slept through genocide at the dawn of the twenty-first century. The U.S. media has done an inadequate job of covering international news; therefore, the American public often does not know what is happening abroad before a crisis erupts, then they are caught off guard and left to ponder why the crisis occurred and what their country's next move should be. The media usually does an adequate job of covering a crisis; however, by that time, it is too late for preventative action to be taken.

The media in the United States is big business; therefore, news coverage is often influenced by what sells, rather than by what needs to be covered, to keep the American public informed about world events. The media tends to cover local, national, and trivial events, while international affairs are often relegated to the back pages or ignored.

To test this thesis, I conducted surveys of newspapers from different regions of the country during the four periods of genocide covered in this book. Ten newspapers were selected at random from the West, Midwest, East, and the South for the year in which genocide began in each country: 1992 (Bosnia), 1994 (Rwanda), 1998 (Kosovo), and 2003 (Darfur). One edition of each newspaper was chosen for every month of the selected years. They were examined to see if they carried stories about international news, other than the crises listed above, on their front pages. Stories that appear on the front page of a newspaper are often viewed by the public as the most important, and, therefore, are the most widely read.

THE DATA

The data consists of 480 editions of various newspapers from four regions of the country (West, Midwest, East, and the South). As mentioned above, ten newspapers were selected from each of the four years, and one edition of that newspaper was selected from each month. In other words, twelve editions of ten different newspapers (120 editions) were used for each year of a survey. The results of the surveys are listed below and an appendix with the editions of the newspapers is included at the back of the book (Appendix A).

THE YEAR OF THE CRISIS IN BOSNIA

The newspapers used to examine the first year of the survey, 1992, were the *Seattle Post-Intelligencer*, the *Detroit Free Press*, the *Houston Chronicle, Portland Oregonian*, the *Austin American Statesman*, the *Chicago Sun Times*, the *Worcester Telegram*, the *Arizona Star*, the *Tulsa World*, and the *Philadelphia Inquirer*. The following results were obtained from the survey of the 120 editions of these newspapers.

1992 Survey of Ten Newspapers

The following results were obtained from newspapers with at least one international story other than Bosnia on the front page.

Yes	No
21.6%	78.3%

The survey for 1992 showed that only 21.6 percent of the newspapers surveyed carried stories regarding international affairs on the front page. This provides evidence, for the hypothesis stated above, that the U.S. media does not focus on international news. The newspapers in the survey tended to focus almost exclusively on domestic stories.

When the newspapers are considered on a regional basis, the survey shows that there is a difference in how newspapers in different regions of the country cover international affairs as well. The survey for 1992 revealed the following information.

Regional Breakdown of the Ten Newspapers in the 1992 Survey

Below is the regional breakdown for 1992. The figures below show the percentage of newspapers with at least one international story on the front page out of the total from that particular region.

West	2.8%
Mid-West	16.7%
East	33.3%
South	36.1%

The newspapers in the South tended to do the best job of covering international events, followed by the East and the Midwest. The coverage by newspapers in the West was poor in this survey—a dismal 2.8 percent.

THE YEAR THE CRISIS BEGAN IN RWANDA

The survey of newspapers from 1994 showed some changes from 1992, plus some similarities. Overall, the coverage of international events was more extensive in 1994 than 1992; however, there was still a notable regional difference in the coverage of such events. The newspapers used in this survey were the *Buffalo News*, the *Pittsburgh Post Gazette*, the *Akron Beacon*, the *Pentagraph* (Illinois), the *Denver Post*, the *Riverside Press-Enterprise*, the *Miami Herald*, the *Raleigh News Observer*, the *Wichita Eagle*, and the *Birmingham News*.

1994 Survey of Ten Newspapers

Listed below are the results of the survey of newspapers with at least one international story on the front page other than Rwanda.

Yes	No
43.3%	56.7%

There was a notable increase of 19 percent in the coverage of international stories in 1994. Nevertheless, the percentage of stories covered on the front page during this year was far from impressive. A regional breakdown of the newspapers included in the survey for 1994 shows an overall improvement for every region of the country.

Regional Breakdown of the Ten Newspapers in the Survey for 1994

Below is a regional breakdown for the newspapers used in this survey from the various regions with at least one international story on the front page that was other than Rwanda.

West	20.8%
Midwest	41.6%
East	75%
South	38.8%

The regional breakdown shows that only East Coast newspapers did a consistent job of covering international events. East Coast coverage was notably stronger than in any other part of the country, as it was in 1992. Overall, coverage did tend to increase in all regions of the country, but the news coverage still fell short of what it should be for newspapers located in a preeminent power of the world.

YEAR THE CRISIS BEGAN IN KOSOVO

The survey for 1998 consisted of the *Sarasota Herald*, the *Dallas Morning News*, the *Albuquerque Journal*, the *Long Beach Press Telegraph*, the *Providence Journal*, the *Boston Globe*, the *Cincinnati Post*, the *Miami Star Tribune*, the *Tampa Tribune*, and the *Washington Post*. The results of the survey for 1998 revealed that front-page coverage of international news showed a slight decline from 1994.

1998 Survey of Ten Newspapers

Newspapers that had at least one international story on the front page other than Kosovo were fewer in number than in 1994.

Yes	No
37.5%	62.5%

The results show a continuous pattern of low coverage given to international news on the front page. Domestic news continued to get the lion's share of the coverage.

The regional breakdown for 1998 shows a shifting pattern in the coverage of international news. Coverage of international news on the front page increased in the West, but it declined in the rest of the country.

Regional Breakdown of the Ten Newspapers in the Survey for 1998

West	33.3%
Midwest	16.6%
East	50%
South	36.1%

This regional breakdown also revealed that the newspapers in the East continued to devote more coverage to international news on their front page than newspapers in other regions of the country. Newspapers in other regions of the country seemed to be focusing more of their attention on domestic stories.

The scope of each year of this survey is notably limited; however, combining all three years of the survey and 480 editions of newspapers from various regions is sufficient for generalizations to be made.

THE YEAR THE CRISIS BEGAN IN DARFUR

Genocide began in Darfur in 2003; therefore, this survey consisted of newspapers from that year. The newspapers included in this survey were the *New York Daily News*, the *Boston Herald*, the *Union Leader* (New Hampshire), the *San Francisco Chronicle*, the *San Diego Union*, the *St. Louis Post-Dispatch*, the *Cedar Rapids Gazette*, the *Atlanta Journal-Constitution*, the *Richmond Times*, and the *Charleston Post & Courier*.

2003 Survey of Ten Newspapers

The results of the survey of newspapers with at least one international news story other than Darfur on the front page are listed below.

Yes	No
32.5%	67.5%

The survey for 2003 shows that the trend of neglecting international news has continued into the twenty-first century. More than two-thirds of the newspapers in the survey tended to treat international news as if it was insignificant. A regional breakdown of the newspapers reveals a decline in the coverage of international news in some regions of the country and an increase in others.

Regional Breakdown of the Ten Newspapers in the Survey for 2003

West	66.7%
Midwest	50%
East	2.7%
South	33.3%

East Coast papers have traditionally devoted more space to international news than to other regions. In 2003 some East Coast papers devoted more space to domestic stories. Mostly likely, this was for commercial reasons. Newspaper circulation has declined in recent years. More domestic stories may be one way of maintaining circulation. However, the survey shows a major increase in the coverage of international news by West Coast papers and Midwest papers.

RESULTS FROM ALL YEARS OF THE SURVEY

The survey shows how many newspapers had at least one international story on the front page, other than the genocide in Bosnia, Rwanda, Kosovo, and Darfur, during the years of the crises.

Yes	No
33.5%	66.5%

Results from the combined survey show that the U.S. press has done an inadequate job of covering international news. It has failed to point out links between domestic and foreign policy, and has not adequately exposed the American people to what is happening in the world. This failure is widespread, as can be witnessed by the overall regional composite of all years of the survey.

REGIONAL COMPOSITE OF ALL YEARS

The figures below are a regional breakdown of newspapers with at least one international story on the front page that was not related to the genocide covered in the case studies. The percentage figures were calculated from the total number of newspapers from each region.

West	29.6%
Midwest	31.5%
East	38.3%
South	34%

This breakdown of 480 newspapers confirms the findings of the individual yearly surveys. The U.S. press, in all regions of the United States, has done an inadequate job of covering international news.

Nevertheless, it remains doubtful whether or not the American public will be interested in reading about people to whom they do not relate. For example, in 1988, Saddam Hussein used poison gas against the Kurds in his country. This blatant violation of the Geneva Conventions was widely publicized by the U.S. news media. However, there was no demand among citizens in the United States that the U.S. government cease military assistance to this tyrant, so Iraq continued to receive U.S. military aid. Similarly, after the Gulf War of 1991, the *Los Angeles Times*[1] and other newspapers reported that U.S. military forces had buried thousands of Iraqi forces alive in trenches in violation of U.S. Army policy. The American public did not seem to notice, nor did they seem to care, that the war had been won. What good is information if those who receive it do not want to hear the message?

Conclusion

The U.S. press has done an inadequate job of covering international news. News coverage in the United States tends to be parochial and trivial. International news is often relegated to the back pages of newspapers or ignored.

International news is usually not covered on most of the front pages of U.S. newspapers unless there is an ongoing crisis; otherwise, news is treated like a business. Newspapers tend to provide readers with stories they think the readers want, rather than with the information readers need to be well-informed citizens.

The surveys in this chapter also demonstrated that there is some regional variation in the coverage of international news. Historically, East Coast papers have tended to do a better job covering international news than newspapers in other parts of the country. However, this has now changed, as East Coast papers seek a commercial advantage in a market of declining readers.

If the American people are to play a significant role in the formation of U.S. foreign policy, they need to be better informed about what is going on in the world; therefore, U.S. newspapers need to devote more coverage to international affairs. The intellect of the American people should not be taken for granted by only putting parochial and trivial stories on the front pages of U.S. newspapers.

On the other hand, if the American people are to become better informed about what is going on in the world, they must demand better news coverage. As long as newspapers that focus on local and trivial events sell, this is the type of newspaper that will be printed. If the American people demand more comprehensive coverage of the news, they can have it—it is strictly a matter of economics. They are getting the news that sells; therefore, they should stop buying until news coverage becomes more comprehensive.

Chapter 10

International Relations and Education

We are the world; we are the children.

—*Lyrics by Michael Jackson, composed for USA Africa*

Introduction

There is a sense of irony to the lyrics above. U.S. recording artists and actors wanted to do something about starvation in Africa. As a result, they composed and recorded a song to raise money for that cause. They felt that they could make a difference in the lives of the starving and the needy. Today, young people in the United States are not educated about what is going on in the world and do not feel that they can make a difference. U.S. education has failed to elevate students above their immediate circumstances to get them to embrace the world as their own. Instead, U.S. students look inward instead of raising their heads, opening their eyes, seeing the world, and realizing that they are a part of it.

The United States is a global power, the only superpower in the post–Cold War era, yet U.S. students are taught nothing about global obligations. They are taught that they are citizens of the United States, but not citizens of the world, and that being a superpower carries added responsibilities.

They are aware that they can make a difference in the lives of people when there is a natural disaster, such as the tsunami that struck Southeast Asia in December 2004 and the earthquake that struck Haiti in 2010. Nevertheless, they are often unaware that they can also shape U.S. foreign policy. They have not learned from the Vietnam War that a highly motivated and politicized public can change the course of U.S. foreign policy. On the one hand, students are unaware of the public's ability to shape U.S. foreign policy, because U.S. schools have failed as institutions of higher learning and as institutions of empowerment. On the other hand, the U.S. government has learned, from its Vietnam War experience, that it can keep a free hand in the formation of foreign policy, as long as it can stave off the point of critical mass, where the concerns of the public grow and it demands action or change. As a result, students in the United States are not conscious of the potential impact they can have on U.S. foreign policy.

THE EVOLUTION OF THE COLD WAR AND POST–COLD WAR EDUCATION IN AMERICA

The purpose of this section is not to give a history of education in the United States during the Cold War and post–Cold War eras. It is to provide an explanation of why U.S. schools have failed as effective agents of political socialization.

Life Adjustment Education

After World War II, the education establishment in the United States began to focus on "Life Adjustment Education." The central focus of this idea was to help students develop social skills and become "good citizens." The end of World War II meant that troops would be demobilizing and youths would need help adjusting to civilian life. Moreover, the education establishment was also concerned about the growing role of government agencies in the education and training of American youth. New Deal programs, such as the Civilian Conservation Corps (CCC) and the National Youth Administration, were viewed as rivals by the education establishment, which had become a powerful interest group and successfully lobbied for the abolition of these government programs so it could direct the future of U.S. youth.

Life adjustment education is anti-intellectual. It was argued that only 20 percent of U.S. students would go to college and that another 20 percent would take up trades or become skilled workers. It was assumed that the remaining 60 percent of the students would become housewives and blue-collar workers who did not need to know math, science, history, or study the classics. As Diane Ravitch has said, "Life adjustment education was based on the assumption that 60 percent of the nation's youth lacked the brains for either college or skilled occupations."[1]

Life adjustment education failed to educate students. Its main emphasis was social conformity rather than intellectual development. Regardless of whether one is going to college or not, clerks, mechanics, and blue-collar workers still need to be able to make informed decisions. Essentially, students were taught to be followers and not leaders, because most of them were viewed as inferior people and were being conditioned to fit into inferior political/social roles. This was the type of education that the younger part of generation VIII and generation IX (the baby boomers) often received. They were not encouraged to look beyond their immediate political communities or to think about international politics. This was something that was considered to be out of their league and to be left in the hands of government decision-makers. The abdication of decision-making in foreign policy–making by the American public meant that politicians did not have to worry about public opinion as much in the international arena as in the domestic arena, unless an international crisis developed that hit the front pages of the nations' newspapers and disrupted the lives of the public (e.g., the Korean War and later the Vietnam War). Prior to reaching the point of critical mass, the populace was not concerned with international issues. As a result of life adjustment education, people were taught that it was better to do what they were told and to get along well with others rather than to ask questions.

There was criticism of schools from many quarters. The launch of Sputnik in 1957 exposed the weakness of U.S. education, but this was a minor storm that was soon to blow over and life adjustment education continued unabated for most U.S. students.

Education in the 1960s

During this era, most students were not taught how they were connected to the world or how events in other countries can affect them socially, politically, or economically. As the Cold War raged, and global communications improved, there was a critical need for students to know what was going on in the world. The 1960s brought forth social and political upheavals, yet the changes brought forth in education were not earth-shattering. They were merely minor reforms and not an improvement or expansion in the curriculum. One has to wonder, if this was the case, then what led to the political activism of the 1960s and the protest against the War in Vietnam? It was not the educational system that led to this heightened awareness and growth in political involvement on the part of the United States' youth.

Political activism occurred in the 1960s because the point of critical mass alluded to earlier was reached. When the War in Vietnam ended so did student activism and students' concerns about the conduct of U.S. foreign policy. In the 1960s, the movement away from an academic curriculum continued. During this era, there was a demand to make education relevant, to democratize the classroom, and to make schools the platform for the personal growth of students.

> The demand for relevance in curriculum encouraged students to turn inward and pursue their own interest; the necessity of appealing to students' interest also spurred schools and colleges to "market" courses with alluring titles as if students were consumers in a vast educational marketplace.[2]

Students were not viewed as students but consumers in a market. Teachers were not teachers but "facilitators" of knowledge. Once more, we see that there was no effort made for students to engage in critical thinking.

The Vietnam War was something of an aberration. Students became aware of what was happening in Southeast Asia and concerned about the United States' involvement in Vietnam, not as a result of what they had learned at schools but because the Vietnam War was an event that, over time, touched them personally. At the height of the war, the United States had 500,000 troops involved in active combat in Vietnam. However, this does not accurately reflect the extent of the United States' involvement in Vietnam. Over the course of the war, three million U.S. citizens were rotated in and out of Vietnam. Since this affected so many people, especially the young, activism was the end result. The Vietnam War was an event that touched young Americans personally, because they could be drafted for military service. This helped to stir young Americans into action and mobilize public opinion against the war. Ultimately, this affected the country's decision to withdraw from Vietnam. Young Americans saw a direct connection between U.S. foreign policy and how it could affect their lives. This was a rare moment. Students had reached this stage of political awareness without the assistance of the schools. In fact, one might even say that they reached it in spite of the schools; however, this state of heightened awareness among U.S. students was not to last.

The '70s

In the 1970s, U.S. political leaders sought to avoid the mistakes they had made in the 1960s. They sought to avoid long-term military commitments, so as not to arouse the public's concern. Military adventures were to be short-term. This, and the adoption of an all-volunteer military, was sufficient to deflect the attention of students away from foreign policy matters. The movement away from intellectual rigor in U.S. education that had begun in previous eras continued in the 1970s.

> Enrollment in "general track" had jumped in the 1960s "from 12.0 percent in the late 1960s to 42.5 percent in the late 1970s," ... and the general track had become "the dominant student track in high school." Neither academic or vocational, the general track consisted of courses such as driver education, general shop, remedial studies, consumer education, training for marriage and adulthood, health education, typing, and home economics.[3]

Of course, there was an outcry about what was happening in the schools, but the reaction to the criticism was not to strengthen the curriculum, it was to set minimum standards. In such instances, the minimum becomes the standard and it becomes a self-defeating policy.

The '80s and Beyond

The students of the 1980s fared no better than their predecessors. Social promotion, grade inflation, and dumbing down the curriculum continued during this period. The development of the students' ability to think independent thoughts, reason, and communicate effectively still did not constitute the primary focus of the educational process.

> Changes in the curriculum in pursuit of relevance accentuated narcissistic themes. Social studies courses focused on immediate personal and social issues; chronological history and civic knowledge, which required students to think about worlds larger than their own acquaintances, were relegated to minor departments.[4]

By the 1980s, "academic credit was offered for courses such as cheerleading, student government, and mass media."[5] With an educational system like this, students were not taught about the world, their role in the world, or about the intricacies of U.S. foreign policy. As far as they were concerned, what happened "over there" (abroad) did not matter, because they did not believe it affected them. Instead of being players in international politics, they became bystanders.

Darfur as an Aberration

The student movement to "Save Darfur" that developed on college campuses in 2004 seems to contradict the argument being made above. The movement to "Save Darfur," like student activism against the War in Vietnam, was an aberration and not the result of what students learned in class. It was the direct result of their involvement with American pop culture. As stated in Chapter 7, student activism on this issue was a direct outgrowth of the movie *Hotel Rwanda*. Moreover, messages about genocide in Darfur subsequently began to reach them via the Internet, a mode of communication that most students use on a routine basis.

However, what is notable is that in 2004 saving Darfur was a cause célèbre for college students. Today, the young have abandoned the cause. Saving Darfur was a fad for many students. Most have now moved on. Their passion faded as Darfur faded from the headlines.

Reasons for the Failure of American Education

Education in the United States no longer serves to enlighten. It has simply become another task that one has to accomplish to get the pot of gold at the end of the rainbow. We no longer seek to understand ourselves and others, or to question our own motives or those of our national leaders. In essence, education in the United States has failed. It has failed to lift us up to a higher point of understanding. It has failed to break down barriers of race and ethnicity. Most important of all, it has failed to give us a better understanding of people who are not like us, and it has not taught us how to relate to them. But why have we failed?

We have failed because we are constantly turning our vision inward. As long as we are looking inward, we can never look out. We can never see the world, or understand it. How can one's eyes be opened and one be enlightened if one has an educational system that reinforces cultural narcissism? We are not the world but a part of it.

Over the years, as "progressive education" evolved, the goal of "progressive education" seemed to be to keep students from acquiring knowledge. It was as if knowledge was a sacred item placed on the shelf and locked away from the students, while schools diverted their attention to other endeavors. Is it any wonder that Americans often do not relate to the world because they know nothing of it and because they often do not relate to each other?

Part IV

Looking toward the United Nations for a Solution

Chapter 11

Why United Nations Reforms Will Not Change the Status Quo

Introduction

The United Nations has been a successful organization; nevertheless, it is on the brink of becoming an irrelevant organization like the League of Nations, which ceased to be viable because it failed to protect weak states from aggressors. Today, the United Nations has failed to protect people in Third World countries from the tyrants within their borders who violate human rights and perpetuate genocide. Will the United Nations suffer the same fate as the League of Nations? It is possible. In recent years, some of its failures have led to calls for a complete overhaul of the organization. There have been charges of financial and administrative mismanagement, failed peacekeeping missions, and an inability to respond promptly during a crisis. Moreover, the Security Council reflects the world order that existed after World War II, rather than the world order that exists today. The United Nations seems overburdened. During the fall of 2000, UN Secretary-General Kofi Annan held the Millennium Summit to breathe new life into the organization. Secretary-General Annan sought to make world leaders renew their commitment to the UN Charter and the Universal Declaration of Human Rights. It was the largest gathering of world leaders ever. By most outward indications, the summit was a success; however, the proposed reforms will not work. The UN reforms fail to address the source of the problem. They do not alter the dynamics of human relations. The reforms did not include a blueprint to bridge the cultural gap between the West and the Third World to prevent genocide in the future; therefore the reforms are doomed to fail.

Without bridging the cultural gap that exists between developed and developing countries, all of the recommended reforms will remain a hollow intellectual exercise. The problems the United Nations has faced in recent years are problems of perception, motivation, and action. Very often when quick, firm, and decisive action is required in the Third World, there is little or no response from the United Nations, unless the country in peril is perceived as having strategic or economic value for one of the five permanent members of the Security Council. Today, whether one lives or dies often depends on where one lives. As a result, the United Nations has an uneven record of saving the lives of those in need. It has created an Orwellian nightmare. According to the Universal Declaration of Human Rights, all are equal, but according to the Security Council, some people are more equal than others. Bridging the cultural gap entails altering one's perception of others and viewing them as being equal and worthy of life itself.

The proposed reforms at the Millennium Summit also ignored the potential role that the United Nations Educational, Scientific, and Cultural Organization (UNESCO) can play in narrowing the cultural divide between countries during the new millennium. This was a major oversight that should be corrected. This chapter will review administrative reforms, peacekeeping, Security Council reforms, and the Millennium Summit. It will show what needs to be done so the United Nations does not become an irrelevant organization like the League of Nations.

UNITED NATIONS ADMINISTRATIVE REFORMS

The United Nations began to come under attack in the 1980s for corruption and administrative incompetence. In many Western countries the United Nations was viewed as a "vast sprawling bureaucracy." The U.S. Congress responded to these charges by passing the Kassebaum Amendments. In 1985 Senator Nancy Kassebaum (Republican-Kansas) introduced Section 143 of Public Law (P.L.) 99–93. It required the United States' assessed contributions to the United Nations, and its specialized agencies, to be reduced from 25 percent to 20 percent of the budget for those agencies in the fiscal year 1987. The reduction was to continue for subsequent years until the United Nations granted voting rights on budgetary matters proportionate to budget contributions.

The United States thought that Third World countries that constitute a majority in the General Assembly arrived at budgetary matters in an arbitrary manner.

In response to this action by the U.S. Congress, the General Assembly adopted Resolution 41/213. It called for a more streamlined, less complex, and top-heavy staff. In addition, it also sought to reduce duplication of activities. Subsequently, Congress also passed another Kassebaum Amendment, Section 409 of P.L. 103–236. It gave the president discretionary authority to withhold 20 percent of the funds appropriated for UN contributions if the United Nations did not institute consensus-based budget policies to assure that attention was paid to major financial contributors.

What was at stake was more than trying to improve the administration of the United Nations. What was taking place was a tug-of-war for the control of the United Nations. The United Nations was engulfed in a clash between the United States and its Western European allies and the Third World. The United States had effectively lost control of the United Nations, and was trying to use the power of its purse to regain it.

The United States used to dominate the affairs of the United Nations. Of the fifty-one states that joined the United Nations in 1945, thirty-nine were U.S. allies, and only five were allies of the Soviet Union.[1] And in 1950, thirty-seven out of the sixty states could be classified as U.S. allies.[2] Moreover, from 1945 to 1965, the United States did not cast a single veto in the Security Council while the Soviet Union cast 103 vetoes. During the first twenty years of the United Nations, the United States never cast a veto at the United Nations because it never had to defend its position. Over time, decolonization became a reality. In 1960, sixteen African countries entered the United Nations. However, after 1965, the United States found itself on the losing end most of the time; as the world changed, so did the United Nations. This diversified body began to focus the United Nations' attention on issues such as racial justice, dignity, and equality.[3] From 1978 to 1987, the General Assembly passed over 120 resolutions dealing with the Republic of South Africa.[4] By the mid-1980s, the United States was only in agreement with the General Assembly 14.3 percent of the time. The Cold War was still going on, and it was the United States' primary concern, while most of the members of the General Assembly wanted a New International Economic Order.

This was more than a struggle for control of the United Nations between the haves and the have-nots of the world. It was a conflict of values and that in turn affected the perception of the UN members. On the one hand, Western countries have been insensitive to the goals and aspirations of the Third World majority who want to change the structure of the current international system, because they believe that it is controlled by and benefits Western countries at the expense of the developing world. Some in the West viewed leaders of developing countries as being insignificant players on the international scene. In *Nuclear Weapons and Foreign Policy*, Henry Kissinger wrote:

> the independence movements, almost without exception, provided poor preparation for an understanding of the elements of power in international relations. Based in the dogmas of late nineteenth century liberalism, especially pacifism, the independence movement relied more on an evaluation of power factors, and to this day their claim to superior spirituality remains the battle cry of Asian nationality.[5]

On the other hand, Third World countries have been insensitive to the need for efficient administration. The United Nations has been less than a model of Weberian bureaucratic efficiency. Prior to the 1990s, the UN bureaucracy was subject to fraud, mismanagement, and patronage, according to a report by Richard Thornburg, the former UN undersecretary general for administration and management. This meant little to the Third World majority at the United Nations. The spoils system personifies the bureaucracy many Third World countries, but the corruption was criticized by Western countries that did not want to see their financial resources wasted. Moreover, it was especially tough for the United States as it watched the General Assembly pass measures it opposed, such as Resolution 3379 that stated that Zionism was racism.

Nevertheless, the UN bureaucracy has been unfairly attacked by many of its western critics. Erskin Childers and Brian Urquart have pointed out that the United Nations serves the interest of 5.5 billion people but has a staff the size of the civil service of Wyoming, a state that has a population of about 545,000. Moreover, its staff is smaller than the civil service of Stockholm, Sweden, which has a population of 672,000.[6]

Secretary-General Kofi Annan attempted to close the cultural gap between developed countries and developing countries by initiating administrative reforms that met the demands of the United States for greater accountability, while maintaining many of the goals and aspirations of the Third World majority.

Secretary-General Annan's Administrative Reforms

Secretary-General Annan's reforms had a twofold purpose. They sought to streamline the administration of the organization to make it more efficient and to placate the United States so its organizational support would be maintained. To transform the United Nations into a model of rational decision-making, he recommended reforms to the General Assembly in his report "Renewing the United Nations: A Programme for Reform." In his report, Secretary-General Annan made the following recommendations:

- The establishment of the position of Deputy Secretary-General;
- The establishment of a Senior Management Group;
- Development and strengthening of the Executive Committee;
- Decentralizing decision making;
- Establishment of a Revolving Credit Fund of $1 billion;
- Integration of the twelve Secretariat units into five;
- Ensuring that all staff have requisite skills;
- Improving the Organization's ability to deploy peacekeepers rapidly;
- Strengthening post-conflict peace-building;
- Zero-based budgeting.[7]

In the fall of 1997, these recommendations were approved by the General Assembly, but these reforms will do no good unless those who foot the bill for the United Nations respect the organization, are willing to pay their dues, and are willing to prevent and stop genocide. Thus, one can clearly see that administrative reforms are not enough. There must also be reforms in the perception of the organization in the United States, which had been $1.7 billion in arrears in 1999. Without the bridging of the cultural gap, UN reforms will become meaningless because dues will be withheld and the critical support the United Nations needs will not be forthcoming from the United States, which is crucial for the survival of the United Nations. This will be demonstrated in the next section.

UNITED NATIONS PEACEKEEPING

Peacekeeping has been defined as supplementing the self-help international system. Peacekeepers may uncover facts, monitor borders, supervise disarmament or demobilization of forces, maintain security, conduct elections, and provide temporary administrations for countries.[8] In the post–Cold War era, peacekeeping has become one of the United Nations' primary functions. During the Cold War, it was difficult to set up peacekeeping operations because of the rift between the United States and the Soviet Union.

The Cold War was a cultural conflict. According to Max Weber, capitalism was an outgrowth of the Protestant Reformation. Marxism, by contrast, was the outgrowth of the economic deprivation suffered by the Soviet Union and Eastern Europe. In effect, the Cold War was a supranational cultural war that enveloped people and their societies. However, once the Cold War was over, it should have been easier for members to agree on peacekeeping missions, but this was often not the case. The Cold War helped to mask the cultural rift between Western countries and the Third World. Though the cultural rift is not as extensive as the Cold War between the United States and the Soviet Union, the tension that exists between developed countries and Third World countries can potentially hamper the functioning of the organization.

A War of Indifference exists between developed and developing countries. The West only views a Third World country as being significant if it is located in a strategic area or has natural resources that are crucial to the West. As a result, when action is needed during a crisis, it is often not forthcoming because the country in need of a peacekeeping mission or military intervention is not of strategic value to any of the permanent members of the Security Council. Therefore, geography and natural resources are often the determining factor as to whether one lives or one dies.

The indifference of the permanent members of the Security Council to the Third World can be witnessed by briefly examining how it has responded or failed to respond to crises in nonstrategic areas. One such area is Liberia. The response of the Security Council to the crisis in Liberia was typical of its response to Africa. It stood by and watched as the government collapsed and 1.3 million people became refugees. The Economic Community of West Africa (ECOWAS) sent in troops to keep the peace. The western international community was conspicuously silent about the massive loss of life in Liberia, but a chorus of condemnation was heard from the western world when five American nuns were murdered in October 1992 by the National Patriotic Front of Liberia (NPLF). No such condemnation was heard from the western world or the Security Council when 3,000 Liberians were killed in October and early November 1992. Similarly, when the troops ECOWAS deployed in Liberia were attacked in the western region of Liberia during the early months of 1993, all that the Security Council did was to pass a resolution in April to condemn the attack. A more effective means of dealing with the crisis would have been to threaten intervention by UN forces if the attacks continued.

Furthermore, the nonchalant attitude of the Security Council toward Africa could also be witnessed during the crisis in Rwanda and Darfur as well. The crisis in Rwanda in 1994 was a modern-day holocaust that could have been prevented. In *Shake Hands With the Devil*, General Romo Dallaire, the head of the UN Assistance Mission for Rwanda (UNAMIR), stated that he had received intelligence reports about the storage locations of weapons in Rwanda. However, the UN headquarters in New York tied his hands and thus prevented him from seizing weapons that were later used to kill civilians and endanger the lives of UN peacekeepers. Dallaire was hemmed in by the United Nations' narrow rules of engagement (ROE) that were written during the Cold War era to prevent a conflict between the superpowers. Today, the United States is the only superpower remaining. In this post–Cold War era of genocide, UN peacekeeping commanders need broader authority to deter or stop genocide. Rwanda became a killing field where one million people perished and two million were displaced from their homes, but the Security Council failed to intervene. The inaction of the United Nations during this crisis is hard to explain, because the precedent for intervention when genocide was in progress had been set by the Security Council during the Gulf War. The Security Council passed Resolution 688 on April 5, 1991, to justify further action against Saddam Hussein when he was engaged in genocide against the Kurds in northern Iraq. The cowardice that the United Nations displayed in Rwanda is reprehensible. The United Nations needs to get over its "Somalia syndrome," due to which it cuts and runs at the first sign of danger.

In May 1999, Secretary-General Annan commissioned a study to review the actions of the United Nations during the genocide in Rwanda. The panel released its finding in December 1999. The report titled "Report of the Independent Inquiry into the Actions of the United Nations during the 1994 Genocide in Rwanda" stated:

> The overriding failure of the United Nations before and during the genocide in Rwanda can be summarized as a lack of resources and a lack of will to take on the commitment, which would have been necessary to prevent or to stop the genocide.[9]

This was, at best, an effort by Secretary-General Annan to clean up the mess made by the Security Council by looking at the facts acknowledging the shameful behavior of the Security Council, especially the permanent members, and to move on in the hope that it will not happen again.

The Organization of African Unity (now the African Union) also commissioned a study into the events that transpired in Rwanda in 1994. The report "Rwanda: The Preventable Genocide" stated:

> At the UN, the Security Council, led unremittingly by the United States, simply did not care enough about Rwanda to intervene appropriately. What makes the Security Council's betrayal of its responsibility even more intolerable is that the genocide was in no way inevitable. First, it could have been prevented entirely. Then even once it was allowed to begin, the destruction could have been significantly mitigated. All that was required was a reasonably-sized international military force with a strong mandate to enforce the Arusha agreements. Nothing of the kind was ever authorized by the Security Council either before or during the genocide.[10]

The report also declared:

> We urge all those parties that have apologized [like the United States] for their role in the genocide, and those who have yet to apologize, to support strongly our call for the secretary-general to appoint a committee to determine reparations owed by the international community to Rwanda.[11]

Peacekeeping, or the lack of it, has been an area of notable failure for the United Nations in recent years. The United Nations was slow to react in Bosnia, Kosovo, and Darfur. Its peacekeeping mission in Sierra Leone was also not successful.

To rectify the problems with UN peacekeeping missions, Secretary-General Annan convened a panel to review UN peacekeeping operations. The report "Report of the Panel on United Nations Peace Operations" made the following recommendations:

- The need to distinguish between aggressor and victim;
- The Secretariat to keep the Security Council informed;
- New information gather and analysis entity to support the Secretary-General and the Executive Committee on Peace and Security;
- Rapid deployment;
- Clear credible and achievable mandates.[12]

The recommendations are logical, and, if implemented, could make a difference but unfortunately they will not. Better equipped and better trained peacekeepers are needed to improve UN peacekeeping. When UN peacekeepers arrived in Sierra Leone, they were ill-equipped for the mission. Moreover, some U.S. peacekeeping forces in Kosovo were charged with abuse. The U.S. forces were trained for combat and did not have the requisite skills needed to keep the peace in the Balkans. What good does it do to make recommendations and to implement them if one's perception of the people that it will impact does not change? In other words, nothing has changed to alter the attitude of the United States and the other western countries toward making a commitment to halting genocide when it occurs. Therefore, action appears to be unlikely even if the recommendations are implemented.

Some of the harshest words regarding UN peacekeeping have been spoken by Lt. Gen. Romeo Dallaire, who commanded the UN peacekeeping forces in Rwanda. He said, "I believe that we are going to see a continued scenario of disasters in regions that are not of great interest to the white man" if attitudes at the United Nations do not change.[13] To paraphrase Shakespeare, the fault lies not in the United Nations but in ourselves. The United Nations is controlled by its member states and is highly influenced by the permanent members of the Security Council, especially the United States. The analysis of UN peacekeeping by William Durch in *The Evolution of UN Peacekeeping* revealed that the cooperation of the United States is essential for a successful peacekeeping mission. The cooperation of the United States is also essential in peacemaking operations as well. There was a notable reliance on the United States by NATO in Kosovo.

The United Nations must also work toward ending racism and indifference in the way it deals with refugees. According to the Office of the UN High Commissioner for Refugees, only $31.75 per capita was available for African refugees in 1999. On the other hand, $265.5 per capita was available for refugees in Kosovo. "U.N. officials and aid workers say they must give European refugees used to cappuccino and CNN a higher standard of living to maintain the refugees' sense of dignity and stability."[14] Without a resulting change in attitude, UN reforms will be meaningless.

SECURITY COUNCIL REFORM

At the end of World War II, the leaders of the Allied Powers made themselves the overlords of the world by entrenching themselves in the Security Council of the United Nations as permanent members. But the world has undergone substantial changes since the end of

World War II. Countries that were once colonies have now gained their independence and Japan and Germany have become industrial giants, but these changes are not reflected in the Security Council. Currently, the United States, the United Kingdom, the People's Republic of China, France, and Russia serve on the Security Council as permanent members. The ten nonpermanent seats are divided as following: five seats are reserved for the Afro-Asian bloc, two for Latin America, one for Eastern Europe, and two for Western Europe and other areas, but this system is undemocratic. It is not representative of the diversity that exists in the General Assembly.

Moreover, the current structure of the Security Council is ill-equipped to take into consideration the concerns of the world, since it is reluctant to intervene when Western interests are not at stake. This means that if Third World countries cannot legitimize their problems in terms of Western interest, they may not be addressed at all. One need not be reminded of what happened in Bosnia, Rwanda, Kosovo, and Darfur. Issues involving human rights and justice are just as important as Western strategic and economic interests.

A number of Security Council reforms have been proposed at the United Nations. A few of them will be reviewed here briefly.

The United States

The United States favors the addition of five permanent seats to the Security Council. One permanent seat could go to Germany and the other to Japan. The other permanent seats may go to Africa, Asia, Latin America, and the Caribbean. With the possible creation of one additional nonpermanent seat, the Security Council could be limited to twenty-one seats. This position is known as "the quick fix" and is rejected by most of the Third World as being undemocratic.[15] It makes some concessions to Third World countries for greater representation on the Security Council, but its main focus is on maintaining the maximum efficiency of the Council.

Countries with a Similar Position

Poland: Supports Germany and Japan as permanent members. It also supports permanent regional representation for Africa, Asia, Latin America, and the Caribbean. And the creation of a nonpermanent seat for Eastern Europe.[16]

Hungary: Same position as the United States.[17]

Cambodia: Same position as the United States but with limitations on the veto.[18]

Russia: The Federation believes that Security Council expansion should be limited to twenty or twenty-one seats. The enlargement should include industrialized and developing countries. Russia supports India as a permanent member from the developing countries and the selection of permanent members from Latin America and Africa.[19]

Uzbekistan: It supports the creation of two additional permanent seats for Germany and Japan and three nonpermanent seats. Any expansion of the Security Council would be limited to twenty-one seats.[20]

Nordic countries: Norway, Finland, Denmark, Sweden, and Iceland believe that five new permanent seats should be created. Africa, Asia, and the Latin American/Caribbean region should be represented among the new permanent members. The Security Council could be expanded to twenty-three seats.[21]

Ireland: The Republic supports Japan and Germany as permanent members and appropriate candidates from developing countries. It believes that an expanded Security Council should be limited to twenty-one seats.[22]

Belgium: Wants the Security Council enlarged in both categories. It thinks the Security Council should be enlarged to twenty-one members.[23]

Georgia: Supports the creation of two additional permanent seats that would be occupied by Germany and Japan and four nonpermanent seats that would be occupied by representatives from Africa, Asia, Latin America/Caribbean, and Eastern Europe.[24]

Paraguay: The representative from Paraguay said any expansion of the Security Council should include two industrial countries that are global contributors and representatives from the Latin American/Caribbean region, Asia, and Africa.[25]

The United Kingdom: The United Kingdom of Great Britain and Northern Ireland favors permanent seats for Germany and Japan. In addition it supports permanent regional seats for Latin America, Africa, and Asia.[26]

Laos: The Laos People's Democratic Republic favors having two new permanent members from industrialized countries and permanent seats for Asia, Africa, and the Latin American/Caribbean region. And Eastern Europe should have representation as a nonpermanent member.[27] In the past, Laos has also supported India as a permanent member.[28]

North Korea: The Democratic People's Republic of Korea supports the creation of two permanent seats for developed countries and three from developing countries based on geography.[29]

Philippines: Wants to explore the "2 + 3 formula" and other plans for expanding nonpermanent seats.[30]

Kazakhstan: Supports Germany and Japan as permanent members and three permanent seats for countries from Asia, Africa, and the Latin American/Caribbean region.[31]

Armenia: Has voiced support for five new permanent members of the Security Council. Those seats should be occupied by countries from Africa, Asia, and the Latin American/Caribbean region, and Germany and Japan should also be permanent members. The expansion of nonpermanent seats should include Eastern Europe.[32]

The Non-Aligned Movement

The countries of the Non-Aligned Movement (NAM) have adopted a common position on the expansion of the Security Council. They believe that an additional eleven seats on the Security Council should be created to enhance geographical representation and to democratize the Council.[33] In other words, the Security Council should be expanded to twenty-six seats. It has not been specified if the seats should be permanent or nonpermanent. The following countries have spoken out in support of the NAM position at the United Nations: Botswana,[34] Cameroon,[35] Zimbabwe,[36] Syria,[37] Cuba,[38] Iran,[39] Myanmar,[40] Singapore,[41] Angola,[42] South Africa,[43] Kuwait,[44] Ghana,[45] Sri Lanka,[46] Pakistan,[47] Egypt,[48] Colombia,[49] Sudan,[50] Guyana,[51] Lebanon,[52] Tunisia,[53] and Viet Nam.[54] The main support for this position comes from developing countries.

Intermediate Positions

Countries in this category have varying positions. They have taken a stand that lies between the goal of the United States of minimizing the expansion of the Security Council to maintain efficiency and that of Third World Countries that want increased democracy by expanding the Council.

France: France wants an increase in the number of permanent and nonpermanent seats. It wants to allocate one permanent seat each to Germany and Japan. It also wants to allocate three permanent seats to developing countries and new nonpermanent seats to developing countries to improve geographical representation. It wants Security Council membership to be limited to twenty five seats.[55]

Bulgaria: Believes that adding five permanent and five nonpermanent seats to the Council will restore its credibility. It does not seem to object to Germany and Japan being added as permanent members.[56]

Ukraine: Wants to see the Security Council expanded to make the number of seats twenty-four to twenty-six. The expansion would include an increase in permanent and nonpermanent members. The Ukraine supports Germany's and Japan's bids to become permanent members of the Council and permanent seats for Africa, Asia, and Latin America. It also believes that the underrepresentation of Eastern Europe should be addressed.[57]

Croatia: Has adopted the position that five new permanent seats should be created along with four new nonpermanent seats. It has stated that two of the permanent seats should go to industrialized countries and that three should go to developing countries. From the new nonpermanent seats, one each should go to Africa, Asia, the Latin American/Caribbean region, and Eastern Europe.[58]

Czech Republic: Believes that five permanent seats should be added to the Security Council along with four to five nonpermanent seats. One of the nonpermanent seats would be allocated to Eastern Europe, and the permanent seats would be rotated on a regional basis.[59]

Japan: Supports the expansion of the Council to twenty-four members. It advocates the creation of five additional permanent seats and four nonpermanent seats.[60] Japan also believes that it should become a permanent member: "Japan, with the endorsement of many countries, was prepared to become a new permanent member of the Security Council."[61]

Kyrgyzstan: Supports the expansion of permanent and nonpermanent members on the Security Council, and believes that Germany and Japan should be added as permanent members. It also believes that developed and developing countries should be represented in both categories and that expansion should be limited to twenty-five seats.[62]

Australia: Stands for the expansion of the Security Council to twenty-five members. Australia believes that Germany and Japan should be included as permanent members and that there should be permanent seats for underrepresented regions.[63]

Fiji: Wants to see five new permanent seats created on the Security Council and seven new nonpermanent seats. Japan, Germany, Asia, Africa, and the Latin American/Caribbean region would be allocated seats as permanent members. And Africa and Asia would be allotted two nonpermanent seats. Eastern Europe, Latin America/Caribbean, and Western Europe would be allocated one of the new nonpermanent seats.[64]

Germany: Is in favor of the creation of four additional nonpermanent seats and five permanent seats. It believes that two permanent seats should go to industrialized countries and that three should go to "the South."[65]

Senegal: Seeks a compromise between limiting the Council to twenty-one seats, like the United States, in the name of efficiency and NAM's suggestion of expansion to twenty-six seats.[66]

Austria: Permanent and nonpermanent seats on the Security Council should increase to make the total Council membership twenty-five seats. It also advocates that Germany and Japan be admitted to the Council as permanent members, and "it equally supported a qualified member from 'the South.'"[67]

Romania: Believes that the Security Council should have twenty-five seats. It also supports the admission of Germany and Japan as permanent members.[68]

Slovenia: Has stated that there should be five new permanent seats on the Security Council and that Germany and Japan should each be allocated a seat. It believes that the Council should be expanded to include twenty-five members.[69]

Canada: Favors the addition of six to ten new nonpermanent seats.[70]

Uruguay: Wants an increase of the permanent and nonpermanent members of the Council to encompass twenty-five members.[71]

The Italian Plan

Italy has developed a plan that garnered some support among Third World Countries because it would help to make the Security Council more democratic. The Italian Plan calls for the creation of ten new nonpermanent seats that would rotate among thirty countries selected by the General Assembly.[72] It is supported by Italy, by NAM as a fallback position, and by Turkey.[73]

The African Union Plan

The African Union (AU) has adopted a proposal for the reform of the UN Security Council. It has taken the position that Africa should be allotted two permanent seats on the Security Council and that the countries chosen to fill those seats should be determined by African countries themselves.[74] This position has the nearly unanimous backing of African states. Although most also support the position of NAM, it should be pointed out that these positions are not mutually exclusive—they are mutually inclusive.

The League of Arab States

The League of Arab States, better known as the Arab League, has devised a plan to increase the representation of Arab states on the Security Council. It has adopted the position that at least one permanent seat on the Security Council and two nonpermanent seats should go to Arab countries, since they represent 12 percent of the United Nations' membership.[75]

The Organization of Islamic Conference

This organization consists of fifty-six countries. One of its most prominent members, Iran, has stated that Islamic countries are entitled to one permanent seat on the Security Council since Islamic countries have more than one billion people.[76]

Convergence and Divergence of Thought on Reform

At first glance, it seems that the various countries and blocs have wide and varying views on Security Council reform. Most of the countries that support the U.S. plan are overwhelmingly European. The AU Plan, the NAM Plan, and the Italian Plan derive support from virtually the same base of developing countries. However, there are more similarities between the plans than differences. All of them are in concurrence that the Security Council needs to be expanded. The plans are only about five seats apart on the size of the Security Council. And, most countries, with the exception of the five permanent members, believe that the veto should be abolished or curtailed. The United Nations has been grappling with this issue on a constant basis since 1993, yet it has not arrived at a consensus. This seems incomprehensible given the relative closeness of the various plans.

There is more to this debate than haggling over a few seats on the Security Council. What the divergent positions reveal is a cultural divide that exists between the member states. Most of the developing states want a greater voice in the affairs of the Council, but the permanent members, especially the United States, want to keep changes to a minimum. In theory they could simply split their differences; however, the cultural divide between them seems so wide that they do not know how to cross it. The cultural gap can be narrowed if the parties are willing to cross the bridge.

Crossing the Bridge to Security Council Reform

The reason for the United Nations' inability to deal with many post–Cold War problems is that it was not set up to handle them. The United Nations does not reflect the current world order. That means that the United Nations, especially the Security Council, should be reorganized.

Reorganizing the Security Council

One reform that would make the United Nations more democratic would be the elimination of the permanent members' veto power. This would prevent one nation from stopping action when there is a consensus, and action would be swifter if resolutions could be passed in the Security Council by mustering a majority vote instead of the requisite two-thirds majority that is currently needed.

If the reforms mentioned above are adopted, an important problem would remain: the tyranny of the majority. The justification for the aforementioned reforms is that they make the United Nations more democratic; however, this process would be undermined if a permanent group arose that was constantly able to ignore the interest and concerns of the minority. That is why a rule similar to U.S. Senate Rule 22 should be adopted. This rule allows the minority to have their day and to protect their rights via the filibuster. And, like Senate Rule 22, the UN measure should allow debate to be cut off with a three-fifths vote. This measure would have the dual purpose of making the United Nations more democratic, while keeping in mind James Madison's warning, from Federalist Paper No. 10, that democracy is more that just simply majority rule and must also protect minority rights.[77]

If the United Nations is reformed in the manner prescribed above, it can remain a vital organization well into the twenty-first century, but if reforms are not enacted, its future will remain in doubt, because it does not reflect the world's interest and reacts slowly in a crisis. Realistically, the reforms are not likely to be enacted since the United States foots one-fourth of the United Nation's budget and is not likely to weaken its own position in the organization. And, Chapter 18, Article 108 of the UN Charter states that any changes in the charter are subject to veto by the five permanent members. They are not likely to weaken their position either, but one can always hope that they will.

THE MILLENNIUM SUMMIT

The Millennium Summit was the largest gathering of world leaders ever. They gathered at the United Nations in an attempt to breathe new life into the organization so it could function more effectively in the new millennium. The reforms put forth and approved at the Summit were far-reaching and comprehensive.

The reforms were aimed at mending the regional biases that exist at the United Nations, recommitting it to the principles embodied in its charter and the Universal Declaration, and at shoring up peacekeeping. To that end, the Millennium Summit passed a declaration, and the Millennium Assembly passed a resolution. The declaration "Security Declaration on Ensuring an Effective Role for the Security Council in the Maintenance of International Peace and Security, Particularly in Africa" did the following:

- Reaffirmed the determination to give equal priority to the maintenance of peace and security in every region;
- Underlined the importance of rapid deployment;
- Stressed that perpetrators of crimes against humanity, genocide, war crimes, and other serious violations be brought to justice.[78]

Likewise the Millennium Assembly's resolution (A/55/l.2), the "United Nations Millennium Declaration," stressed:

- Faith in the U.N. and its Charter;
- A collective responsibility to uphold human dignity;
- Tolerance;
- Freedom from dehumanizing conditions such as poverty;
- Reaffirmation of faith in the United Nations.[79]

Secretary-General Annan seemed committed to making these goals a reality. At the Summit, he said:

> No amount of resolutions or statements can change reality. Only action can—prompt, unified and effective action, pursued with skill and discipline to halt the conflict and restore the peace. Only such determined action can restore the reputation of the United Nations as a credible force for peace and justice.[80]

It appeared that a "Kofi Doctrine" had emerged. At the summit, President Clinton also stated:

> One essential lesson of the last century is this: there are times when the international community must take a side—not merely stand between sides. For when good and evil collide, even-handedness can be an ally of evil.[81]

He then went on to say:

> We need better machinery to ensure UN peacekeepers can be rapidly deployed, with the right training and equipment, the ability to project credible force, and missions well-defined by a well functioning headquarters. To meet this challenge, we must also more effectively deploy civilian police to UN missions.[82]

A "Clinton Doctrine" appeared to be emerging as well. The two doctrines dovetailed. The "Kofi-Clinton Doctrine" seemed to be predicated on the idea that military force must be used to prevent or stop massive human rights violations such as genocide when they occur. These two leaders seemed to have finally understood what it would take to make the United Nations a credible force again. Nevertheless, this doctrine was not implemented in Darfur. The "War of Indifference" still prevails. The reforms of the Millennium Summit were well-thought-out and necessary but are insufficient, because they did not include a blueprint for changing existing attitudes. For this to be done, additional reforms are necessary.

SUPPLEMENTARY REFORMS

The United Nations has not been effective at preventing or stopping genocide. In the area of human rights, the United Nations has lost credibility. Gross violators of human rights such as Cuba, Zimbabwe, Libya, Belarus, and China were members of the UN Human Rights Commission, which was responsible for promoting respect and the observation of human rights of all people. The inclusion of Sudan, a country committing genocide, in such a body made a mockery of human rights and called the credibility of the United Nations as an organization promoting human rights into question. Therefore, Kofi Annan replaced the Human Rights Commission with a smaller Human Rights Council. Its purpose is to evaluate the fulfillment of human rights by all states. Every member comes up for review on a periodic basis, and members are elected by a two-thirds majority of the General Assembly.

Annan's reforms are an improvement over the previous system, but more far-reaching reforms are needed to prevent and stop genocide. The current reforms will not prevent gross violators from being seated on the Human Rights Council. First, measures must be taken so that only countries that respect human rights are seated on the Council. Second, when the Office of the UN High Commissioner for Refugees receives information about genocide, it should send a report to the Human Rights Council. After receiving the report, the Human Rights Council should be able to call a worldwide Genocide Watch. Third, if the Council concurs that genocide is occurring, it should forward a report to the Security Council, which could trigger a worldwide Genocide Alert. Fourth, if diplomacy fails to bring genocide to an end, then the Security Council should be authorized to deploy troops from a standing army to end the genocide. This would empower the United Nations by presenting a deterrent to genocide, and give it the means to stop genocide once it occurs. In recent years the United Nations has been irrelevant in both endeavors.

Other supplementary reforms will also help the United Nations to improve the organization. The Convention on the Elimination of All Forms of Racial Discrimination requires all the countries that have signed it to prepare a report that is sent to the United Nations Committee on Racial Discrimination in Geneva, Switzerland. Countries that have signed the convention are to analyze their own practices to determine if they are living up to the convention. The reports submitted by the United States are candid in discussing both its strengths and its shortcomings and should serve as a role model for other countries.

All countries should be encouraged to ratify the convention, and the reports should be expanded to require countries to report on what they are doing to solve racial and ethnic problems. If there are recurring racial or ethnic problems within a country, it should be asked to attempt new solutions. Most ethnic and racial conflicts are based on the distribution of goods and political power within a society. Therefore, altering the status quo would be a logical step to solving such problems.

To that end, the United Nations Educational, Scientific and Cultural Organization (UNESCO) should be invited to play a leading role in the effort to educate and prevent genocide and human rights violations from occurring. Moreover, there should be annual UN summits that follow up on the reforms approved at the Millennium Summit. The representatives from each country at the annual summit would give an oral report about the progress that their country was making toward eradicating ethnic and racial problems. Time would be allotted for questions from other countries. This would help to create peer pressure and focus worldwide publicity on countries where there is recurring ethnic and racial strife. This would give them an incentive to solve their problems and avoid the international spotlight. Not showing up for the annual summit would only cause more attention to be focused upon a country that was violating human rights.

Besides focusing on the eradication of racial and ethnic problems *within* countries, the above-mentioned approach should also be used for dealing with racial and ethnic problems *between* countries. One of the notable problems that was discussed at the Millennium Summit was the uneven distribution of the benefits of globalization. The annual summits, likewise, could be used as forums to find solutions to globalization, debt, and new strategies for economic development. Solving these problems would go a long way toward solving many of the problems of developing countries and ending the Cold War between the Third World and the West. However, developing countries should not fall into the trap of believing that economic growth will solve their social problems. It will not. In some cases it will make them worse if the benefits of economic development are not spread among the various racial and ethnic groups within a country. The standard of living in Yugoslavia was, in some cases, ten times higher than the standard of living in many African countries, yet Yugoslavia still fell apart.

These are a few suggestions that will hopefully help the United Nations to change the attitudes of some of its members. The year 2001 was designated as the Year of Dialogue among Civilizations by the General Assembly. Let us hope that a civil dialogue takes place in the future so that a Huntingtonian "clash of civilizations" can be avoided. Until the attitude of the international community changes, UN reforms will be meaningless.

CONCLUSION

Most of the proposals put forward to reform the United Nations are well-thought-out and will go far in improving the administration, peacekeeping, and effectiveness of the organization. Nevertheless, a major obstacle remains: the reforms do nothing to change the attitudes and prejudices of member states. This is a major oversight. Therefore, there is no reason to believe that the United Nations will operate differently in the future. For lives to be saved and for the organization to be effective, attitudes, especially among the Western states, need to change. This is especially true for the United States where some members of Congress hold the United Nations in contempt. The United Nations cannot be effective without the cooperation of the United States, which needs to combat its neoisolationism, continue to pay its dues, and remember that it is not the world but a vital part of it.

Change is possible. President Clinton and Secretary-General Annan learned from Rwanda, and began to demonstrate a strong commitment that will enable the United Nations to play a vital role in the next millennium. However, in Darfur that effort fell short. Sometimes experience is a hard teacher, but learn we must.

CONCLUSION: GENOCIDE IN THE AGE OF OBAMA

Genocide continues to occur because mankind has not reconciled itself to the differences that exist among people. Differences based on race, aspects of culture, and economic development have led to the development of an international cultural, racial, and economic hierarchy. The human rights of people living in developed western countries are dually protected. Their government and the governments of other developed countries recognize their humanity. If expatriates from developed countries are mistreated abroad, they can seek relief by appealing to the diplomatic corps from their mother country; moreover, they have been extended the protection of international law. International society recognizes them as human beings worthy of its protection. The rights, privileges, and immunities embodied in the UN Charter and the Universal Declaration of Human Rights applies to them.

On the other hand, while international society recognizes the states governed by Third World people, neither their governments, nor international society, have recognized most of the people of the Third World as individuals who are entitled to human rights. European Muslims are the newest members of international society. In the 1990s, action was taken to halt genocide against them in Bosnia and Kosovo. However, no corresponding action was taken to halt genocide against Africans in Rwanda and Darfur. Genocide in Darfur continues unabated. A racist hierarchy of life exists.

International society has sent an explicit message to President Obama that those who look like him are relegated to the bottom of the pyramid and can be destroyed. Obviously, this is unacceptable to him, but how will he respond? So far, he has not. As this is being written, the United States is facing its worst economic crisis since the Great Depression. This has consumed most of his effort, but respond he must.

When Kofi Annan was the secretary-general of the United Nations, he proposed various reforms for the organization (see the list at the end of this chapter). These reforms will appease the United States and its allies, but, unfortunately, they do not go far enough. They do not lay the groundwork to prevent or stop genocide from occurring in the future; therefore, genocide is destined to occur again unless further changes are also initiated.

One of the ideas promoted by this book was reform of the Security Council to reflect the diversity and richness of world cultures. It was assumed that this would also prevent the material interests of the five permanent members from determining whether lives would be sacrificed or spared in Third World countries. It is obvious that this is also not enough to halt genocide.

The tragic events in Darfur mirror those in Bosnia, Rwanda, and Kosovo. These events happened for one reason, and one reason only: the world did not care enough to stop them. It also becomes clear that such tragic events are destined to happen again in the future unless President Obama leads the way and includes all the people of the Third World as members of international society.

What is important is that people, regardless of where they live or what culture they come from, be valued for their intrinsic worth. The United States should take the lead in this process, because it has the operational resources at its disposal to save lives. Unless this happens, the current era of genocide will continue, and we will see hand-wringing in the West instead of action.

We have also been lulled into a state of complicity with the illusion that justice has been done for the victims of genocide. Indictments and sentences have been given to many who were responsible for genocide in recent years. Radovan Karadzic and Radko Mladac have been indicted. Slobodan Milosevic was indicted, but died while in custody. Also, the UN tribunal for war crimes at The Hague issued its final indictment for Ljube Boskovski, Macedonia's former interior minister. It seems as if justice is now being done. But such thinking soils the memories of the victims of genocide. At least, we must remember that they should not have died in the first place, and that many of the deaths could have been prevented if we had only cared enough. If we had only broadened our concept of the national interest to include the preservation of human lives, genocide would not have occurred. In the long run, we need to care about others who are different from ourselves, and note that saving human lives is in the national interest of everyone.

The improvements in mass communication have brought us closer to having a common culture; unfortunately, it has not brought us closer to having a common humanity. As long as there is indifference to human suffering, the spirit of Adolf Hitler lives. Because the United States went to sleep, the age of genocide began at the dawn of the twenty-first century. This nightmare will only end when the United States wakes up.

UN Reforms Proposed by Kofi Annan, the Former Secretary-General

Freedom from Want

- Establishment of a timetable for providing 0.7 percent of gross national income for development by 2015.
- Provide immediate duty-free and quota-free market access for the least developed nations' exports.

Freedom from Fear

- Pledge full compliance with treaties on nuclear nonproliferation and biological and chemical weapons conventions.
- Agree on a definition of terrorism so an antiterrorism convention can be concluded by 2006.
- Request that the Security Council adopt a resolution that defines principles for when force and preemptive action can be used.
- Agree to create a commission for peace-building to help stabilize and develop postconflict societies.

Freedom to Live in Dignity

- Embrace the "responsibility to protect" as a basis for intervention in cases of genocide and crimes against humanity when a government cannot or will not protect its citizens.
- Create a democracy fund to help countries seeking to bolster their democracy.

Strengthen the United Nations

- Reach consensus on how to expand the Security Council to make it more broadly representative of the international community.
- Create a human rights council whose members abide by the highest standards.
- Strengthen international oversight and endorse management reforms to make the Secretariat more accountable, transparent, and efficient.
- Adopt a plan to revitalize the General Assembly by streamlining its agenda, community structure, and debate procedures.[1]

Appendix A

The newspapers listed below were used in the survey in Chapter 5. "Yes" indicates that an edition of a newspaper carried a story on the front page regarding international politics other than Bosnia in 1992, other than Rwanda in 1994, and other than Kosovo in 1998. Similarly, "no" indicates that a newspaper did not carry an international story on its front page other than Bosnia in 1992, Rwanda in 1994, Kosovo in 1998, and Darfur in 2003.

1992

Seattle Post-Intelligencer: January 15 (no), February 17 (no), March 30 (no), April 18 (no), May 22 (no), June 8 (no), July 16 (no), August 7 (no), September 19 (no), October 14 (no), November 21 (yes), and December 3 (no).

Detroit Free Press: January 30 (yes), February 19 (no), March 21 (no), April 17 (no), May 14 (no), June 25 (no), July 24 (no), August 17 (yes), September 4 (no), October 19 (no), November 24 (no), and December 11 (yes).

Houston Chronicle: January 24 (yes), February 4 (yes), March 16 (yes), April 19 (no), May 22 (yes), June 20 (no), July 30 (no), August 27 (yes), September 2 (no), October 24 (no), November 7 (no), and December 5 (yes).

Portland Oregonian: January 1 (no), February 19 (no), March 7 (no), April 13 (no), May 19 (no), June 5 (no), July 17 (no), August 13 (no), September 14 (no), October 1 (no), November 28 (no), and December 19 (no).

Austin American Statesman: January 3 (no), February 21 (yes), March 21 (no), April 24 (yes), May 17 (no), June 5 (yes), July 15 (yes), August 8 (yes), September 10 (no), October 16 (no), November 21 (no), and December 3 (no).

Chicago Sun Times: January 16 (yes), February 5 (no), March 22 (no), April 21 (no), May 30 (no), June 7 (no), July 4 (no), August 15 (no), September 16 (no), October 1 (no), November 16 (no), and December 11 (no).

Worcester Telegram: January 2 (yes), February 20 (no), March 6 (no), April 23 (no), May 10 (no), June 26 (no), July 21 (yes), August 30 (no), September 19 (no), October 4 (no), November 1 (no), and December 29 (yes).

Tulsa World: January 27 (yes), February 20 (no), March 17 (no), April 3 (no), March 22 (no), June 11 (no), July 1 (no), August 11 (no), September 16 (yes), October 25 (no), November 3 (no), and December 26 (no).

Arizona Star: January 19 (no), February 20 (no), March 1 (no), April 14 (no), May 23 (no), June 1 (no), July 18 (no), August 20 (no), September 10 (no), October 26 (no), November 2 (no), and December 30 (no).

Philadelphia Inquirer: January 5 (no), February 4 (no), March 16 (no), April 5 (no), May 9 (yes), June 1 (yes), July 26 (yes), August 5 (yes), September 1 (no), October 9 (yes), and December 25 (no).

1994

The Buffalo News: January 26 (yes), February 1 (no), March 29 (yes), April 20 (yes), May 28 (yes), June 14 (yes), July 31 (yes), August 18 (yes), September 21 (yes), October 25 (yes), November 1 (no), and December 2 (yes).

The Pittsburgh Post-Gazette: January 3 (yes), February 21 (yes), March 6 (no), April 8 (yes), May 12 (yes), June 5 (yes), July 18 (yes), August 5 (yes), September 6 (yes), October 3 (yes), November 17 (no), and December 21 (no).

Akron Beacon: January 16 (yes), February 26 (yes), March 9 (no), April 24 (yes), May 31 (no), June 3 (yes), July 26 (yes), August 18 (no), September 30 (yes), October 19 (no), November 14 (yes), and December 6 (no).

The Pantagraph: January 7 (no), February 3 (no), March 22 (no), April 4 (no), May 1 (no), June 19 (no), July 25 (no), August 20 (yes), September 11 (no), October 17 (yes), November 19 (yes), and December 21 (no).

Denver Post: January 23 (no), February 21 (yes), March 28 (no), April 19 (no), May 14 (no), June 17 (no), July 12 (yes), August 8 (no), September 30 (no), October 5 (no), November 22 (yes), and December 20 (yes).

The Press-Enterprise: January 17 (no), February 4 (no), March 12 (no), April 13 (no), May 16 (no), June 1 (no), July 16 (no), August 27 (no), September 19 (yes), October 18 (no), November 15 (no), and December 4 (no).

Miami Herald: January 3 (no), February 17 (no), March 28 (yes), April 27 (yes), May 29 (yes), June 4 (yes), July 22 (yes), August 6 (yes), September 24 (yes), October 3 (yes), November 8 (yes), and December 15 (yes).

Raleigh News Observer: January 1 (no), February 11 (no), March 3 (no), April 19 (no), May 8 (no), June 12 (no), July 17 (no), August 31 (no), September 5 (no), October 16 (no), November 8 (no), and December 20 (no).

Wichita Falls Eagle: January 23 (no), February 14 (no), March 19 (yes), April 24 (no), May 7 (yes), June 26 (no), July 2 (yes), August 14 (no), September 5 (yes), October 12 (yes), November 3 (no), and December 21 (no).

Birmingham News: January 18 (no), February 9 (no), March 5 (no), April 2 (no), May 28 (no), June 12 (no), July 20 (no), August 5 (no), October 13 (yes), November 9 (no), and December 6 (no).

1998

Sarasota Herald: January 30 (yes), February 4 (no), March 10 (no), April 12 (no), May 21 (no), June 7 (no), July 5 (no), August 17 (yes), September 22 (yes), October 19 (no), November 4 (no), and December 6 (no).

Dallas Morning News: January 9 (no), February 8 (no), March 13 (no), April 10 (yes), May 5 (yes), June 19 (yes), July 4 (yes), August 22 (yes), September 30 (yes), October 26 (yes), November 15 (yes), and December 23 (no).

San Jose Mercury News: January 13 (yes), February 23 (yes), March 26 (no), April 29 (no), May 8 (yes), June 14 (yes), July 2 (yes), August 13 (yes), September 2 (yes), October 14 (no), November 2 (yes), and December 6 (no).

Long Beach Press Telegram: January 29 (no), February 21 (no), March 20 (no), April 9 (no), May 13 (no), June 1 (yes), July 10 (no), August 19 (no), September 12 (no), October 5 (no), November 23 (yes), and December 28 (no).

Providence Journal: January 12 (no), February 10 (no), March 21 (no), April 5 (no), May 13 (no), June 21 (no), July 2 (no), August 4 (no), September 3 (no), October 20 (no), November 10 (no), and December 2 (no).

Boston Globe: January 16 (yes), February 14 (no), March 10 (no), April 21 (yes), May 12 (yes), June 26 (yes), July 18 (yes), August 25 (yes), September 27 (no), October 8 (no), November 17 (yes), and December 6 (yes).

Cincinnati Post: January 6 (no), February 7 (no), March 14 (no), April 4 (no), May 1 (no), June 29 (yes), July 2 (no), August 17 (yes), September 25 (no), October 7 (no), November 2 (no), and December 11 (no).

Minneapolis Star Tribune: December 17 (no), January 17 (yes), February 8 (no), March 19 (no), April 25 (no), May 28 (yes), June 2 (no), July 23 (no), August 3 (no), September 1 (no), October 21 (no), and November 4 (no).

Tampa Tribune: January 14 (no), February 20 (no), March 3 (no), April 9 (no), May 16 (yes), June 24 (no), July 10 (no), August 15 (yes), September 5 (no), October 11 (no), November 26 (no), and December 10 (no).

Washington Post: January 3 (yes), February 29 (yes), March 6 (no), April 15 (yes), May 9 (yes), June 6 (no), July 1 (yes), August 18 (yes), September 28 (yes), October 20 (yes), November 7 (yes), and December 22 (yes).

2003

Atlanta Journal-Constitution: January 25 (no), February 10 (yes), March 16 (no), April 7 (yes), May 23 (yes), June 29 (yes), July 1 (yes), August 19 (no), September 23 (yes), October 18 (yes), November 19 (no), and December 15 (yes).

Boston Herald: January 22 (no), February 27 (no), March 3 (yes), April 14 (no), May 2 (no), June 18 (no), July 23 (no), August 4 (no), September 11 (no), October 12 (no), November 6 (no), and December 13 (no).

Charleston Post & Courier: January 20 (no), February 23 (no), March 28 (no), April 1 (no), May 13 (no), June 4 (no), July 17 (yes), August 1 (no), September 21 (no), October 6 (no), November 12 (no), and December 7 (no).

Cedar Rapids Gazette: January 31 (no), February 27 (no), March 5 (no), April 10 (yes), May 17 (no), June 18 (no), July 22 (no), August 19 (no), September 1 (no), October 26 (no), November 20 (yes), and December 28 (no).

New York Daily News: January 27 (no), February 3 (no), March 29 (no), April 15 (no), May 23 (no), June 17 (no), July 7 (no), August 2 (no), September 9 (no), October 6 (no), November 28 (no), and December 4 (no).

Richmond Times: January 18 (yes), February 13 (no), March 19 (no), April 1 (no), May 30 (no), June 23 (no), July 2 (no), August 18 (no), September 15 (no), October 8 (no), November 10 (no), and December 7 (no).

St. Louis Post: January 2 (yes), February 13 (yes), March 22 (no), April 9 (yes), May 18 (yes), June 2 (yes), July 20 (yes), August 5 (yes), September 24 (yes), October 8 (no), November 29 (yes), and December 30 (yes).

San Diego Union: January 4 (yes), February 8 (yes), March 22 (yes), April 21 (yes), May 10 (yes), June 6 (yes), July 31 (yes), August 8 (yes), September 26 (yes), October 17 (yes), November 7 (yes), and December 20 (yes).

San Francisco Chronicle: January 1 (yes), February 25 (no), March 8 (yes), April 28 (yes), May 14 (no), June 9 (no), July 26 (no), August 17 (no), September 25 (no), October 22 (no), November 18 (no), and December 15 (yes).

Union Leader: January 6 (no), February 1 (no), March 23 (no), April 11 (no), May 31 (no), June 28 (no), July 4 (no), August 20 (no), September 23 (no), October 30 (no), November 18 (no), and December 3 (no).

Appendix B

Listed below are the names of individuals and the positions they held in the Sudanese government in 2004 when they supervised and controlled the activities of the Janjaweed. Therefore, the following individuals are responsible for the genocide in Darfur:

> Ali Osman Taha, the first vice president; Major General Salah Abdallah Ghosh, the director general, Government of Sudan Security; Dr. Nafie Ali Nafie, the former external intelligence chief; Major General Al Tayeb Mohanmed Hheir, the presidential security advisor; Abdalhamid Musa Kasa, the minister of commerce; Abdalrahim Mohammed Hussein, the minister of interior; Major General Adam Hamid Musa, the governor of southern Darfur; Brigadier Mohamed Ahmed Ali, the Riot Police director, who led police attacks on internally displaced persons at Mayo Camp right out in Khartoum in mid-March; Mohamed Yousef Abdala, the Humanitarian Affairs state minister; and Abdella Safi el Nur, the cabinet minister and the general coordinator of Janjaweed are guilty, along with members of the Command and Coordinating Council of the Janjaweed such as Lieutenant Colonel Sukeirtalah, the leader of Janjaweed-Geneina; Ahmed Mohammed Harun, a commander and the state minister of the interior; Osman Yusif Kibir, the governor of Darfur; El Tahir Hassan Abbud, National Congress Party (NCP); Mohammed Salih Al Sunusi Baraka, a member of the National Assembly; Mohammed Yusif El Tilet, a minister of the Western Darfur state; and Major General Hussein Abdalla Jibril, a member of the National Assembly.

In the field command, the following individuals are responsible for genocide:

> Brigadier Musa Hilal; Brigadier Hamid Dhawai; Brigadier Abdal Wahid, Kabkabiya sector; Brigadier Mohammed Ibrahim Ginesto; Major Hussein Tangos; and Major Omer Baabas.[1]

Notes

Introduction

1. Ali A. Mazrui, *The African Condition* (New York: Cambridge University Press, 1980), 23–45.
2. Basil Davidson, *The Story of Africa* (London: Mitchell Beazley, 1984), 219.
3. Steven L. Spiegel, *World Politics in a New Era* (Fort Worth: Harcourt Brace College Publishers, 1995); and Ali A. Mazrui, *The African Condition* (New York: Cambridge University Press, 1980), 23–398.
4. Glenn P. Hastedt and Kay Knickrehm, *Dimensions of World Politics* (New York: Harper Collins Publishers, 1991), 397.
5. See John F. Kennedy, *Why England Slept* (New York: Doubleday and Company, 1961).
6. *Washington Post National Weekly Edition*, September 6, 1999.

Chapter 1

1. Dale C. Tatum, *Who Influenced Whom?: Lessons from the Cold War* (Lanham, MD: University Press of America, 2002), 57–97.
2. Tatum, "Preaching Smith but Practicing Keynes," *Peace Review*, vol. 8, no. 12 (April–June 2006): 241.
3. Samuel P. Huntington, "Clash of Civilizations," *Foreign Affairs* (Summer 1993).
4. Ali A. Mazrui, *The Africans: A Triple Heritage* (Boston: Little Brown and Company, 1983), 181.
5. Omari H. Kokole, "STABEX Anatomized," *Third World Quarterly*, vol. 3, no. 3 (July 1981): 687–702.
6. See Ali A. Mazrui, *Cultural Forces in World Politics* (Portsmouth, NH: Heinemann, 1990), 67–82.
7. Charles Hugh Smith, "Arab Oil Money and U.S. Treasury Bonds: Quid Pro Quo?," available at http://www.oftwominds.com/blogs/quidproquo.html (accessed on October 10, 2005).
8. Tatum, "Preaching Smith but Practicing Keynes," 239.

CHAPTER 2

1. See Robert Sheer, *With Enough Shovels: Reagan, Bush, and Nuclear War* (New York: Random House, 1982).
2. Theodore C. Sorensen, *Kennedy* (New York: Harper & Row Publishers, 1965), 245.
3. President George W. Bush, President's Daily Briefing, "Bin Laden Determined to Strike in U.S.," August 6, 2001, declassified April 10, 2004.
4. *Public Papers of the Presidents: George W. Bush—2005,* vol. 1 (Washington, DC: Government Printing Office, 2006), 66.
5. President George W. Bush, "Remarks to the American Jewish Committee," May 14, 2001, *Public Papers of the Presidents: George W. Bush,* vol. 1 (Washington, DC: Government Printing Office, 2002), 487.
6. "Transcript: Vice Presidential Debate," Case Western Reserve University, Cleveland, Ohio, October 5, 2004, from *Washington Post,* October 6, 2004.
7. United Nations Security Council, "Report of the International Commission of Inquiry on Darfur to the United Nations Secretary-General," Geneva, January 25, 2005.
8. Kofi Annan, "Lessons of the Iraq War Underscore Importance of UN Charter—Annan," September 16, 2004 (New York: UN News Center, United Nations).

CHAPTER 3

1. *Judgement at Nuremburg,* directed by Stanley Kramer (United Artists, 1961).
2. One who commits genocide.

CHAPTER 4

1. See William J. Durch, ed., *The Evolution of UN Peacekeeping* (New York: St. Martin's Press, 1993).
2. *The Universal Almanac 1995* (Kansas City, MO: Universal Press Syndicate Company, 1994), 489.
3. Alain Destexhe, *Rwanda and Genocide in the Twentieth Century* (New York: New York University Press, 1995), 40.
4. Gerard Prunier, *The Rwanda Crisis: History of a Genocide* (New York: Columbia University Press, 1995), 7.
5. Destexhe, op. cit.
6. Ibid.
7. Ibid.
8. Arthur Jay Klinghoffer, *The International Dimension of Genocide in Rwanda* (New York: New York University Press, 1998), 6.

9. Destexhe, op. cit., 43; and Ali A. Mazrui, *A World Federation of Cultures: An African Perspective* (New York: The Free Press, 1976), 57.
10. Human Rights Watch, "The Organization," *Leave None to Tell the Story,* available at http://www.hrw.org/en/reports/1999/03/01/leave-none-tell-story.
11. Ibid., 3–4.
12. Ibid., 8.
13. David B. Guralnik, ed., *Webster's New World Dictionary of the American Language* (New York: Simon and Schuster, 1960), 582.
14. Ali A. Mazrui, *Cultural Forces in World Politics* (Portsmouth, NH: Heinemann, 1990), 55–56.
15. "Letter to Congressional Leaders on Evacuation of United States Citizens in Rwanda," *Public Papers of the Presidents: Administration of William J. Clinton*, Vol. I (Washington, DC: Government Printing Office, 1996), 678.
16. "Ignoring Genocide," *Leave None to Tell the Story*, op. cit., 9–10.
17. "Radio Address on the Situation in Rwanda," *Public Papers of the Presidents: Administration of William J. Clinton*, op. cit., 807.
18. *USA Today*, May 31, 1994.
19. "Ignoring Genocide," op. cit., 2.
20. United Nations Security Council Resolution 912, adopted on April 21, 1994, at its 3,336th Meeting.
21. Destexhe, op. cit., ix.
22. Ibid.; and Scott R. Feil, *Preventing Genocide in Rwanda: How the Early Use of Force Might Have Succeeded in Rwanda* (New York: Carnegie Corporation, 1998), 1, 3.
23. Klinghoffer, op. cit., 91.
24. Destexhe, op. cit., 50; Prunier, op. cit., 96–97.
25. Destexhe, op. cit.
26. *The New York Times*, May 12, 1994.
27. Prunier, op. cit., 91.
28. *The New York Times*, May 21, 1994.
29. *The New York Times*, May 25, 1994.
30. *The New York Times*, May 21, 1994.
31. United Nations Security Council Resolution 918, adopted on May 17, 1994, at its 3,377th Meeting.
32. *The New York Times*, June 1, 1994.
33. *The New York Times*, June 10, 1994.
34. United Nations General Assembly, "Convention on the Prevention and Punishment of the Crime of Genocide," December 9, 1948, A/RES/260.
35. Ibid.
36. Ibid.
37. "Statement on the Closing of the Embassy in Rwanda," *Public Papers of the Presidents: Administration of William J. Clinton*, op. cit., 1257.

38. Interview on CNN's "Global Forum with President Clinton," May 3, 1994, *Public Papers of the Presidents: Administration of William J. Clinton*, op. cit., 830.
39. United Nations Security Council Resolution 929, adopted on June 22, 1994, at its 3,392nd Meeting.
40. *Africa South of the Sahara 1999* (London: Europa Publications Limited, 1998), 850; *The New York Times*, July 5, 1994.
41. *The New York Times*, op. cit.
42. Remarks by Henry Hyde in the House of Representatives, Wednesday, January 26, 1994, *Congressional Record*, Vol. 144 (Washington, DC: Government Printing Office, 1994): HR3744.
43. Remarks by Robert J. Dole, Wednesday, January 26, 1994, 103rd Congress, 2nd Session, *Congressional Record*, Vol. 140, (Washington, DC: Government Printing Office, 1994): S180.
44. Ibid.
45. Remarks by John L. Mica, U.S. House of Representatives, Wednesday, May 18, 1994, 103rd Congress, 2nd Session, *Congressional Record*, Vol. 140, op. cit., H3530.
46. Remarks placed in the *Congressional Record* by Connie Morella, U.S. House of Representatives, Tuesday, May 24, 1994, 103rd Congress, 2nd Session, *Congressional Record*, Vol. 140, op. cit., H3904.
47. Remarks by Paul Simon, U.S. Senate, Tuesday, April 26, 1994, 103rd Congress, 2nd Session, *Congressional Record*, Vol. 140, op. cit., S4900.
48. Remarks by Daniel P. Moyhihan, U.S. Senate, Friday, June 10, 1994, 103rd Congress, 2nd Session, *Congressional Record*, Vol. 140, op. cit., S6791.
49. Remarks by David Durenburger, U.S. Senate, Thursday, June 16, 1994, 103rd Congress, 2nd Session, *Congressional Record*, Vol. 140, op. cit., S7052.
50. Quoted in *The New York Times,* May 25, 1994.
51. "Ignoring Genocide," op. cit., 16.
52. "Request for Protection of Informant," Cable from General Dallaire, UNAMIR to New York.
53. *The New York Times*, March 26, 1998.
54. John F. Kennedy, *Why England Slept* (New York: Doubleday and Company, 1961), 26.

CHAPTER 5

1. "Bosnia-Hon. Steny H. Hoyer (Extension of Remarks-September 23, 1993)," in *Congressional Record*, vol. 139, September 23, 1993 (Washington, DC: Government Printing Office, 1993): E2246.
2. The administration of President George Herbert Walker Bush will be referred to as the Bush I administration, given the selection of his son

George Walker Bush by the Supreme Court in 2000. The administration of George Walker Bush will be referred to as the Bush II administration in subsequent chapters.

3. The term generation VIII refers to the eighth generation since the American Revolutionary War.
4. The term generation IX refers to the ninth generation since the American Revolutionary War.
5. Out There News, "Bosnia: Can You Blame History," available at http://www.outtherenews.com (accessed on June 7, 2000).
6. *Boston Globe*, May 3, 1995.
7. Degos D. Kostich, *The Land and Peoples of the Balkans* (Philadelphia: J.B. Lippincott Company, 1962), 106.
8. Susan L. Woodward, *Balkan Tragedy* (Washington, DC: The Brookings Institute, 1995), 37.
9. Ibid., 48.
10. Ibid., 51.
11. Laura Silber and Allan Little, *Yugoslavia: Death of a Nation* (New York: Penguin Books, 1997), 31.
12. Clinton Rossiter, ed., *The Federalist Papers* (New York: Mentor Books, 1961).
13. Laura Silber and Allan Little, op. cit., 209–10.
14. Ibid., 128; and Misha Glenny, *The Fall of Yugoslavia: Third Balkan War* (New York: Penguin Books, 1996), 60.
15. Laura Silber and Allan Little, op. cit., 86.
16. Misha Glenny, op. cit., 154; Silber and Little, op. cit., 208.
17. Glenny, op. cit., 154.
18. Silber and Little, op. cit., 209.
19. Silber and Little, op. cit., 212–13.
20. Woodward, op. cit., 216; Glenny, op. cit., 142; and Silber and Little, op. cit., 86, 208.
21. Silber and Little, op. cit., 86.
22. Woodward, op. cit., 136.
23. David B. Guralnik, ed., *Webster's New World Dictionary* (New York: Simon and Schuster, 1984), 1175.
24. Glenny, op. cit., 151.
25. Tim Kidder, Elizabeth Terney, Rachel Whittaker, and Hilary Young, "A War Torn Region: Bosnia-Herzegovina, Croatia, and Yugoslavia," April 25, 1997, available at http://www.earlham.edu/~pols/ps17971/terneel/rape.html.
26. Adil Kulenovic, "Interview With Vladimir Srebrov, a founding member of the Serb Democratic Party," *Vereme* (Belgrade), October 30, 1995.
27. *Croatian Herald*, July 28, 1992.
28. Ali A. Mazrui, *A World Federation of Cultures* (New York: The Free Press, 1976), 212.
29. *Newsday*, August 2, 1992.

30. Ibid.
31. Ibid.
32. Silber and Little, op. cit., 248.
33. David Rohde, *Endgame* (Boulder, CO: Westview, 1998), 200.
34. Gail Armstrong and Patricia Forestier, "Ending the Balkan Nightmare," *Freedom Magazine*, vol. 31, issue 2: 15.
35. Mazrui, op. cit., 57.
36. Keith Doubt, *Sociology after Bosnia and Kosovo: Recovering Justice* (Lanham, Maryland: Roman and Littlefield, 2000), 19.
37. Glenny, op. cit., 45–60; Silber and Little, op. cit., 119–32.
38. Associated Press, July 24, 1993.
39. Woodward, op. cit., 27.
40. Glenny, op. cit., 134.
41. Ibid., 151.
42. Silber and Little, op. cit., 201.
43. Ibid., 150–52.
44. *Boston Globe*, October 22, 1992.
45. Alan Fogelquist, "How the War Started," available at http://sadik.net/bosnia/start.html.
46. *Boston Globe*, August 10, 1992.
47. *Congressional Record,* Senate, July 24, 1992, vol. 138 (Washington, DC: Government Printing Office, 1992): S10282.
48. *Congressional Record*, Senate, June 11, 1992, vol. 138, op. cit., S8118.
49. *Congressional Record*, Senate, June 4, 1992, vol. 138, op. cit., S7575.
50. *Congressional Record*, Senate, April 29, 1992, vol. 138, op. cit., S5815.
51. *Congressional Record*, House of Representatives, May 21, 1992, vol. 138, op. cit., E1509.
52. *Congressional Record*, House of Representatives, June 16, 1992, vol. 138, op. cit., H4745.
53. *Congressional Record*, House of Representatives, July 8, 1992, vol. 138, op. cit., H6142.
54. *Congressional Record*, Senate, August 11, 1992, vol. 138, op. cit., S12107.
55. Robert S. Hirschfield, ed., *The Power of the Presidency: Concepts and Controversy* (Chicago: Aldine Transaction, 1973), 201.
56. *The New York Times,* April 8, 1993.
57. *U.S. News and World Report*, August 2, 1993.
58. *New York Times*, September 28, 1992.
59. Ibid.
60. *Wall Street Journal*, May 13, 1993.
61. "The President's News Conference," June 17, 1993, *Public Papers of the Presidents: William J. Clinton—1993*, vol. 1, 869.
62. "The President's News Conference," April 23, 1993, *Public Papers of the Presidents: William J. Clinton—1993*, vol. 1, 484.
63. Ivo H. Daadler, *Getting to Dayton* (Washington, DC: The Brookings Institute, 2000), 5–36.

64. Silber and Little, op. cit., 331.
65. "Interview With Foreign Journalist," July 2, 1993, *Public Papers of the Presidents: William J. Clinton—1993*, vol. 1, 989.
66. *Congressional Record*, Senate, May 19, 1993, vol. 139 (Washington, DC: Government Printing Office, 1993), S6071.
67. "Interview With the Italian Media," May 27, 1994, *Public Papers of the President of the United States: William J. Clinton—1994*, vol. 1 (Washington, DC: Government Printing Office, 1995), 1000.
68. Woodward, op. cit., 312.
69. Harry S. Truman, "Presidential Power," speech given on May 8, 1954, in New York, NY, speaking as a guest of honor on his birthday.
70. U.S. Senate Select Committee on Intelligence, "U.S. Actions Regarding Iranian and Other Arms Transfers to the Bosnian Army, 1994–1995, *Report of the Select Committee on Intelligence*, United States Senate together with Additional Views," November 1–22, 1996; and Christopher Cox, Chairman, House Republican Policy Committee Policy Perspective, "Clinton Vetoed Congress' Bill to Help Bosnia While Encouraging Iran to Do So, Instead Giving Iran a Foothold in Europe," April 26, 1996, available at http://www.fas.org/irp/news/1996/hrpc_iranalt.htm.
71. *Boston Globe*, November 30, 1994.
72. *Congressional Record*, Senate, July 29, 1992, vol. 138, op. cit., S10556.
73. *Congressional Record*, Senate, June 29, 1993, vol. 139, S8208.
74. *Congressional Record*, Senate, June 6, 1995, vol. 141 (Washington, DC: Government Printing Office, 1995), S7743–S7746; and *Boston Globe*, June 7, 1995.
75. *Congressional Record*, Senate, June 7, 1995, vol. 141, op. cit., S7880.
76. "Statement by President Clinton on Veto of Lifting of Bosnia Arms Embargo," August 11, 1995, The White House, Office of the Press Secretary, *Public Papers of the President of the United States: William J. Clinton—1995*, vol. 2 (Washington, DC: Government Printing Office, 1996), 1254.
77. *Boston Globe*, April 28, 1993.
78. This plan was referred to as the Invincible Plan because it was negotiated aboard the HMS Invincible in 1993. The plan called for the division of Bosnia into three regions among the Serbs, Croats, and Muslims of Bosnia-Herzegovina.
79. *Wall Street Journal*, December 17, 1991.
80. Silber and Little, op. cit., 310.
81. Rohde, op. cit., passim, 204–15.
82. *The New York Times*, August 4, 1992.
83. *Newsweek*, June 6, 1995.

CHAPTER 6

1. See Noel Malcolm, *Kosovo: A Short History* (New York: New York University Press, 1998); and Miranda Vickers, *Between Serb and Albanian: A History of Kosovo* (New York: Columbia University Press, 1998).
2. Malcolm, op. cit., 85.
3. Ibid., 73.
4. Malcolm, op. cit., 131–34; Vickers, op. cit., 24–25.
5. Ibid., 130.
6. Ibid., 253–54; Vickers, op. cit., 77.
7. Malcolm, op. cit., 258.
8. Vickers, op. cit., 93.
9. See Chapter 5 on Bosnia for more details.
10. Vickers, op. cit., xiii.
11. Malcolm, op. cit., 267.
12. Snezzana Trifunovska, *Yugoslavia through Documents: From Its Creation to Dissolution* (Dordrecht: Martinus Nijhoff Publishers, 1994), 212.
13. Ibid.
14. Vickers, op. cit., 146.
15. For details on Tito's break with the Soviet Union, see Chapter VIII of Dale C. Tatum, *Who Influenced Whom?: Lessons from the Cold War* (Lanham, MD: University Press of America, 2002).
16. Julie A. Mertus, *Kosovo: How Myths and Truths Started a War* (Berkeley, CA: University of California Press, 1999), 68.
17. Ibid., 70.
18. Ibid., 20.
19. Malcolm, op. cit., 337.
20. Peter R. Prifti, *Confrontation in Kosova: The Albanian Serb Struggle, 1969–1999* (Boulder, CO: Eastern European Monograph Series, 1999), 56
21. Mertus, op. cit., 46.
22. Laura Silber and Allan Little, *Yugoslavia: Death of a Nation* (New York: Penguin Books, 1997), 38.
23. Ibid.
24. Tim Judah, *Kosovo: War and Revenge* (New Haven, CT: Yale University Press, 2000), 50.
25. Silber and Little, op. cit., 72.
26. Vickers, op. cit., 248.
27. Carole Rogel, *The Breakup of Yugoslavia and Its Aftermath* (Westport, CT: Greenwood Press, 2004), 77.
28. *The New York Times*, December 28, 1992; *Washington Post*, April 18, 1999.
29. UN General Assembly, "The Convention on the Prevention and Punishment of the Crime of Genocide," December 9, 1948, A/RES/260.
30. *Washington Post*, June 28, 1999.
31. "Questioning Kosovo," The Pew Research Center, May 14, 1999.

32. The constitutionality of the War Powers Resolution is questionable. In *INS v. Chadha* (1983), the U.S. Supreme Court ruled that Congress cannot compel the executive branch to take action by passing a concurrent resolution, because it violates the system of checks and balances.
33. See Honorable C.W. Bill Young, "The Republic of Hungary and the Republic of Bosnia and Herzegovina," March 19, 1998, House of Representatives, Extensions, *Congressional Record*, vol. 144 (Washington, DC: Government Printing Office, 1998): E421–E422.
34. Honorable Judd Gregg, "Kosovo," April 20, 1999, Senate, *Congressional Record*, vol. 145 (Washington, DC: Government Printing Office, 1999): S3893.
35. Romeo Dallaire, *Shake Hands With the Devil: The Failure of Humanity in Rwanda* (New York: Carol & Graf Publishers, 2005), 522.
36. Honorable Joseph Biden, "Resolution of the Kosovo Problem," June 17, 1998, Senate, *Congressional Record*, vol. 144, op. cit., S64463.
37. The Honorable Chuck Hagel, "United States Foreign Policy," September 30, 1999, Senate, *Congressional Record*, vol. 145 (Washington, DC: Government Printing Office, 1999): S11143.
38. "Peacekeeping Operations in Kosovo Resolution," March 11, 1999, House, *Congressional Record*, vol. 145, op. cit., H1184.
39. Honorable James Inhofe, "The Kosovo Quagmire," March 23, 1999, Senate, *Congressional Record*, vol. 145, op. cit., S3094.
40. Thomas Hobbes, *The Leviathan: Or the Matter, Forme and Power of a Commonwealth Ecclesiasticall and Civil* (New York: Collier Books, 1968), 136.
41. United Nations International Law Commission, Second Session, "The Principles of the Nuremberg Tribunal, 1950," June 5–July 29, 1950, Document A/1316.
42. Ibid.
43. Remarks to the Regional Federal Officials, October 27, 1998, *Public Papers of the Presidents: William J. Clinton*, vol. 2 (Washington, DC: Government Printing Office, 1999), 1880.
44. John F. Kennedy, *Why England Slept* (New York: Doubleday and Company, 1961), 17–18.

CHAPTER 7

1. These remarks were delivered at the Darfur Emergency Summit at the Graduate Center of the City University of New York, July 14, 2004. The summit was sponsored by the American World Jewish Congress and the U.S. Holocaust Memorial Museum.
2. A failed state is defined as one that is unwilling to cope or seek a solution to its problems, and uses a portion of its population as scapegoats to gain some legitimacy among a segment of the population.

3. Fergus Nicholl, "Three Empires on the Nile: Ismail Pasha, General Gordon, The Mahdi and Lord Kitchner in Peter," in *The Kenna Handbook of Sudan,* ed. Peter Gwynvay Hopkins (London: Kegan Paul, 2007), 126.
4. Ann Mosley Leach, *Sudan: Contested National Identities*(Bloomington, IN: Indiana University Press, 1998), 29.
5. Ibid., 15.
6. Amir H. Idris, *Conflict and Politics of Identity in Sudan* (New York: Palgrave Macmillan, 2005), 34.
7. Ibid., 28; and Gerard Prunier, *Darfur: The Ambiguous Genocide* (Ithaca, NY: Cornell University Press, 2005), 4–5.
8. Prunier, op. cit., 4.
9. Douglass H. Johnson, *The Root Cause of Sudan's Civil Wars* (Oxford: James Curry, 2004), 3.
10. See David Easton, *A Systems Analysis of Political Life* (New York: John Wiley and Sons, 1965); David Easton, *A Framework of Political Analysis* (Englewood Cliffs, NJ: Prentice-Hall, 1965); Karl W. Deutsch, *The Nerves of Government: Models of Political Communication and Control* (New York, NY: The Free Press of Glencoe, 1963); and Gabriel Almond and G. Bingham Powell, eds., *Comparative Politics Today: A World View* (New York: Longman, 1996).
11. Johnson, op. cit., 3.
12. See Dale C. Tatum, "Preaching Smith but Practicing Keynes," *Peace Review*, vol. 18, no. 2 (April–June 2006): 237–43.
13. Norman Anderson, *Sudan in Crisis: The Failure of Democracy* (Gainesville, FL: University Press of Florida, 1999), x, 7.
14. Lesch, op. cit., 5.
15. Jerome Tubiana, "Darfur: A Conflict for Land?," in *War in Darfur: And the Search for Peace*, ed. Alex de Waal (London: Global Equity Initiative, 2007), 70.
16. Johnson, op. cit., 3.
17. *The Observer*, August 1, 2004.
18. Tubiana, op. cit., 77.
19. Ibid., 74.
20. Prunier, op. cit., 50.
21. Professor David Hoile, "Darfur in Perspective," available at www.darfurinperspective.com.
22. Richard Lobban, "The Three Towns of Sudan," in de Waal, op. cit., 8.
23. Prunier, op. cit., 92–93, 107.
24. Albert Memmi, *The Colonizer and the Colonized* (Boston: Beacon, 1965), 52.
25. Ibid., 91.
26. United Nations Security Council, "Report of the International Inquiry to the United Nations Secretary General," Geneva, January 25, 2005.

27. UN General Assembly, "The Convention on the Prevention and Punishment of the Crime of Genocide," December 9, 1948, A/RES/260.
28. United Nations, "Report of the International Commission of Inquiry on Darfur to the United Nations Secretary-General," January 25, 2005, 56.
29. Ibid., 63.
30. Ibid., 65.
31. Ibid., 84.
32. Ibid.
33. Ibid., 74.
34. Amnesty International, "Sudan: Arms Continuing to Fuel Serious Human Rights Violations in Darfur," AFR/019/2007, 5–6.
35. Ibid., 7.
36. Ibid., 15.
37. Ibid., 16.
38. "Report," op. cit., 63–64.
39. "Sudan," op. cit., 8.
40. *Los Angeles Times*, January 9, 2008.
41. "Report Confirms Sudan's Use of Slavery," June 7, 2002, House of Representatives, *Congressional Record*, vol. 148 (Washington, DC: Government Printing Office, 2002): E1002.
42. *Sudanese Peace Act*, Public Law 107-245-October 21, 2002.
43. Honorable Frank R. Wolf, "Stop the Killing in Sudan," April 2, 2004, [Extensions], House of Representatives, *Congressional Record*, vol. 150 (Washington, DC: Government Printing Office, 2004): E518.
44. Prunier, op. cit., 133.
45. Honorable John McCain, May 6, 2004, Executive Session, Senate, *Congressional Record*, vol. 150, op. cit., S4969.
46. Honorable Frank R. Wolf, "Genocide in Sudan," June 8, 2004, [Extensions], House of Representatives, *Congressional Record*, vol. 150, op. cit., E1070.
47. Ibid.
48. Honorable Richard Durbin, "Conflict in Sudan," May 17, 2004, Senate, *Congressional Record*, vol. 150, op. cit., S5530–S5531.
49. Honorable Joseph Biden, "Responding to the Crisis in Darfur," July 20, 2004, *Congressional Record*, vol. 150, op. cit., S8447.
50. Honorable Thomas G. Tancredo, "Declaring Genocide in Darfur, Sudan," *Congressional Record*, vol. 150, op. cit., H6526.
51. Honorable Frank R. Wolf, "Documenting the Atrocities in Darfur," September 9, 2004, [Extensions], House of Representatives, *Congressional Record*, vol. 150, op. cit., E1577.
52. Honorable Charles B. Rangel, "Assisting the Peacekeeping Effort in Darfur," November 17, 2004, [Extensions], House of Representatives, *Congressional Record*, vol. 150, op. cit., E2031.
53. Ibid.

54. "Comprehensive Peace in Sudan Act of 2004," November 19, 2004, House of Representatives, *Congressional Record*, vol. 150, op. cit., H10035.
55. March 2, 2005, Senate, *Congressional Record*, vol. 151 (Washington, DC: Government Printing Office, 2005), S1939.
56. Honorable Frank R. Wolf, "The War in Darfur," February 9, 2005, [Extensions], House of Representatives, *Congressional Record*, vol. 151, op. cit., E201.
57. Ibid., E202.
58. "The Crisis in Darfur," December 8, 2005, House of Representatives, *Congressional Record*, vol. 151, op. cit., H11224.
59. Honorable Charles B. Rangel, "United States Executive Action on Darfur: More is Needed," May 5, 2005, [Extensions], House of Representatives, *Congressional Record*, vol. 151, op. cit., E887.
60. Rebecca Hamilton and Chad Hazlet, "'Not on Our Watch': The Emergence of the American Movement for Darfur," in de Waal, op. cit., 350.
61. Ibid., 350–51.
62. Honorable Jerrold Nedler, "Darfur Peace and Accountability Act of 2006," April 27, 2006, [Extension], House of Representatives, *Congressional Record*, vol. 152 (Washington, DC: Government Printing Office, 2006), E656.
63. "Darfur Peace Agreement in Sudan," March 25, 2006, Senate, *Congressional Record*, vol. 152 (Washington, DC: Government Printing Office, 2006): S5212.
64. "Darfur," February 16, 2007, Senate, *Congressional Record*, vol. 153 (Washington, DC: Government Printing Office, 2007): S2161.
65. "Sudan," May 10, 2007, Senate, *Congressional Record*, vol. 153 (Washington, DC: Government Printing Office, 2007): S5922.
66. Honorable Frank R. Wolf, "Missed Opportunities on Human Rights," December 10, 2008, [Extensions], House of Representatives, *Congressional Record*, vol. 154 (Washington, DC: Government Printing Office, 2008): E2362.
67. Analysis by Wayne Schneider, General Council, New York Teachers' Retirement System and Cornelia Chebinou, Washington Director, National Association of State Auditors Comptrollers and Treasures, "The Sudan Accountability and Divestment Act of 2007."
68. Paul Kennedy, *Strategy and Diplomacy* (London: George Allen and Unwin, 1983), 15–16.
69. George W. Bush, "Remarks to the Jewish Committee," May 14, 2001, *Public Papers of the Presidents: George W. Bush*, vol. 1 (Washington, DC: Government Printing Office, 2002): 487.
70. Honorable Frank R. Wolf, "Missed Opportunities on Human Rights," op. cit.

71. Johnson, op. cit., 177.
72. Prunier, op. cit., 139–40.
73. President George W. Bush, "President Bush Discusses Genocide in Darfur, Implements Sanctions," Office of the Press Secretary, February 14, 2006, The White House.
74. President George W. Bush, "Interview of President by Matt Frei, BBC World News America," Office of the Press Secretary, February 14, 2008.
75. President George W. Bush, "The Bush Record: President Bush's Freedom Agenda Helped to Protect the American People," January 12, 2009, The White House.
76. Prunier, op. cit., 140.
77. UN General Assembly, "The Convention on the Prevention and Punishment of the Crime of Genocide," December 9, 1948, A/RES/260.
78. Susan B. Rice and Gayle E. Smith, "The Darfur Catastrophe," *Washington Post*, May 30, 2004.
79. *Sudan Tribune*, January 3, 2007.
80. Institute for Securities Studies, South Africa, August 5, 2009, available at www.iss.co.za/af/profiles/Sudan/cpaprov.htm.

CHAPTER 8

1. Thomas Patterson, J. Garry Clifford, and Kenneth J. Hagen, *American Foreign Relations: A History Since 1895* (Boston: Houghton Mifflin Company, 2000), 39.
2. Robert K. Merton, *Social Theory and Structure* (New York: Free Press of Glemcoe, 1957), 310.
3. William R. Slomanson, *Fundamental Perspectives on International Law* (Belmont: Wadsworth/Thomas Learning, 2000), 85.
4. Skyne Uku-Wertimer, "International Dimensions of Crimes Against Humanity: Ethnic Cleansing, Genocide, and Pogrom," presented at the International Studies Association 50th Convention, New York, NY, February 15–18, 2009.
5. Thomas Hobbes, *Leviathan: Or the Matter Forme and Power of a Commonwealth Ecclesiasticall and Civil* (New York: Collier Books, 1968), 136.
6. The names and the positions held by these individuals will be listed in Appendix B at the end of the book.

CHAPTER 9

1. *Los Angeles Times*, September 12, 1991.

CHAPTER 10

1. Diane Ravitch, *Left Back: A Century of Failed School Reform* (New York: Simon and Schuster, 2000), 329.
2. Ibid., 392.
3. Ibid., 405.
4. Ibid., 406.
5. Ibid., 408.

CHAPTER 11

1. Inis Claude, *Swords into Plow Shares* (New York: Random House, 1964), 470.
2. Glen P. Hasted and Kay Knickerem, *Dimensions of World Politics* (New York: Harper Collins, 1991).
3. Omari H. Kokole, "Black Africa and the Nuclear Factor" (PhD dissertation, Dalhousie University, Halifax, Nova Scotia, 1988), 16.
4. Omari H. Kokole, *Dimensions of Africa's International Relations* (Delmar, New York: Caravan Press, 1993), 32.
5. Henry Kissinger, *Nuclear Weapons and Foreign Policy* (New York: Harper and Brothers, 1957), 261.
6. Erskine Childers and Brian Urquart, *Renewing the United Nations System* (Uppsala, Sweden: Dag Hammarskjold Foundation, 1994), 28.
7. United Nations General Assembly, Fifty-First Session, Agenda Item 168, "Renewing the United Nations," July 14, 1997, A/51/950.
8. William J. Durch, ed., *The Evolution of UN Peacekeeping* (New York: St. Martin's Press, 1993), 3.
9. United Nations, "Report of the Independent Inquiry into the Actions of the United Nations during the 1994 Genocide in Rwanda," December 15, 1999, S/1999/1257.
10. African Union, International Panel of Eminent Personalities, "Rwanda: The Preventable Genocide," July 7, 2000.
11. Ibid.
12. United Nations General Assembly, Security Council, Fifty-Fifth Session, "Report of the Panel on United Nations Peace Operations," August 21, 2000, A/55/305-S/2000/809.
13. *National Post* (Canada), September 5, 2000.
14. *Los Angeles Times*, May 21, 1999.
15. UN General Assembly, "General Assembly Continues to Debate on Security Council Reform With Focus on Changing Veto, Permanent Membership," Press Release GA/9692, December 20, 1999; "Security Council Reform Should Redress Long-Standing Imbalance in Geographical Representation, General Assembly Is Told, Press Release," Press Release GA/9373, December 4, 1997; and "Germany

and Japan Must Be Part of Any Increase in Permanent Membership of Security Council, United States Tells General Assembly," Press Release GA/9147, October 30, 1996.

16. General Assembly, "General Assembly Concludes Consideration of Security Council Reform," Press Release GA/9693, December 20, 1999; and General Assembly, "General Assembly Hears of Frustration at Lack of Progress in Three-Year Effort Towards Reform of Security Council," Press Release GA/9145, October 29, 1996.
17. Ibid.
18. Ibid.
19. General Assembly, "General Assembly Continues Debate on Security Council Reform with Focus on Changing Veto, Permanent Membership," Press Release GA/9692, December 20, 1999; "General Assembly Opens Debate on Security Council Reform, Including Increase in Membership and Equitable Representation," Press Release GA/9508, November 19, 1998; and "Without Consensus Support, Enlargement of the Security Council Would Be 'Flawed from the Start,' Assembly Told," Press Release GA/9374, December 5, 1997.
20. General Assembly, "Concludes Consideration of Security Council Reform," op. cit.
21. General Assembly, "Norway Proposes Five New Permanent Seats on the Security Council as General Assembly Continues Debate on Reform Efforts," Press Release GA/9146, October 30, 1996; General Assembly, "Security Council Reform Should Redress Long-Standing Imbalances in Geographical Representation, General Assembly is Told," Press Release GA/9373, December 4, 1997; and General Assembly, "Draft Saying Security Council Reform Possible Only by Article 108 of the United Nations Charter Called 'Divisive and Damaging,'" Press Release GA/9510, November 20, 1998.
22. General Assembly, "General Assembly Concludes Consideration of Security Council Reform"; General Assembly, "Without Consensus Support, Enlargement of Security Council Would Be 'Flawed From the Start,'" Press Release GA/9374; General Assembly, "Norway Proposes Five New Permanent Seats on the Security Council as General Assembly Continues Debate on Reform Efforts," Press Release GA/9146, October 30, 1996; and ibid.
23. General Assembly, "Security Council Reform Should Redress Long-Standing Imbalances in Geographical Representation, General Assembly is Told," Press Release GA/9373, December 4, 1997.
24. General Assembly, "General Assembly Concludes Consideration of Security Council Reform," Press Release GA/9693, December 20, 1999.
25. General Assembly, "General Assembly Concludes Consideration of Security Council Reform," op. cit.

26. *The Guardian*, Tuesday, September 5, 2000; General Assembly, "General Assembly Continues Discussion of Security Council Reform," GA/9689, December 16, 1999; General Assembly, "Draft Saying Security Council Reform Possible Only in Article 108 of United Nations Charter Called 'Divisive and Damaging,'" Press Release GA/9510, November 20, 1998; and General Assembly, "Germany and Japan Must Be Part of Any Increase in Permanent Membership of Security Council, United States Tells General Assembly," Press Release GA/9147, October 30, 1996.
27. General Assembly, "General Assembly Continues Debate on Security Council Reform With Focus on Changing Veto, Permanent Membership," op. cit.
28. General Assembly, "Norway Proposes Five New Permanent Seats on the Security Council as General Assembly Continues Debate on Reform Efforts," op. cit.
29. Ibid.
30. Ibid.
31. General Assembly, "Draft Saying Security Council Reform Possible Only by Article 108 of the United Nations Charter Called 'Divisive and Damaging,'" op. cit.
32. General Assembly, "Legal Implications of Draft Reform Could Damage Charter, Germany Tells Assembly Debate Focusing on Enlarging Council Membership," Press Release GA/9509, November 20, 1998.
33. Non-Aligned Movement, "Communiqué Ministerial Meeting of the Coordinating Bureau of the Non-Aligned Movement," Cartagena de Indias, Colombia, May 19–20, 1998.
34. General Assembly, " General Assembly Concludes Consideration of Security Council Reform," op. cit.
35. Ibid.
36. General Assembly, "Norway Proposes Five New Permanent Seats on Security Council As General Assembly Contributes to Debate on Reform Effort," op. cit.; and ibid.
37. General Assembly, "General Assembly Continues Debate on Security Council Reform With Focus on Changing Veto, Permanent Membership," op. cit.; and General Assembly, "Security Council Reform Should Redress Long-Standing Imbalance in Geographical Representation, General Assembly Is Told," op. cit.
38. General Assembly, "General Assembly Continues Discussion of Security Council Reform," op. cit.; and General Assembly, "Without Consensus Support, Enlargement of the Security Council Would Be 'Flawed From the Start,' Assembly Told," op. cit.
39. Ibid.
40. Ibid.
41. General Assembly, "General Assembly Opens Debate on Security Council Reform, Including Increase in Membership and Equitable Representation," Press Release GA/9508, November 19, 1998.

42. General Assembly, "Interest of Smaller Nations Should Be Protected in Reform Proposals of the Security Council, Australia Tells Assembly," Press Release GA/9375, December 5, 1997.
43. General Assembly, "Without Consensus Support, Enlargement of Security Council Would Be 'Flawed From the Start,' Assembly Is Told," Press Release GA/9374, December 5, 1997.
44. General Assembly, "Norway Proposes Five New Permanent Seats on the Security Council as General Assembly Contributes to Debate on Reform Efforts," op. cit.; ibid.
45. Ibid.
46. Ibid.
47. General Assembly, "Security Council Reform Should Redress Long-Standing Imbalances in Geographical Representation, General Assembly Is Told," op. cit.; General Assembly, "Draft Saying Security Council Reform Possible Only by Article 108 of United Nations Charter Called 'Divisive and Damaging,'" op. cit.
48. General Assembly, "Norway Proposes Five New Permanent Seats on Security Council as General Assembly Continues Debate on Reform Efforts," op. cit.; and ibid.
49. General Assembly, "Legal Implication of Draft on Security Council Reform Could Damage Charter," op. cit.; General Assembly, "General Assembly Hears of Frustration at Lack of Progress in Three Year Effort toward Reform of Security Council," Press Release GA/9145, October 29, 1996; and ibid.
50. General Assembly, "Security Council Reform, U.N. Regional Grouping and Geopolitical Realities among Issues Addressed as Assembly General Debate Continues," Press Release GA/9314, September 29, 1997.
51. General Assembly, "Germany and Japan Must Be Part of Any Increase in Permanent Membership of Security Council, United States Tells General Assembly," Press Release GA/9147, October 30, 1996.
52. General Assembly, "Draft Saying Security Council Reform Possible Only by Article 108 of United Nations Charter Called 'Divisive and Damaging,'" op. cit.
53. Ibid.
54. General Assembly, "Legal Implications of Draft on Security Council Reform Could Damage Charter," op. cit.
55. General Assembly, "Without Consensus Support, Enlargement of the Security Council Would Be 'Flawed from the Start,'" op. cit.; and General Assembly, "Draft Saying Security Council Reform Possible Only by Article 108 of the United Nations Charter Called 'Divisive and Damaging,'" op. cit.
56. General Assembly, "General Assembly Continues Debate on Security Council Reform with Focus on Changing Veto, Permanent Membership," op. cit.
57. General Assembly, "General Assembly Continues Discussion of Security Council Reform," Press Release GA/9689, December 16, 1999.

58. General Assembly, "Germany and Japan Must Be Part of Any Increase in Permanent Membership of Security Council," op. cit.; ibid.
59. Ibid.
60. General Assembly, "Assembly Adopts Text on Bosnia and Herzegovina; Takes up Security Council Reform," Press Release GA/9688, December 16, 1999.
61. General Assembly, "Security Council Reform Essential to United Nations Reorganization, Prime Minister of Japan Tells General Assembly," Press Release GA/9098, September 24, 1996.
62. General Assembly, "Interest of the Smaller Nations Should Be Protected in Reform Proposals for Security Council, Australia Tells Assembly," Press Release GA/9375, December 5, 1997.
63. General Assembly, "Need for Fair Geographical Representation on the Security Council Stressed as Assembly Concludes Phase of Reform Debate," op. cit.; and ibid.
64. General Assembly, "Reform Should Redress Long-Standing Imbalances in Geographical Representation," op. cit.; and General Assembly, "Need for Fair Geographical Representation on Security Council Stressed as Assembly Concludes Phase of Reform Debate," Press Release GA/9151, November 1, 1996.
65. General Assembly, "Increase in Number of Permanent Security Council Seats Will Serve Interest of Only Few Countries, Italy Tells General Assembly," Press Release GA/9372, December 4, 1997.
66. Ibid.
67. Ibid.
68. General Assembly, "Germany and Japan Must Be Part of Any Increase in Permanent Membership of Security Council," op. cit.
69. General Assembly, "Norway Proposes Five New Permanent Seats on Security Council as General Assembly Continues Debate on Reform Efforts," op. cit.
70. Ibid.
71. General Assembly, "Developing Countries Need Stronger Presence on Reformed Security Council," Press Release GA/9317, September 30, 1997.
72. General Assembly, "Affirmative Votes from Two Thirds of Its Members Will Be Required for Decision on Security Council Reform, Assembly Decides," Press Release GA/9511, November 23, 1998; and General Assembly, "General Assembly Hears of Frustration at Lack of Progress in Three-Year Effort towards Reform," op. cit.
73. General Assembly, "Norway Proposes Five New Permanent Seats on Security Council as General Assembly Continues Debate on Reform Efforts," op. cit.
74. Organization of African Unity, "African Common Position on Security Council Reform," September 29, 1994.

75. General Assembly, "Affirmative Vote from Two Thirds of Its Members Will Be Required for Decision on Security Council Reform, Assembly Decides," op. cit.; General Assembly, "Draft Saying Security Council Reform Possible Only by Article 108 of United Nations Charter Called 'Divisive and Damaging,'" op. cit.; and General Assembly, "Security Council Reform Should Redress Long-Standing Imbalance in Geographical Representation, General Assembly Is Told," Press Release GA/9373, December 4, 1997.
76. General Assembly, "General Assembly Continues Discussion of Security Council Reform," Press Release GA/9689, December 16, 1999; and General Assembly, "Draft Saying Security Council Reform Possible Only by Article 108 of United Nations Charter Called 'Divisive and Damaging,'" op. cit.
77. Clinton Rossiter, ed., *The Federalist Papers* (New York: Mentor, 1961), 78.
78. United Nations Security Council, Resolution 1318 (2000), "Security Declaration on Ensuring an Effective Role for the Security Council in the Maintenance of International Peace and Security, Particularly in Africa," adopted by the Security Council at its 4194th Meeting, on September 7, 2000.
79. United Nations General Assembly, "United Nations Millennium Declaration," September 8, 2000, A/55/L2.
80. *New York Times*, September 8, 2000.
81. President William J. Clinton, Millennium Summit, September 6, 2000, United Nations, New York.
82. Ibid.

CONCLUSION

1. *Los Angeles Times*, March 19, 2005.

APPENDIX B

1. *Congressional Record* 151 (May 13, 2005): H3005.

Bibliography

A. Primary Sources

Amnesty International. "Sudan: Arms Continuing to Fuel Serious Human Rights Violations in Darfur." AFR/019/2007.

Bush, President George W. "Statement of the President." Office of the Press Secretary, The White House, October 21, 2002.

———. "United States Helps Refugees in Darfur: Fact of the Day." U.S. Department of State and U.S. Agency for International Development, July 8, 2004.

———. "President's Statement on Violence in Darfur, Sudan." Office of the Press Secretary, The White House, September 9, 2004.

———. "President Bush Welcomes NATO Secretary General to the White House." Office of the Press Secretary, The White House, June 1, 2005.

———. "President Discusses Global War on Terror at Kansas State University." Office of the Press Secretary, The White House, January 23, 2006.

———. "Executive Order: Blocking Property of Persons in Connections with the Conflict in Sudan's Darfur Region." Office of the Press Secretary, The White House, April 27, 2006.

———. "Fact Sheet: Darfur Agreement: A Step toward Peace." Office of the Press Secretary, The White House, May 8, 2006.

———. "President Discusses Peace Agreement in Sudan: The Roosevelt Room." Office of the Press Secretary, The White House, May 8, 2006.

———. "Executive Order: Blocking Property of and Prohibiting Transactions with the Government of Sudan." Office of the Press Secretary, The White House, October 13, 2006.

———. "President Bush Discusses Sudan with Special Envoy and Makes Remarks on North Korea." The Office of the Press Secretary, The White House, October 31, 2006.

———. "Notice: Continuation of the National Emergency with Respect to Sudan." Office of the Press Secretary, The White House, November 1, 2006.

———. "Fact Sheet: Stop the Genocide in Darfur." Office of the Press Secretary, The White House, April 18, 2007.

———. "Fact Sheet: Fighting Genocide in Darfur." Office of the Press Secretary, The White House, May 29, 2007.

———. "President Bush Discusses Genocide in Darfur, Implements Sanctions." Office of the Press Secretary, The White House, May 29, 2007.

———. "President Bush Meets with United Nations Secretary General Ban Ki-Moon." Office of the Press Secretary, The White House, July 17, 2007.

———. "Fact Sheet: A Mission of Liberation around the World: President Bush Calls on Members of the United Nations General Assembly to Work toward Standards of the Universal Declaration of Human Rights." Office of the Press Secretary, The White House, September 25, 2007.

———. "President Bush Participates in United Nations Security Council Meeting on Africa." Office of the Press Secretary, The White House, September 25, 2007.

———. "Statement by the President." Office of the Press Secretary, The White House, December 31, 2007.

———. "Interview of the President in Roundtable with the Foreign Print Media." Office of the Press Secretary, The White House, January 4, 2008.

———. "Building a Better Future through Trusting and Empowering the American People: President Bush Delivers 2008 State of the Union Address, Says Congress and the Administration Must Come Together to Achieve Results." White House Office of Communications, January 28, 2008.

———. "Interview of President by Matt Frei, BBC News America." Office of the Press Secretary, The White House, February 14, 2008.

———. "Setting the Record Straight: President Bush Committed to Strengthen Democracy throughout Africa." Office of the Press Secretary, The White House, February 22, 2008.

———. "President Meets with Darfur Advocates: The Roosevelt Room." Office of the Press Secretary, The White House, April 26, 2006.

———. "Notice: Continuation of the National Emergency with Respect to the Situation in or in Relation to Sudan." Office of the Press Secretary, The White House, October 30, 2008.

———. "Fact Sheet: Leading the Global Response to the Crisis in Darfur." Office of the Press Secretary, The White House, December 11, 2008.

———. "100 Things Americans May Not Know about the Bush Administration Record." White House Office of Communications, January 2009.

———. "Memorandum for the Secretary of State. Subject: Waiver of Reimbursement under the United Nations Participation Act to Support the United Nations/Africa Union Mission in Darfur." Office of the Press Secretary, The White House, January 5, 2009.

———. "Policies of the Bush Administration 2001–2009." White House Office of Communication, January 2009.

———. "Executive Orders Issued by President George W. Bush." The White House, January 9, 2009.

———. "The Bush Record: President Bush's Freedom Agenda Helped to Protect the American People." The White House, January 12, 2009.

Clinton, President William J. "Millennium Summit Speech." United Nations, New York, September 6, 2000.

Congressional Record. Vol. 138. Washington, DC: Government Printing Office, 1992.

———. Vol. 140. Washington, DC: Government Printing Office, 1994.
———. Vol. 141. Washington, DC: Government Printing Office, 1995.
———. Vol. 148. Washington, DC: Government Printing Office, 2002.
———. Vol. 150. Washington, DC: Government Printing Office, 2004.
———. Vol. 151. Washington, DC: Government Printing Office, 2005.
———. Vol. 152. Washington, DC: Government Printing Office, 2006.
———. Vol. 153. Washington, DC: Government Printing Office, 2007.
———. Vol. 154. Washington, DC: Government Printing Office, 2008.
———. Vol. 155. Washington, DC: Government Printing Office, 2009.

Foreign Relations of the United States 1951. Volume IV, *Europe: Political and Economic Developments*. Washington, DC: United States Government Printing Office, 1985.

General Assembly. "Draft Resolution Referred by the General Assembly at its Fifty-Fourth Session, United Nations Millennium Declaration." A/55/L.2.

———. "Resolution Adopted by the General Assembly." 52/12. "Renewing the United Nations: A Programme for Reform." A/RES/52/12, November 12, 1997.

———. "Resolution Adopted by the General Assembly." 53/22. "United Nations Year of Dialogue among Civilizations." A/RES/53/22, November 16, 1998.

———. "United Nations Reform: Measures and Proposals, A Millennium Assembly, the United Nations system (Special Commission) and a Millennium Forum." A/52/850, March 31, 1998.

———. "United Nations Reform: Measures and Proposals, Renewing the United Nations: A Programme for Reform." A/51/950/add.7, December 9, 1997.

———. "United Nations Reform: Measures and Proposals, The Millennium Assembly of the United Nations: Thematic framework for the Millennium Summit." A/53/948, May 10, 1999.

Hadley, Stephen. "Statement by National Security Advisor Stephen Hadley." Office of the Press Secretary, The White House, January 5, 2009.

House of Representatives. U.S. Congress. *Slavery in Mauritania and Sudan: Joint Hearing before the Subcommittee on International Operations and Human Rights and Africa of the Committee on International Relations.* 104th Cong., 2nd sess., March 13, 1996.

Human Rights Watch. *Leave None to Tell the Story: Genocide in Rwanda.* March 1999.

Kulenovic, Adil. "Interview with Vladimir Srebrov, a Founding Member of the Serb Democratic Party." October 30, 1995.

McClellan, Scott. "Press Briefing by Scott McClellan." Office of the Press Secretary, The White House, March 16, 2006.

Perino, Dana. "Press Gaggle by Dana Perino." Office of the Press Secretary, The White House, February 19, 2008.

Powell, Secretary of State Colin L. "The Crisis in Darfur." Written Remarks, Senate Foreign Relations Committee, September 9, 2004.

Public Papers of the Presidents of the United States: William J. Clinton—1993. Vol. 1. Washington, DC: Government Printing Office, 1994.

Public Papers of the Presidents of the United States: Willam J. Clinton—1994. Vol. 1. Washington, DC: Government Printing Office, 1995.

Public Papers of the Presidents of the United States: William J. Clinton—1995. Vol. 2. Washington, DC: Government Printing Office, 1996.

Public Papers of the Presidents of the United States: William J. Clinton—1998. Vol. 2. Washington, DC: Government Printing Office, 1999.

Public Papers of the Presidents of the United States: George W. Bush—2001. Vol. 1. Washington, DC: Government Printing Office, 2002.

Report of the Select Committee on Intelligence. November 1996.

Request for Protection of Informant. Cable from General Dallaire, UNAMIR to New York.

Sudanese Peace Act. Public Law 107-245-October 21, 2002.

Trifunovska, Snezana. *Yugoslavia through Documents: From Its Creation to Its Dissolution.* Dordrecht: Martinus Nijhoff Publishers, 1994.

Truman, Harry S. "Presidential Power." Speech on May 8, 1954. "United Nations Convention on the Prevention and Punishment of the Crime of Genocide." Adopted by Resolution 260 (III) A of the United Nations General Assembly on December 9, 1948.

United Nations. "Report of the Independent Inquiry into the Actions of the United Nations during the 1994 Genocide in Rwanda." December 15, 1999.

———. "We the Peoples. Millennium Forum Declaration and Agenda for Action, Strengthening the United Nations for the 21st Century." May 22–26, 2000.

———. "Report of the Panel on United Nations Peace Operations." August 21, 2000.

———. "Report of the International Commission of Inquiry on Darfur to the United Nations Secretary-General." January 25, 2005.

United Nations Educational, Scientific, and Cultural Organization. Draft Resolution, "Preparations By UNESCO for the United Nations Year of Dialogue Among Civilizations." Submitted by the Islamic Republic of Iran, 30/C/COM.IV/DR.2*. November 3, 1999.

———. Draft Resolution, "Preparations By UNESCO for the United Nations Year of Dialogue Among Civilizations." Submitted by Pakistan, 30/C/COM.IV/DR.10*. November 9, 1999.

———. "Preparation by UNESCO of the United Nations Year of Dialogue." March 16, 2000.

United Nations Security Council. "Security Council Declaration on Ensuring an Effective Role for the Security Council in the Maintenance of International Peace and Security, Particularly in Africa." September 7, 2000.

United Nations Security Council Resolution 688. Adopted on April 5, 1991 at its 2,982nd Meeting.

United Nations Security Council Resolution 846. Adopted on June 22, 1993 at its 3,244th Meeting.

United Nations Security Council Resolution 872. Adopted on April 5, 1993 at its 3,288th Meeting.
United Nations Security Council Resolution 912. Adopted on April 21, 1994 at its 3,336th Meeting.
United Nations Security Council Resolution 914. Adopted on April 27, 1994 at its 3,369th Meeting.
United Nations Security Council Resolution 918. Adopted on May 17, 1994 at its 3,377th Meeting.
United Nations Security Council Resolution 929. Adopted on June 22, 1994 at its 3,392nd Meeting.
United Nations Security Council Resolution 1160. Adopted on March 31, 1998 at its 3,868th Meeting.
United Nations Security Council Resolution 1199. Adopted on September 23, 1998 at its 3,930th Meeting.
United Nations Security Council Resolution 1203. Adopted on October 24, 1998 at its 3,937th Meeting.
The U.S. and the Genocide in Rwanda: Evidence of Inaction. The National Security Archives, August 20, 2001.
U.S. Congress. Senate. Select Committee on Intelligence. *U.S. Actions Regarding Iranian and Other Arms Transfers to the Bosnian Army, 1994–1994: Report of the Select Committee on Intelligence Together with Additional Views*. November 1996.
U.S. Department of State. *Erasing History: Ethnic Cleansing in Kosovo*. May 1999.
———. "Initial Report of the United States of America to the United Nations Committee on the Elimination of Racial Discrimination." September 2000.
U.S. Department of State, Bureau of European Affairs. "Background Notes: Bosnia." August 1999.
U.S. Department of State, Bureau of International Organizational Affairs. "Clinton Administration Policy on Reforming Multilateral Peace Operations." PDD25, February 22, 1996.
U.S. Department of State, Bureau of Public Affairs. "The Dayton Peace Agreement." December 11, 1995.
Wiesel, Elie. "On the Atrocities in Sudan." At the Emergency Summit at the Graduate Center of the City University of New York on July 14, 2004.

B. Books

Akol, Lam. *Southern Sudan: Colonial Resistance and Autonomy*. Trenton, NJ: The Red Sea Press, 2007.
Almond, Gabriel, and G. Bingham Powell, eds. *Comparative Politics Today: A World View*. New York: Longman, 1996.
Andersen, Roy R., Robert F. Seibert, and Jon G. Wagner. *Politics and Change in the Middle East: Sources of Conflict and Accommodation*. Upper Saddle River, New Jersey: Prentice Hall, 2001.

Anderson, G. Norman. *Sudan in Crisis: The Failure of Democracy.* Gainsville, FL: University Press of Florida, 1999.

Bates, Robert H. *When Things Fell Apart.* New York: Cambridge University Press, 2008.

Blechman, Barry, and Stephen S. Kaplan, eds. *Force without War.* Washington, DC: The Brookings Institute, 1978.

Bull, Hedley, and Adam Watson, eds. *The Expansion of International Society.* Oxford: Clarendon, 1984.

Calvocoressi, Peter. *World Politics 1945–2000.* New York: Pearson Longman, 2001.

Campbell, John C. *Tito's Separate Road.* New York: Harper and Row, 1967.

Childers, Erskine, and Brian Urquart. *Renewing the United Nations System.* Uppsala, Sweden: Dag Hammarskjold Foundation, 1994.

Clarke, Richard. *Against All Enemies: Inside America's War on Terror.* New York: Free Press, 2004.

Claude, Inis. *Swords Into Plow Shares.* New York: Random House, 1964.

Collins, Robert O. *A History of Modern Sudan.* Cambridge: Cambridge University Press, 2008.

Daadler, Ivo H. *Getting to Dayton.* Washington, DC: The Brookings Institute, 2000.

Dallaire, Lt. Gen. Romo. *Shake Hands with the Devil: The Failure of Humanity in Rwanda.* New York: Carol and Graf, 2005.

Davidson, Basil. *The Story of Africa.* London: Mitchell Beazley, 1984.

Destexhe, Alain. *Rwanda and Genocide in the Twentieth Century.* New York: New York University Press, 1995.

Deutsch, Karl W. *Nationalism and Social Communication: An Inquiry into the Foundations of Nationality.* Cambridge, MA: MIT Press, 1966.

———. *The Nerves of Government: Models of Political Communication and Control.* New York: The Free Press of Glencoe, 1963.

———. *Politics and Government: How People Decide Their Fate.* Boston: Houghton Mifflin Company, 1974.

de Waal, Alex, ed. *War in Darfur: And the Search for Peace.* London: Global Equity Initiative, 2007.

Djilas, Milovan. *Conversations with Stalin.* New York: Harcourt, Brace, and World, 1962.

———. *Tito.* New York: Harcourt Brace Jovanovich, 1980.

Doubt, Keith. *Sociology after Bosnia and Kosovo: Recovering Justice.* Lanham, Maryland: Rowman and Littlefield, 2000.

Durch, William J., ed. *The Evolution of UN Peacekeeping.* New York: St. Martin's Press, 1993.

Easton, David. *A Framework for Political Analysis.* Englewood Cliffs, NJ: Prentice-Hall, 1965.

———. *A Systems Analysis of Political Life.* New York: John Wiley and Sons, 1965.

Essien, Kwame, and Toyin Falola. *Culture and Customs of Sudan*. Westport, CT: Greenwood Press, 2009.

Eubank, Keith. *The Origins of World War II*. New York: Thomas Y. Crowell Company, 1979.

Feil, Scott R. *Preventing Genocide in Rwanda: How the Early Use of Force Might Have Succeeded in Rwanda*. New York: Carnegie Corporation, 1998.

Fogelquist, Alan. *Handbook of Facts on the Break-up of Yugoslavia, International Policy and the War in Bosnia-Herzegovina*. Ann Arbor, MI: AEIOU Publishing, 1993.

Fox, Annette Baker. *The Power of Small States*. Chicago: The University of Chicago Press, 1959.

Galbraith, Peter W. *The End of Iraq: How American Incompetence Created a War without_End*. New York: Simon and Schuster, 2006.

George, Alexander, and Richard Smoke. *Deterrence in American Foreign Policy*. New York: Columbia University Press, 1974.

Glenny, Misha. *Fall of Yugoslavia: The Third Balkan War*. New York: Penguin, 1996.

Gourevitch, Philip. *We Wish to Inform You That Tomorrow We Will Be Killed with Our Families: Stories from Rwanda*. New York: Picador, 1998.

Guralink, David B., ed. *Webster's New World Dictionary of the American Language*. New York: Simon and Schuster, 1984.

Handel, Michael. *Weak States in the International System*. Totowa, NJ: Frank Cass and Company Limited, 1984.

Harris, George. *Troubled Alliance*. Washington, DC: American Enterprise Institute for Public Policy Research, 1972.

Hastedt, Glenn P., and Kay Knickrehm. *Dimensions of World Politics*. New York: Harper Collins Publishers, 1991.

Hobbes, Thomas. *Leviathan: Or the Matter, Forme and Power of a Commonwealth Ecclesiasticall and Civil*. New York: Collier, 1968.

Hofstede, Geert. *Culture and Organizations: Software of the Mind*. New York: McGraw-Hill, 1997.

Hopkins, Peter Gwynvay, ed. *The Kenna Handbook of Sudan*. London: Kegan Paul, 2007.

Hosmer, Stephen T. *The Conflict over Kosovo: Why Milosevic Decided to Settle When He Did*. Santa Monica, CA: Rand, 2001.

Huntington, Samuel P. *The Clash of Civilizations*. New York: Simon and Schuster, 1996.

Idris, Amir H. *Conflict and Politics of Identity in Sudan*. New York: Palgrave Macmillan, 2005.

Jacobson, Harold K. *Networks of Interdependence: International Organizations and the Global Political System*. New York: McGraw-Hill Publishing, 1984.

Jacoby, Susan. *The Age of American Unreason*. New York: Pantheon, 2008.

Johnson, Douglass H. *The Root Causes of Sudan's Civil Wars*. Oxford: James Curry, 2004.

Jok, Jok Madut. *Sudan: Race, Religion, and Violence.* Oxford: Oneworld Publications, 2007.

Judah, Tim. *Kosovo: War and Revenge.* New Haven: Yale University Press, 2000.

Kaplan, Robert D. *Balkan Ghost: A Journey through History.* New York: St. Martin's Press, 1993.

Kaplan, Stephen S. *The Diplomacy of Power.* Washington: The Brookings Institute, 1981.

Kennedy, John F. *Why England Slept.* New York: Doubleday and Company, 1961.

Kennedy, Paul. *Strategy and Diplomacy.* London: George Allen and Unwin, 1983.

Kissinger, Henry A. *Nuclear Weapons and Foreign Policy.* New York: Harper and Brothers, 1957.

Klinghoffer, Arthur Jay. *The International Dimension of Genocide in Rwanda.* New York: New York University Press, 1998.

Kokole, Omari H. *Dimensions of Africa's International Relations.* Delmar, NY: Caravan, 1993.

Kostich, Degos D. *The Land and Peoples of the Balkans.* Philadelphia, PA: J. B. Lippincott, 1962.

Lambeth, Benjamin. *NATO's Air War for Kosovo: A Strategic and Operational Assessment.* Santa Monica, CA: Rand, 2001.

Lasswell, Harold D. *The Analysis of Political Behavior: An Empirical Approach.* London: Routledge and Kegan Paul, 1951.

———. *Politics: Who Gets What, When, How.* New York, NY: World Publishing Company, 1972.

Lasswell, Harold D., and Abraham Kaplan. *Power and Society: A Framework for Political Inquiry.* New Haven, CT: Yale University Press, 1951.

Lesch, Ann Mosley. *Sudan: Contested National Identities.* Bloomington, IN: Indiana University Press, 1998.

Locke, John. *Two Treatises of Government.* Cambridge: Cambridge University Press, 2005.

Malcolm, Noel. *Kosovo: A Short History.* New York: New York University Press, 1998.

Mazrui, Ali A. *The African Condition.* New York: Cambridge University Press, 1980.

———. *Africa's International Relations.* Boulder, CO: Westview, 1977.

———. *Cultural Forces in World Politics.* Portsmouth, NH: Heinemann, 1990.

———. *A World Federation of Cultures.* New York: The Free Press, 1976.

Memmi, Albert. *The Colonizer and the Colonized.* Boston: Beacon Press, 1965.

Merton, Robert K. *Social Theory and Structure.* New York: Free Press of Glemcoe, 1957.

Mertus, Julie A. *Kosovo: How Myths and Truths Started a War.* Berkeley: University of California Press, 1999.

Mingst, Karen, and Margaret P. Karnes. *The United Nations in the Post–Cold War Era.* Boulder, CO: Westview, 2000.

Morgenthau, Hans J. *Politics among Nations.* New York: Alfred A. Knopf, 1967.

Neuman, Stephanie, and Robert E. Harkavy, eds. *Arms Transfers in the Modern World.* New York: Praeger, 1980.

Norris, John. *Collision Course: NATO, Russia, and Kosovo.* Westport, CT: Praeger, 2005.

Organski, A. F. K. *World Politics.* New York: Alfred A. Knopf, 1968.

Patterson, Thomas, J. Garry Clifford, and Kenneth Hagen. *American Foreign Relations: A History Since 1895.* Boston: Houghton Mifflin, 2000.

Pierre, Andrew J. *The Global Politics of Arms Sales.* Princeton, NJ: Princeton University Press, 1982.

Power, Samantha. *A Problem from Hell: America and the Age of Genocide.* New York: Harper Perennial, 2007.

Prifti, Peter R. *Confrontation in Kosova: The Albanian-Serb Struggle, 1969–1999.* Boulder, CO: Eastern European Monographs, 1999.

Pruiner, Gerard. *Darfur: The Ambiguous Genocide.* Ithaca, NY: Cornell University Press, 2005.

———. *The Rwanda Crisis: History of a Genocide.* New York: Columbia University Press, 1995.

Ravitch, Diane. *Left Back: A Century of Failed School Reforms.* New York: Simon and Schuster, 2000.

Riggs, Robert E., and Jack C. Planto. *The United Nations: International Organization and World Politics.* Belmont, CA: Wadsworth, 1994.

Rogel, Carol. *The Breakup of Yugoslavia and Its Aftermath.* Westport, CT: Greenwood, 2004.

Rohde, David. *Endgame.* Boulder, CO: Westview, 1998.

Roi, Yaacov, ed. *The Limits to Power.* New York: St. Martin's Press, 1979.

Roseneau, James N., ed. *International Politics and Foreign Policy.* New York: Free Press, 1961.

Rossiter, Clinton, ed. *The Federalist Papers.* New York: Mentor, 1961.

Rustinow, Dennis I. *The Yugoslav Experiment 1948–1974.* Berkeley: University of California Press, 1977.

Schelling, Thomas C. *Arms and Influence.* New Haven: Yale University Press, 1966.

Silber, Laura, and Allan Little. *Yugoslavia: Death of a Nation.* New York: Penguin, 1997.

Singer, Marshall. *Weak States in a World of Powers.* New York: Free Press, 1972.

Slomanson, William R. *Fundamental Perspectives on International Law.* Belmont, CA: Wadsworth/Thomas Learning, 2000.

Smith, Anthony D. *The Ethnic Origins of Nations.* Oxford: Basil Blackwell, 1988.

Sorensen, Theodore. *Kennedy.* New York: Harper & Row, 1965.

Spiegel, Steven. *World Politics in a New Era*. Fort Worth, TX: Harcourt Brace College Publishers, 1995.

Tatum, Dale C. *Who Influenced Whom? Lessons from the Cold War*. Lanham, MD: University Press of America, 2002.

Tiefer, Charles. *Veering Right: How the Bush Administration Subverts the Law for Conservative Causes*. Berkeley: University of California Press, 2004.

Totten, Samuel, and Eric Markusen, eds. *Genocide in Darfur: Investigating the Atrocities in the Sudan*. New York: Routledge, 2006.

Ulam, Adam B. *Expansion and Coexistence*. New York: Praeger, 1974.

Vasquez, John. *The Power of Power Politics*. New Brunswick, NJ: Rutgers University Press, 1983.

Vickers, Miranda. *Between Serb and Albanian: A History of Kosovo*. New York: Columbia University Press, 1998.

Vucinich, Wayne, ed. *At the Brink of War and Peace*. New York: Columbia University Press, 1982.

Waltz, Kenneth N. *Man, the State, and War*. New York: Columbia University Press, 1959.

———. *Theory of International Politics*. Reading, MA: Addison-Wesley, 1979.

Wilson, Duncan. *Tito's Yugoslavia*. Cambridge: Cambridge University Press, 1980.

Woodward, Susan L. *Balkan Tragedy*. Washington, DC: The Brookings Institute, 1995.

Zimmerman, Warren. "Yugoslavia: 1989–1996." In *Conference Report: U.S. and Russian Policymaking with Respect to the Use of Force*, edited by Jeremy R. Azrael and Emil A. Payin, 177–99. Santa Monica, CA: Rand Center for Russia and Eurasia, 1996.

C. Articles

Armstrong, Gail, and Patricia Foresiter. "Ending the Balkan Nightmare." *Freedom*, vol. 31, issue 2: 15–20.

Blechman, Barry, Janne E. Nolan, and Alan Platt. "Pushing Arms." *Foreign Policy*, Spring 1982: 138–54.

"Bosnia: Can You Blame History?" *Out There News*. Available at http://www.outtherenews.com (accessed on June 7, 2000).

CRS Issue Brief. "8611: U.N. System Funding: Congressional Issues," December 6, 1996.

Deng, Francis M. "Sudan: A Nation in Turbulent Search of Itself." *The Annals of the American Academy of Political and Social Science*, January 2006: 603, 155.

Donati, Pierpaolo. "Identity and Solidarity in the Complex of Citizenship: The Regional Approach." *Innovation: The European Journal of Social Science*, June 1995, vol. 8, issue 2: 155–73.

Hoile, David. "Darfur in Perspective." Available at Darfur Information.com (accessed on June 5, 2009).

Keohane, Robert O. "The Big Influence of Small States." *Foreign Policy*, Spring 1971: 161–182.

Kidder, Tim, Elizabeth Terney, Rachel Whittaker, and Hilary Young. "A War Torn Region: Bosnia-Herzegovina, Croatia, and Yugoslavia." Available at http://www.earlham.edu/~pols/ps17971/terneel/rape.html (accessed on April 25, 1997).

O'Brian, Ruth. "Speed of the Rwandan Genocide Frazzled an Uninformed Press, Author Says." *The Freedom Forum Online*. Available at http://www.freedomforum.org/ (accessed on November 11, 1998).

Pierre, Andrew J. "Arms Sales: The New Diplomacy." *Foreign Affairs*, winter 1981/82, vol. 60, no. 2: 266–86.

Riedlmayer, Andras. "A Brief History of Bosnia-Herzegovina." *Mostar Online*. Available at http://www.palclub.org/onlineeducationcourses/bosniaandherzegovina.htm.

Snyder, Jr., J. William. "'Command' versus 'Operational Control': A Critical Review of PDD-25." Available at http://www.ibiblio.org/jwsnyder/wisdom/pdd25.html.

Tatum, Dale C. "Preaching Smith But Practicing Keynes." *Peace Review*, vol. 18, number 2, April–June 2006: 237–43.

General Assembly. "General Assembly Takes First Steps toward UN Reform." Department of Public Information, New York, December 27, 2005.

D. Magazines, Newspapers, and Annuals

Africa South of the Sahara 1999. London: Europa Publications Limited, 1998.

Amnesty International. *Amnesty International Report 1995*. New York: Amnesty International, 1995.

———. *Amnesty International Report 1996*. New York: Amnesty International, 1996.

Arab News, April 4, 2009.

Associated Press, January 11, 1994; July 24, 1993; May 27, 1999; and June 3, 1999.

Atlantic Monthly, January 1913.

Boston Globe, October 22, 1992; April 28, 1993; November 30, 1994; and May 3, 1995.

British Ministry of Defense and Foreign and Commonwealth Office. "Kosovo: News, Background and Resources," n.d.

Cable News Network. "Belgium Apologizes for Inaction during Rwanda's 1994 Genocide," April 7, 2000.

———. "Report: Rwandan Genocide Could Have Been Prevented," March 31, 1999.

———. "Rwanda Still Burying Dead Six Years after Genocide," April 6, 2000.

Christian Science Monitor, October 25, 2005; and August 22, 2008.

Council on Foreign Relations. "China, Africa, and Oil," June 6, 2008.

Croatian Herald, July 28, 1992.

Dorman, Michael. "The Killing of Kitty Genovese." *Newsday*, June 10, 1998.

Federation of American Scientists (FAS). "Bosnian Conflict, July 5–17, 1995." Available at http://fas.org/irp/imint/bosnia.htm.

General Assembly. "Affirmative Vote from Two Thirds of Its Members Will Be Required for Decision on Security Council Reform, Assembly Decides." Press Release GA/9511, November 23, 1998.

———. "Assembly Adopts Text on Bosnia and Herzegovina; Takes Up Security Council Reform." Press Release GA/9688, December 16, 1999.

———. "Assembly Proclaims 2001 United Nations Year of Dialogue among Civilizations, Expressing Determination to Facilitate International Discussion." GA/9497, November 4, 1998.

———. "Assembly Seeks Universal Support for International Year of Dialogue." GA/9685, December 10, 1999.

———. "Developing Countries Need Strong Presence on Reformed Security Council." Press Release GA/9317, September 30, 1997.

———. "Draft Saying Security Council Reform Possible Only by Article 108 of the United Nations Charter Called 'Divisive and Damaging.'" Press Release GA/9510, November 20, 1998.

———. "General Assembly Concludes Consideration of Security Council Reform." Press Release GA/9693, December 20, 1999.

———. "General Assembly Continues Discussion of Security Council Reform." Press Release GA/9689, December 16, 1999.

———. "General Assembly Continues to Debate on Security Council Reform with Focus on Changing Veto, Permanent Membership." Press Release GA/9692, December 20, 1999.

———. "General Assembly Hears of Frustration and Lack of Progress in Three-Year Effort towards Reform of Security Council." Press Release GA/9145, October 29, 1996.

———. "General Assembly Opens Debate on Security Council Reform, Including Increase in Membership and Equitable Representation." Press Release GA/9508, November 19, 1998.

———. "Germany and Japan Must Be Part of Any Increase in Permanent Security Council, United States Tells Assembly." Press Release GA/9147, October 30, 1996.

———. "Increase in Permanent Security Council Seats Will Serve the Interest of Only Few Countries, Italy Tells General Assembly." Press Release GA/9372, December 4, 1997.

———. "Interest of Smaller Nations Should Be Protected in Reform Proposals of the Security Council, Australia Tells Assembly." Press Release GA/9375, December 5, 1997.

———. "Legal Implications of Draft Reform Could Damage Charter, Germany Tells Assembly Debate Focusing on Enlarging Council Membership." Press Release GA/9509, November 20, 1998.

———. "Norway Proposes Five New Permanent Seats on the Security Council as General Assembly Contributes Debate on Reform Efforts." Press Relesase GA/9146, October 30, 1996.

———. "Security Council Reform Essential to United Nations Reorganization, Prime Minister of Japan Tells General Assembly." Press Release GA/9098, September 24, 1996.

———. "Security Council Reform Should Redress Long-Standing Imbalance in Geographical Representation, General Assembly Is Told." Press Release GA/9373, December 4, 1997.

———. "Security Council Reform, U.N. Regional Grouping and Geopolitical Realities among Issues Addressed as Assembly General Debate Continues." Press Release GA/93147, October 30, 1996.

———. "Without Consensus Support, Enlargement of the Security Council Would Be 'Flawed from the Start,' Assembly Told." Press Release GA/9374, December 5, 1997.

———. "World Leaders Adopt 'United Nations Millennium Declaration' at Conclusion of Extraordinary Three-Day Summit." GA/9758, September 8, 2000.

The Guardian, September 5, 2000; September 7, 2000; and March 28, 2007.

The Herald, March 5, 2009.

Huffington Post, April 23, 2009; and May 18, 2009.

Human Rights Watch. *World Report 1999.* New York: Human Rights Watch, 1999.

International Herald Tribune, August 3, 2004.

Irish Times, May 26, 1999.

Littlejohns, Michael. "UN Millennium Report Is Good Start: Can Drive Last till September Summit?" *Earth Times News Service*, n.d.

The London Times, September 9, 2000.

Los Angeles Times, May 21, 1999; September 23, 1999; June 9, 2000; September 7, 2001; May 10, 2004; January 9, 2008; April 23, 2008; and March 21, 2009.

Me and Ophelia, July 11, 2004, available at http://meandophelia.blogspot.com/.

Media Intelligence Report, July 28, 1994.

The Nation, December 25, 1995.

National Post (Canada), September 5, 2000.

The New York Times, August 4, 1992; November 9, 1992; April 8, 1993; May 12, 1994; May 21, 1994; May 25, 1994; June 1, 1994; June 10, 1994; July 25, 1994; November 10, 1997; March 26, 1998; September 5, 1998; April 6, 1999; May 5, 1999; July 2, 1999; July 31, 1999; December 10, 1999; March 12, 2000; September 6, 2000; September 7, 2000; September 8, 2000; June 12, 2004; June 23, 2004; March 2, 2005; March 3, 2005; January 1, 2008; and March 31, 2009.

Newsday, August 2, 1992.

Newsweek, June 6, 1995.

Non-Aligned Movement, "Communique Ministerial Meeting of the Coordinating Bureau of the Non-Aligned Movement." Cartagena de Indias, Colombia, May 19–20, 1998.

The Observer, August 1, 2004.

Organization of African Unity. "African Common Position on Security Council Reforms." September 29, 1994.

Organization of the Islamic Conference. "OIC Governmental Group of Experts Formulates Two Draft Universal Documents on Dialogue among Civilizations; Dr. Laraki: Success of the Islamic Ummah in Bringing Together Contemporary Nations." OIC Press Release, February 5, 2000.

Pew Research Center. "Questioning Kosovo," May 14, 1999.

Reuters. "Rwanda Names Military Chief Kagame President," April 17, 2000.

———. "Sudan's Bashir on Second Trip since Warrant," March 25, 2009.

Sudan Human Rights Organization. "Sudan Government Fails to Insure Stability and Peace in Darfur." Press Release, March 1, 2003.

Sudan Tribune, August 3, 2004; October 17, 2004; January 3, 2007; February 18, 2007; May 8, 2007; August 1, 2007; January 2, 2008; July 9, 2008; August 26, 2008; September 14, 2008; January 26, 2009; February 9, 2009; April 1, 2009; April 3, 2009; April 11, 2009; and April 16, 2009.

The Toronto Star, September 18, 2005.

United Nations. "Millennium Report of the Secretary-General of the United Nations," n.d.

———. "Report of the Panel on United Nations Peace Operations," n.d.

———. "Statement by Kofi Annan on Kosovo Crisis." Press Release SG/SM/6997, May 18, 1999.

United Nations Department of Public Information. "Secretary-General Sets Course for Long-Awaited UN Revitalization." January 1998.

United Nations Newservice. "Millennium Summit Adopts Declaration Charting UN's Future." Friday, September 8, 2000.

———. "Security Council Leaders Resolve to Strengthen UN Peacekeeping." Thursday, September 7, 2000.

United Nations Security Council. "Security Council Holds Meeting of World Leaders on Occasion of General Assembly's Millennium Summit." Press Release SC/6919, September 7, 2000.

The Universal Almanac 1995. Kansas City, MO: Universal Press Syndicate Company, 1994.

USA Today, May 31, 1994; and August 31, 2006.

U.S. News and World Report, August 2, 1993.

Wall Street Journal, May 13, 1993.

Washington Post, June 28, 1999; April 4, 2000; May 30, 2004; June 6, 2004; June 13, 2004; June 30, 2004; November 17, 2004; December 27, 2005; April 23, 2006; September 10, 2006; January 1, 2008; and March 5, 2009.

Washington Post National Weekly Edition, September 6, 1999.

E. UNPUBLISHED MATERIAL

Greig, Alison Joanne. "The Role of the Security Council: An Opportunity for Reform." MA thesis, Graduate School of Weber University, Vienna, Austria, 1996.

Hansen, Niles W. "International Cooperation and Regional Policies within Nations." International Institute for Applied Systems Analysis (IIASA), September 1975. Available at http://www.iiasa.ac.at/Admin/PUB/Documents/RM-75-048.pdf.

Kokole, Omari H. "Black Africa and the Nuclear Factor." PhD dissertation, Dalhousie University, Halifax, Nova Scotia, 1988.

National Association of State Retirement Administrators. "The Sudan Accountability Act of 2007." Available at http://www.nasra.org/resources/Act%20of%2007.pdf.

Uku-Wertimer, Skyne. "International Dimensions of Crimes against Humanity: Ethnic Cleansing, Genocide, and Pogrom." Presented at the International Studies Association's 50th convention, New York, NY, February 15–18, 2009.

University for Peace. "Environmental Degradation as a Cause of Conflict in Darfur." Conference proceedings, Khartoum, December 2004.

Zellman, Ariel. "The Janjaweed in Sudan: A Case of Chronic Paramilitarism." Annual convention of the International Studies Association, San Diego, CA, March 23, 2006.

Index